Telecommunication Systems and Applications

Telecommunication Systems and Applications

Edited by
Fraidoon Mazda
MPhil DFH CEng FIEE

With specialist contributions

Focal Press
An imprint of Butterworth-Heinemann
Linacre House, Jordan Hill, Oxford OX2 8DP
A division of Reed Educational and Professional Publishing Ltd

A member of the Reed Elsevier plc group

OXFORD BOSTON JOHANNESBURG
NEW DELHI SINGAPORE MELBOURNE

First published 1996

British Library Cataloguing in Publication Data
Mazda, Fraidoon F
    Telecommunication Systems and Applications
    I. Title
    621.382

ISBN 0 2405 1453 X

Library of Congress Cataloguing in Publication
Mazda, Fraidoon F.
    Telecommunication Systems and Applications/Fraidoon Mazda
    p. cm.
    Includes bibliographical references and index.
    ISBN 02405 145x x
    1. Telecommunications. I. Title
    TK5101.M37 1993   92-27846
    621.382–dc20   CIP
Printed and bound in Great Britain

Contents

Preface

Successful transmission of information is key to the development of any modern telecommunication system and this book describes the various transmission systems and components which are currently used in private and public networks.

The principles of the Synchronous Digital Hierarchy (SDH) are described in Chapter 1, and it is compared with the more traditional Pleisiochronous Digital Hierarchy (PDH).

Chapter 2 introduces the principles of the Integrated Services Digital Network (ISDN) and its implementation in a modern transmission network. Video transmission, both broadcast and cable systems, is described in Chapter 3, which includes an introduction to videophony and videoconferencing.

Chapter 4 briefly reviews telex transmission, which is an established but still used system and this is followed by a more detailed description of facsimile transmission. Although facsimile has been in use for many years it still represents the most common method of transmission of printed text. It has developed over the years and is widely used throughout the world.

Two common transmission components, the modem and the multiplexer, are described in Chapters 6 and 7, and the book concludes with a chapter on the techniques and instruments used to make measurements in telecommunication systems.

Fifteen authors have contributed to this book, all specialists in their field, and the success of the book is largely due to their efforts. The book is also based on selected chapters which were first published in the much larger volume of the *Telecommunications Engineers' Reference Book*.

Fraidoon Mazda
Bishop's Stortford
April 1996

List of contributors

Richard Boulter
BSc (Hons) CEng FIEE
BT Laboratories
(Chapter 2)

Ian Corbett
BSc CEng MIEE
BT Laboratories
(Section 3.5)

David M Davidson
Nortel Ltd
(Chapter 4)

L M Davis
NEC (UK) Ltd
(Chapter 5)

T J Egginton
BSc (Sheffield)
Candalf Digital Comm. Ltd
(Chapter 6)

J R Fox
MA MSc PhD MIEE CEng
BT Laboratories
(Section 3.3)

David Green
Rohde & Schwarz
(Sections 8.6 to 8.11)

Pat Hawker
Formerly IBA Engineering Div.
(Sections 3.1 to 3.2)

J Hoolan
Dowty Communications Ltd
(Chapter 7)

A C Keene
BSc CEng MIEE
Trend Communications Ltd
(Section 8.5)

Gary Law
BSc PhD
Andersen Consulting
(Section 8.4)

Mark Matthews
Nortel Ltd
(Chapter 1)

D G Morrison
MA
BT Laboratories
(Section 3.4)

Hugh Walker
BA (Cantab) MSc
Hewlett-Packard Ltd
(Sections 8.1 to 8.3)

1. The Synchronous Digital Hierarchy

1.1 Introduction

The Synchronous Digital Hierarchy (SDH) is a relatively new standard for multiplexing together many low rate digital traffic channels
into higher rate channels, in order that these low rate channels may
be more efficiently transported around a telecommunications network. Viewed in this way, the SDH is merely a better alternative to
the existing Plesiochronous Digital Hierarchy (PDH), which attempts
to achieve more or less the same results. However, as we shall see
later in this chapter, SDH has evolved to become much more than just
the latest standard for combining and separating traffic channels. Due
to the business pressures confronting the world's Public Telecommunications Operators (PTOs), SDH has developed into a comprehensive set of standards which address all aspects of a
telecommunications transport network. The most important of these
additional aspects concern the performance of traffic paths across the
network, together with the automation of their management. The
result of implementing the SDH standards is that a PTO now has a
consistent mechanism for partitioning, monitoring and controlling
the raw transport capacity of the whole network.

Nevertheless, without some sound business drivers, most PTOs
would view a move from the current, well proven, PDH to the more
advanced SDH as, at best, an interesting academic exercise, and at
worst, a scandalous extravagance. To see why there is such frenetic
activity to changeover to SDH it is necessary to briefly examine the
business environment in which the world's more advanced PTOs are
now operating.

The source of the problem is the PTOs' business customers. These
are the customers from whom the PTOs derive a disproportionately

large percentage of their profits, and who are becoming increasingly dependent on telecom services for their very survival. Not surprisingly, business customers are looking to their use of telecomms to give them a competitive edge and thus, in addition to a straight reduction in tariffs, they are now demanding other things such as lower error rates and higher availability on their existing services, together with the bandwidth flexibility (i.e. channel capacity and routeing capability) that enables the introduction of completely new services. In the past most PTOs operated as monopoly suppliers, and to some extent they could afford to resist these demands. Now, however, liberalisation and deregulation have introduced significant competition into several of these former monopoly markets, especially in the USA, UK and Japan. This competition to supply high quality telecom services to business customers is forcing PTOs to re-examine the cost effectiveness of their existing transmission networks. In particular, they are looking to balance the quality of service delivered to their customers against the capital and operating costs of their networks. The objective of this balance is, of course, to maintain or increase profits.

The disturbing conclusion of most PTOs is that it is not possible to deliver the quality of service demanded by business customers, at the right price, if they continue to operate transmission networks based on the current PDH. Even more disturbing is the fact that this conclusion was reached with full awareness of the falling costs of raw bandwidth i.e. the effects of reduced costs for optical fibres, electro-optic devices and the Application Specific Integrated Circuits (ASICs), which are the heart of any piece of transmission hardware.

1.2 PDH deficiencies

In order to fully appreciate SDH, it is useful to briefly examine some of the limitations of the PDH. These limitations fall under three main headings:

1.   Lack of flexibility. It is more difficult, using PDH based equipment, to drop and insert a low rate channel from a high rate channel, without the use of a 'multiplexer mountain'. The

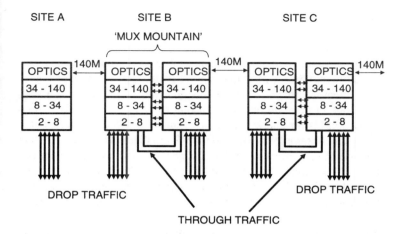

Figure 1.1   The difficulty of accessing a passing 2Mbit/s stream using PDH equipment

normal example given is that of dropping out a 2Mbit/s channel from a passing 140Mbit/s stream. (See Figure 1.1.) The cause of this particular problem lies in the amount of information processing necessary to locate and extract the required traffic channel. The basic PDH multiplexing process involves a bit interleaving operation which obscures knowledge of the individual byte boundaries, and thus leads to an inflexible system. This inflexibility extends beyond drop and insert functionality, to cross connects. These become rather large and cumbersome because the PDH restricts them to use only space switching, as opposed to the much more efficient Time-Space-Time techniques that SDH allows.

2.   Lack of performance. The PDH does not currently have any internationally standardised ways of monitoring the performance of traffic channels at 8Mbits and above. Even at 2Mbit/s, where there is a mechanism (CRC4), it only works when the 2Mbit/s channel has a G.704 frame structure imposed on it. Furthermore, the PDH does not have any agreed management channels or protocol stacks etc. Although some

of the spare bits in the frame alignment words can be, and already are, used to carry management information, the information capacity is somewhat limited (e.g. 22kbit/s @ 34Mbit/s). Worse still, when operating at one of the higher order rates, the PDH makes it difficult to retrieve any management information associated with lower order channels, without a full demultiplexing operation. Finally, even at 2Mbit/s, there is no guarantee of any management information. The usual example here is that of the 2Mbit/s private circuit, leased to the customer as a clear channel i.e. the PTO imposes no G.704 frame structure and the customer has full control over the entire 2.048Mbit/s bandwidth. In this case, there is no room for the PTO to insert any monitoring or control information, hence it cannot tell when the performance of such a circuit drops out of specification. On the other hand, the customer has almost certainly imposed his own frame structure, and therefore can monitor the delivered performance with great accuracy.

3.   Lack of 'Mid-Fibre Meet'. Although the PDH specifies the exact format of the bit stream at the aggregate port of any PDH multiplexer, it puts no such constraints on the bit stream on the line side of a line transmission terminal. (See Figure 1.2.) Consequently, every manufacturer has used his own proprietary line code and optical interface specification, making it impossible for a PTO to interconnect line terminals from two different manufacturers. This operational constraint is destined to become an increasing problem due to the progressive fragmentation of the erstwhile monopoly transmission networks into a patchwork of smaller operations, all of which need to interwork with each other. Without an agreed Mid-Fibre Meet standard, this interworking becomes rather clumsy, as both ends of an interconnecting line system have to be bought from the same manufacturer, and will probably need to be controlled as a pair, rather than independently by each operator. It is interesting to note that Mid-Fibre Meet was one of the original targets for the SDH standard, when it was first proposed in the US as part of the early work on SONET, back

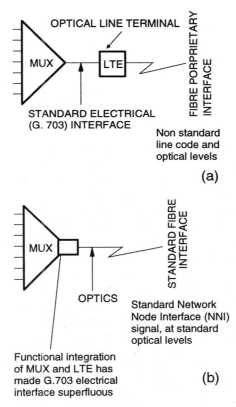

Figure 1.2 Comparison of interfaces needed in PDH and SDH environments: (a) current PDH; (b) SDH

in 1984. (SONET, Synchronous Optical NETwork, is the North American counterpart to SDH. It preceded SDH by some years.)

Of the above three problem areas, it is reasonable to suppose that (3) and to some extent (2) could have been solved by extensions and modifications to the existing PDH standards. In the future, though, it is likely that the sheer quantity of management information needing to be transported around a network will eventually pose an insoluble problem for even a modified/extended PDH, hence any solution to this problem would always be viewed as a stopgap measure.

The problem of traffic path inflexibility is much more difficult to overcome by modifying the PDH. It is tempting to suggest synchronising an entire PDH transmission network, as many PTOs have already done at the 2Mbit/s level. Unfortunately, as well as being progressively more difficult to do at the higher bit rates in the PDH, synchronisation alone does nothing to preserve the byte boundaries within each bit stream. Without any easy method of identifying these byte boundaries, the task of extracting both low order traffic and management channels has not been significantly simplified. As a final nail in the coffin, strict network synchronisation also entails the addition of 'wander' buffers at every multiplexer, in order to accommodate slow variations in the inherent delay of the transmission media (usually optical fibres these days). These buffers themselves give rise to further undesirable transmission delays, which could push some PTOs towards the otherwise unnecessary adoption of costly echo cancellers on 64kbit/s circuits throughout their networks.

1.3 The basis of SDH

Before investigating the SDH standards in detail, it is worth pausing for an overview of what SDH is designed to achieve, and the general way it goes about this task.

As with PDH, SDH is designed to transport isochronous traffic channels and is focused very much on layer one of the well known ISO seven layer OSI protocol hierarchy. Again, like PDH, SDH is based on a hierarchy of continuously repeating, fixed length frames. This contrasts with the majority of competing standards, almost all of which attempt to deliver more efficient use of both transmission and switching plant by employing some form of packetisation of the transported information. Usually, these packets are launched into the network asynchronously and arrive at their destinations with a non-deterministic delay. Consequently, they present something of a problem to delay sensitive voice circuits, which still constitute 80% of all traffic, in even the world's most advanced networks. SDH, on the other hand, was formulated on the premise that despite the pressure to support novel forms of business oriented services, it is of paramount importance to preserve a smooth interworking with the existing PDH networks, most of which were designed to serve the PSTN above all else. At the same time, it was also apparent that the increasingly widespread deployment of optical fibres would rapidly reduce the cost of raw transmission bandwidth, hence there was relatively little pressure to restrict the proportion of bandwidth devoted to multiplexing overheads, as opposed to the traffic payload. Beyond the transport of isochronous traffic channels, and smooth interworking with the existing PDH, the developers of SDH also addressed those weaknesses of the PDH that were identified above. They recognised that it was necessary to adopt not only a synchronous frame structure, but one which also preserved the byte boundaries in the various traffic bit streams. The basic SDH frame structure is one that repeats at intervals of 125µs i.e. it is tailor made for the transport of 64kbit/s channels, or any higher rate channels which are an integer multiple of 64kbit/s. (See Figure 1.3.) In fact, with one rather important exception dealt with in Section 1.4, SDH currently focuses on the transport

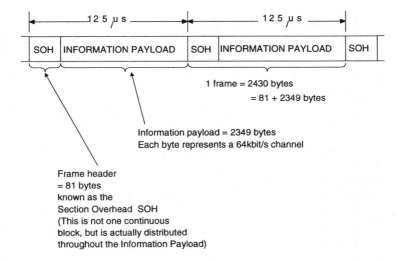

Figure 1.3 The basis of SDH frame structure

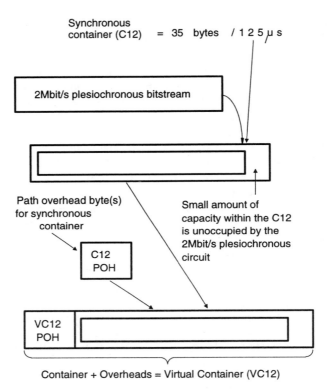

Figure 1.4 Example of the creation of a VC

of 2.048Mbit/s, 34Mbit/s and 140Mbit/s circuits, plus their North American counterparts at 1.5Mbit/s, 6Mbit/s and 45Mbit/s.

The general way that any of these PDH rate circuits are transported by SDH is to map such a circuit into a 'Synchronous Container'. (See Figure 1.4.) A Synchronous Container can be viewed as a subdivision of the basic SDH frame structure, and it consists of a predefined number of 64kbit/s channels. The entire family of Synchronous Containers comprises only a few different types, each of which has been sized to accommodate one or more of the common plesiochronous transmission rates, without wasting too much bandwidth. The operation of mapping a plesiochronous circuit into such a Synchronous Container is very similar to the normal stuffing operation performed in a conventional PDH multiplexer. However, in this case, the plesiochronous channel is being synchronised not to the master oscillator in a PDH multiplexer, but to the frequency of the Synchronous Container, which is, in turn, synchronous to the basic SDH frame structure. (See Figure 1.5.)

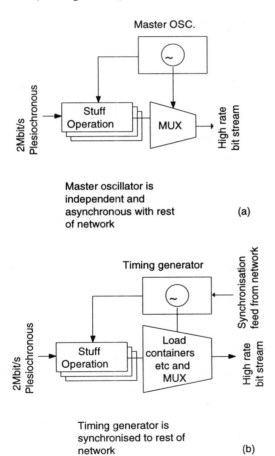

Master oscillator is
independent and
asynchronous with rest   (a)
of network

Timing generator is
synchronised to rest of
network   (b)

Before examining the question of exactly what the SDH frame structure is synchronous with, it is worth digressing to discuss a further operation specified by SDH. This is the attachment of an Overhead, known as the Path Overhead (POH), to each Synchronous Container. (See Figure 1.4.) The idea is that once a plesiochronous circuit has been loaded into a Synchronous Container, this Container has a defined set of POH bytes appended to it, which remain completely unchanged until the Synchronous Container arrives at its destination. The combination of Synchronous Container plus POH is known as a Virtual Container (VC). The VC POH bytes allow a PTO to monitor several parameters, the most important of which is the error rate of the VC between the points at which it was loaded and unloaded with its plesiochronous payload. This provides a PTO with the much sought after end to end performance monitoring that was so difficult using conventional PDH techniques.

Most plesiochronous channels are bi-directional, hence there are usually two continuous streams of VCs travelling in opposite directions between the two end points at which the plesiochronous channel enters and leaves the SDH portion of a network. Viewed in this way, the job of an SDH based network is to load its VCs with (usually) convention PDH channels, and then transport these to their various destinations together with an accurate indication of the quality of the delivered VC payload.

This process of loading containers and then attaching POHs is repeated at several levels in SDH, resulting in the nesting of smaller VCs within larger ones. (See Figure 1.6.) The nesting hierarchy stops when the largest level of VC is loaded into the payload area of a Synchronous Transport Module (STM). These logical STM signals are seen at the interface between any two pieces of SDH equipment, where they can be presented either electrically or, more usually, optically. (See Fig 1.2.) Such an interface is referred to as a Network Node Interface (NNI), because it is usually confined to the internal interfaces within the network, rather than any interface presented to a network user. A User Network Interface (UNI) has also been defined; however, the way in which the payload information in a UNI is mapped into a standard NNI signal is not yet completely defined, and hence it is not widely used. Finally, the reason for the name

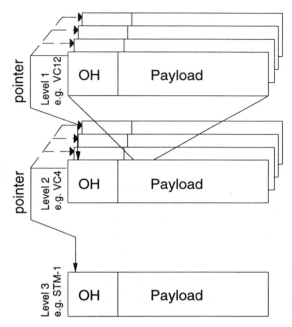

Figure 1.5   General representation of a 3 layer synchronous multiplexer structure

Virtual Container is that unlike the STM signals that appear at the NNI, VC signals are never presented to the outside world. They exist only within pieces of SDH equipment or within STM signals, hence an SDH network element can have NNI and PDH interfaces, but never VC interfaces.

Returning to the question of exactly what is synchronised to what, the basic problem is that, as outlined in Section 1.2, it is very difficult to maintain a complete transmission network in rigid synchronisation for all time. Even if we could tolerate the delays introduced by the addition of the numerous 'wander buffers' necessary to accommodate the slow changes in transmission medium delay, there is no guarantee that different PTOs' networks would all be synchronised to the same master clock. For a network based on the SDH, this problem translates to that of how to synchronously multiplex and demultiplex many individual VCs, which, because they have been created in disparate parts of the same, or even different SDH networks, may have slightly different short term bit rates.

1.3.1 The concept of pointers

The solution adopted by SDH is to associate a pointer with each VC so that when it is multiplexed, along with others, into a larger VC, its phase offset in bytes can be identified relative to some reference point in this larger VC. (See Figure 1.7.) Furthermore, there is also a mechanism for allowing the value of this pointer to change if, for some reason, there is a loss of synchronisation, and the smaller capacity VC is running either slightly slower, or slightly faster than the larger VC. In fact, each of the smaller capacity VCs has its own

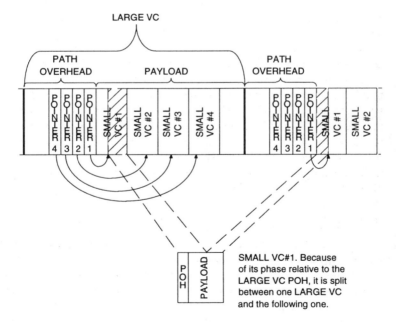

Figure 1.6   Pointers allow small VC to have arbitary phase with respect to large VC

pointer, which can change independently of any of the others. Although the use of these pointers still entails some input buffers, these are very much smaller than would be required if there were no mechanism for changing the phase of a small capacity VC within a larger one, hence the problem of excessive delays can be contained. We now have a picture of an SDH network as one in which the majority of VCs, both large and small, are well synchronised to each other, but, at the same time, there are a few which are not so well synchronised, and every so often the increasing strain of their asynchronism has to be relieved by a byte sized slip relative to the majority of the other VCs in the network. Nevertheless, we retain our ability to locate the management and control information in the VC's POH bytes, because the pointer value associated with VC is recalculated whenever a slip occurs.

The pointer mechanism described above is at the very heart of the SDH standard. It is this mechanism that enables us to construct networks that are nearly, but not completely synchronous, and yet still allows us to easily locate each traffic channel (VC), together with its associated management and control information i.e. POH, but without incurring large penalties in transmission delay. It could be argued that SDH networks are not really synchronous at all, but are actually very tightly controlled asynchronous networks. However, the fact that we have quantised the slips due to this asynchronism means that it is now possible, at any time, to locate and route any of the traffic paths within an SDH network. This, together with network management software, gives us the traffic routeing flexibility that was very difficult to achieve using PDH based equipment. In terms of actual network hardware, it opens the way to the production of economically viable drop and insert multiplexers and cross connects.

1.4 The SDH standards

There are now a dozen or more ITU-T recommendations describing various aspects of SDH, but the centre-piece of the whole group is undoubtedly ITU-T G.707/8/9. These three standards define the SDH multiplexing structure and the ways that non-SDH traffic channels can be mapped into the SDH Virtual Containers. Other standards in the group deal with such things as the functionality of multiplexers (G.781/2/3), the management requirements of such equipment (G.784), and the equivalent recommendations for line systems (G.958). Optical interfaces for all types of SDH equipment are covered in G.957. Further standards address the functionality of synchronous cross connects. Finally there are two more standards which address the way that entire SDH based networks should be constructed in order that they can interwork successfully with other such networks and, even more importantly, so that the management of these networks can be brought under software control. Nevertheless, because of their central role in SDH, we shall concentrate mainly on explaining G.707/8 & 9.

Bearing in mind the nesting of smaller VCs within larger ones, and thence into STMs, the best way to appreciate the details of the SDH multiplexing standards G707/8/9 is to follow the progress of a bi-directional 2Mbit/s plesiochronous circuit, which, for part of its journey, is transported across an SDH based network. (See Figure 1.8.) Such a 2Mbit/s circuit could be a channel between two PSTN switches, or it could be a private leased line which is connecting two

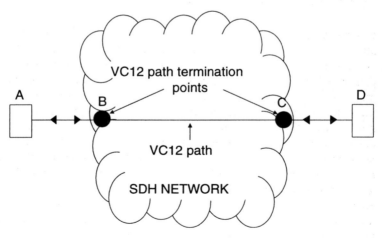

Figure 1.7   2Mbit/s plesiochronous circuit from A to D, which is transported by an SDH network for part of its journey

PBXs. Although the 2Mbit/s circuit is bi-directional, the SDH operations are identical in both directions, hence we shall concentrate on just one direction of transmission, that from A to D.

At point B, where the 2Mbit/s circuit meets the SDH network, the first operation is to take the incoming plesiochronous bit stream and selectively add 'stuffing' bits in order to 'pad-out' this bit stream to the exact rate required to fill the appropriate Synchronous Container. In this case, the Synchronous Container size would be a C12, which is sufficiently large to accommodate a 2Mbit/s plesiochronous bit stream at the limits of its 50 ppm tolerance, together with some additional 'fixed stuffing' bytes. The stuffing of the plesiochronous bit stream should ideally be done relative to the clock to which the whole SDH network is beating; however, as discussed in Section 1.3, there is a chance that the SDH network element (e.g. multiplexer) which is performing the stuffing operation is not quite synchronous with the rest of the network. In this case C12 which it creates is similarly asynchronous.

1.4.1 Path OverHead information

Having mapped the 2Mbit/s bit stream into the C12, the next operation is to generate and attach the Path Overhead byte (POH), which enables this C12 to be identified, monitored for errors and routed through the SDH network. The addition of this POH byte to the C12 creates a Virtual Container 12 (VC12). As mentioned in Section 1.3, the idea is that the POH stays attached to its C12 all the way from the point where it was generated, to the point at which the 2Mbit/s payload exits the SDH network. These two points are the 'Path Termination' points for this VC12, with the continuous stream of VCs between them being referred to as the Path. Between the two path termination points at B and C, there is no legitimate mechanism for altering any of the information in the POH, hence if the receiving path termination detects any discrepancy between the POH and the content of the VC12 payload (i.e. the C12), this indicates that the VC12 payload has somehow become corrupted during its journey across the SDH network. Although path level monitoring is sufficient for a PTO to ascertain what error rate is being inflicted by the SDH network on his customers' 2Mbit/s circuit, it provides no information whatsoever on the source of the errors i.e. which network element has gone faulty. This task is dealt with by the addition of still further overhead information, which will be described shortly. Before this, it is necessary to examine the way in which several VC12s are multiplexed into a higher rate signal.

1.4.2 Multiplexing of Virtual Containers

The general principle of this multiplexing operation is fairly straight forward. Several VC12s, which should, hopefully, be synchronous with one another, are loaded into a larger Synchronous Container, which subsequently has its own POH added, thus creating a larger i.e. higher bit rate, VC. (See Figure 1.6.) In CEPT countries, this operation results in the creation of a VC4, which is large enough to accommodate up to 63 VC12s. Unfortunately, as discussed in Section 1.3, complications arise in this operation, because the network element that is performing this task, may not itself have created all the VC12s. (See Figure 1.9.) This leads to the possibility that not all the VC12s are completely synchronous with one another or, more importantly, with the VC4 into which they are being loaded.

The solution to this problem comes in two parts. Firstly, the internal structure of the VC4 has been purposely designed to allow each VC12 to run slightly faster, or slower, than the VC4 rate. This is done by designating certain bytes in the C4 as overflow bytes (one per VC12) to cope with a VC12 that is running too fast. On the other hand, when a VC12 is running slow, then occasionally, a VC12 byte can be repeated. Secondly, this (hopefully) infrequent change of phase of a VC12 relative to its VC4 is recorded by means of a pointer. A VC4 maintains one pointer for each of the VC12s within its payload, and each pointer registers the offset in bytes between the first byte of the VC4 and the POH byte of a particular VC12. Each pointer is located in a pre-defined position within the VC4, hence once the VC4 POH has been located, it is a simple matter of counting bytes in order to locate each of the 63 pointers to the VC12s. (See Figure 1.10.)

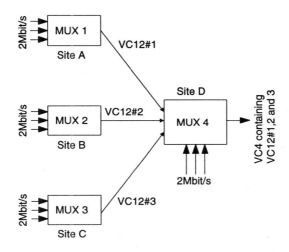

Figure 1.8 Synchronous multiplexing of VC12s into a VC4 when VC12s are created in various places

The trigger for a rephasing of a VC12 relative to its VC4 is when the fill of the VC12 input buffer (into which the incoming VC12 is written prior to loading into the VC4) exceeds a pre-determined threshold. At this point, what appears to be a fairly conventional justification occurs, with either an extra VC12 byte being loaded into the VC4 (into the overflow position mentioned earlier) or, conversely, one byte being repeated. (See Figure 1.11.) Either way, the resulting change of phase of VC12 relative to VC4 is tracked by a corresponding change in pointer value.

Because of the importance of pointers for locating low order VCs (VC12s) within high order VCs (VC4s), the combination of a low order VC plus its pointer is referred to as a Tributary Unit (TU). In

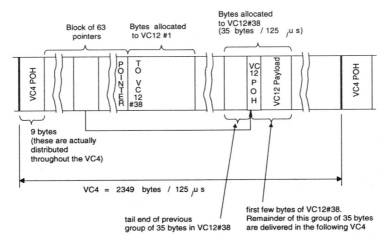

Figure 1.9   Fixed location of VC12 pointers within a VC4

this case, the combination of a VC12 plus its pointer constitutes a TU12.

1.4.3 Channels and Tributary Unit Groups

Having discussed the way in which up to 63 individual TU12s are multiplexed into a VC4, it is now necessary to examine more closely the internal structure of the VC4. For this purpose, it is helpful to consider a VC4 not as a linear string of bytes, but instead, as a two dimensional block of bytes which is arranged as 9 rows, each of 261 bytes. For transmission purposes, this block is serialised by scanning left to right, top to bottom. (See Figure 1.12.) With this structure, a TU12 can be seen to occupy 4, widely separated, 9 byte columns, rather than the contiguous block of bytes, as suggested by Figures 1.10 and 1.11. (See Figure 1.13.) Since a VC4 repeats every 125µs, this implies that a TU12 contains 36 bytes per 125µs i.e. rather more than the 32 bytes nominally required by a plesiochronous 2.048 Mbit/s signal. This, however, is consistent with the need for a TU12 to include a pointer, overflow byte positions, VC12 overhead byte, plesiochronous stuffing etc. Each such group of four columns repre-

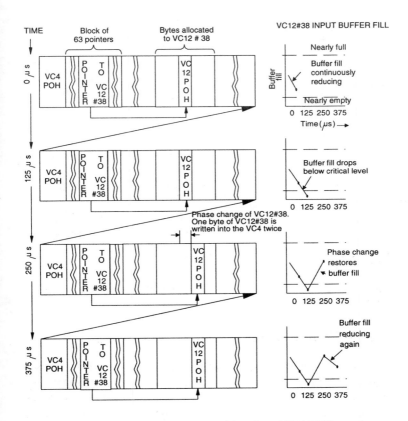

Figure 1.10   Pointer adjustment resulting from VC12#38 running slower than the VC4

sents a separate channel within the VC4 and when a VC12 slips phase relative to the VC4 it slips within its own channel i.e. it does not overflow into another channel, as this would obviously corrupt the data in the other channel. As mentioned earlier, the position of the pointer within this channel is constant, only the VC12 part of the TU12 is allowed to wander in phase.

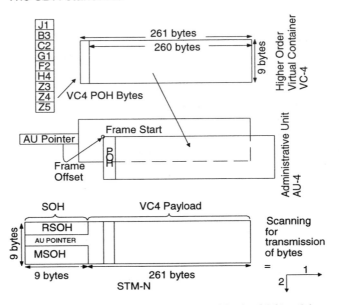

Figure 1.11 Representation of a VC4 as a block of 261 × 9 bytes together with its incorporation within an STM signal

A group of three such TU12 channels within a VC4 is known as a Tributary Unit Group (TUG). As with the concept of a channel, a TUG is not a multiplexing level (such as a VC12) but a group of defined byte positions within a VC4. Some of these positions are reserved for TU pointers, while the others are for the rest of the TUs i.e. the VCs. The reason for introducing the concept of a TUG, instead of sticking with that of a channel, is that, as mentioned in Section 1.3, a C12 and hence VC12, is not the only size of Synchronous Container which has been defined. (See Figure 1.14.) For example, there exists a C2 which is designed to accommodate the North American 6.3Mbit/s plesiochronous rate. In the event of a PTO needing to transport both 2Mbit/s circuits and 6.3Mbit/s ones, they can both be accommodated within the same VC4 by assigning some TUGs to carry groups of three TU12s while other TUGs are assigned to each carry a single TU2.

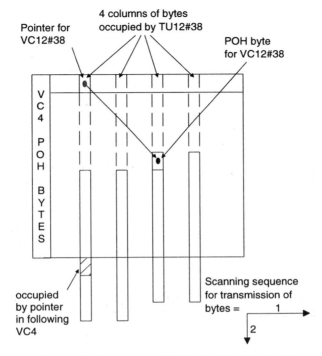

Figure 1.12   Internal structure of VC4 showing fixed pointer locations and distribution of a single TU12 over 4 separate columns

The TUG in this example is known as a TUG2, because at 12 columns of 9 bytes, it is large enough to accommodate a single TU2. Beyond this, a TUG3 has also been defined. This is slightly larger than 7 TUG2s, and designed to accommodate a single 45Mbit/s circuit, after this has been mapped into its appropriate Synchronous Container (in this case, a VC3). A 34Mbit/s signal can also be mapped into a VC3, in an operation that appears somewhat wasteful on bandwidth, as the C3 has been sized for a 45Mbit/s signal. It is interesting to note that, rather than use a more aptly sized container, this bandwidth sacrifice was agreed to by European PTOs in order to reduce the potential network control problem posed by a larger variety of VCs.

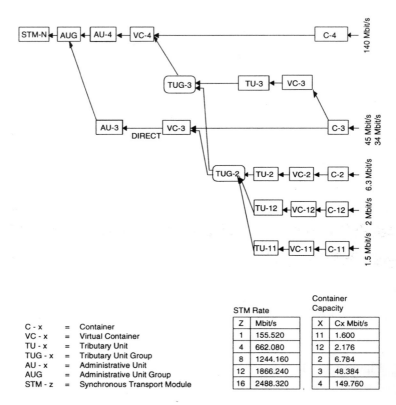

	STM Rate			Container Capacity	
	Z	Mbit/s		X	Cx Mbit/s
C - x = Container	1	155.520		11	1.600
VC - x = Virtual Container	4	662.080		12	2.176
TU - x = Tributary Unit	8	1244.160		2	6.784
TUG - x = Tributary Unit Group	12	1866.240		3	48.384
AU - x = Administrative Unit	16	2488.320		4	149.760
AUG = Administrative Unit Group					
STM - z = Synchronous Transport Module					

Figure 1.13 SDH multiplexing structure

A TUG3 is one third of the payload capacity of a VC4, and together with the TUG2, it constitutes an extremely flexible mechanism for partitioning the payload bandwidth of a VC4. The potentially complicated nature of this partitioning can be better understood by replacing the two dimensional representation of the VC4 payload structure by a three dimensional one. (See Figure 1.15.) For this representation, the order of transmission is left to right, front to back, top to bottom. Figure 1.15 not only shows TU12s and TU3s, as we have already discussed, but also examples of other types of TUs, notably the TU11,

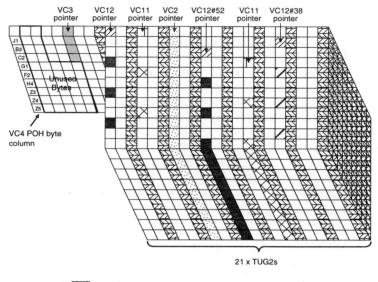

Figure 1.14   Partially filled VC4 with TU structured payload

which is the TU used to accommodate a 1.5Mbit/s (DS1) signal in North America. This payload flexibility extends to alternative mechanisms for constructing a VC4 payload in which, for instance, a normal 140Mbit/s signal is mapped directly into the C4, without any need for recourse to the notion of TUGs. Because of the variety of possible VC4 payloads, part of the VC4 overhead (i.e. the H4 byte) is reserved for indicating the exact structure of this payload. This ability of a single VC4 to carry a mixture of different sized VCs within its payload is considered to be especially useful in the Access portion of the network, where a PTO will not usually have the freedom to dedicate particular VC4s to carrying a single type of lower order VC.

1.4.4 VC4 into a Synchronous Transport Module

Although a VC4 can have its payload constructed in a variety of ways, its POH conforms to the same principles as those of a VC12 i.e. it is generated and attached at the point where the C4 is loaded, and remains unchanged until the C4 is unloaded at its destination. As with the VC12, the VC4 POH is capable of indicating that errors have been introduced into the VC4 payload during its journey, but it is not capable of identifying which network element was responsible. This problem is solved by the addition of yet another set of overhead bytes to the VC4, known as the Section Overhead bytes (SOH). The combination of the SOH plus the VC4 is termed a Synchronous Transport Module (STM), but another way of looking at this structure is to regard the VC4 as fitting neatly into the payload area of the STM. (See Figure 1.12.) Like the VC4, the STM repeats every 125μs. In order to appreciate the structure of an STM, and particularly the SOH, it is best to revert to using the two dimensional representation of a block of bytes. Figure 1.12 shows the standard representation of the smallest STM, known as an STM-1, which has 9 rows of 270 bytes each. This produces a transmission rate of 155.520Mbit/s.

The significance of the STM SOH is that, unlike the VC4 POH, it is generated afresh by every network element that handles the VC4. This handling of the VC4 includes the operations of creating, multi-plexing or routeing within the network, even if such multiplexing or routeing happens to be completely inflexible (e.g. hardwired). When a network element (i.e. line terminal, multiplexer or cross connect) receives an STM, it immediately examines the relevant bytes of the SOH to determine whether any errors have been introduced into the payload i.e. the VC4. Unless this particular network element happens to contain the VC4 path termination point, it subsequently calculates a new, replacement set of SOH bytes which are then attached to the VC4 for onward transmission to the next network element. (See Figure 1.16.)

This section by section monitoring gives the PTO a powerful tool for locating the source of any poor performance within his network, and compliments the capabilities of the VC POHs, which are solely concerned with end to end, rather than section by section (i.e. network

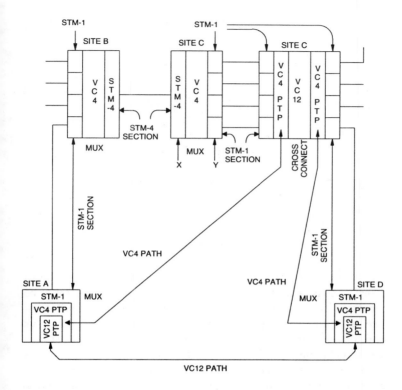

Figure 1.15 VC12 path between sites A and D, showing the VC4 and STM sections involved

element to network element) issues. It could be argued that the POH monitoring is redundant, because the end to end path performance could be synthesised from the individual section indications. However, not only would this be difficult to do, especially if the VC4 journey happened to traverse the networks of more than one PTO, but it would not necessarily detect all the errors in the VC4, because it is quite possible for errors to be generated within the confines of a transited network element i.e. within that portion of a network element between where the old SOH has been removed, and a new one has been added e.g. between X and Y of the mux at site C as shown in Figure 1.16.

Although both the VC POHs and STM SOHs have other duties in addition to the performance monitoring described above, the SOHs shoulder by far the larger part of the burden, hence the reason for the much larger number of bytes in the SOH than, for instance, in a VC4 POH. (See Figure 1.12.) These additional duties include STM alignment function, the carriage of the network management channels, Engineer Orderwire channels, data channels reserved for the PTO and synchronisation signalling channels. Even when these have been accommodated, there is substantial unallocated capacity which is being kept in reserve, to service future network control requirements that have not yet been identified.

1.4.5 Further use of pointers

The use of STMs and their associated SOHs entails a few additional complications beyond those discussed above. An STM may well be generated by a network element which did not have the privilege of also generating the particular VC4 that it is attempting to load. This immediately introduces the possibility of a slight asynchronism between STM and VC4, and, as with the VC12, this problem is also solved by a slip mechanism plus pointer. The pointer bytes occupy defined positions within the SOH and indicate the offset, in bytes, between themselves and the first byte of the VC4 POH. The main difference between this and the VC12 pointer is that when a VC4 slips its phase relative to the STM SOH, it does so by three bytes at a time, rather than the single byte phase change experienced by the VC12.

A second difference between this case, and that of a VC12, is that the combination of a VC4 plus its pointer is known as an Administrative Unit 4 (AU4), rather than a TU4, when the pointer is located in an STM. The AU4 is used in all CEPT countries as the size of traffic block on which networks are planned and operated. There is also an AU3, which is used mainly in North America. This refers to an alternative construction of an STM, whereby the payload consists not of a single VC4, but instead of a group of three VC3s, together with their associated pointers. A further difference between the STM SOH and a VC POH is that the SOH can be divided into two parts, known as the Multiplexer Section OverHead (MSOH) and the Regenerator Section OverHead (RSOH). (See Figure 1.12.) The reason for this is that on long line transmission systems the regenerators do not need to perform the rather costly, and in this case, unnecessary operation of generating and destroying the complete SOH. Instead, only a subset of a SOH is processed, leading to a reduction in gate count, power consumption etc., but still preserving the ability to detect traffic errors and access some management channels. On the other hand, the line terminal equipments process both the RSOH and MSOH. (See Figure 1.17.)

Finally, as with VCs, STMs come in various sizes. As mentioned earlier, the smallest size is termed an STM-1, and can accommodate a single VC4. However, larger sizes exist whose bit rates are integer multiples of the basic STM-1 rate. ITU-T G.707 currently recognises the STM-4 and STM-16, but STM-12 based network elements are also being designed, and it is likely that STM-64 will become a de facto standard in the near future. For all these higher rate STMs, the construction mechanism is the same: the payload is produced by straight byte interleaving of the tributary VC4s, while the SOH is

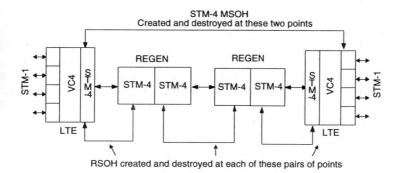

Figure 1.16   Line transmission system showing the multiplexer section overhead (MSOH) operating between LTEs, while only the regenerator section overhead (RSOH) is recalculated between each pair of regenerators

constructed in a more complicated way, particularly in relation to the way the error checking bytes are calculated.

1.4.6 Other sizes of VCs and payloads

The above description of the loading of a 2Mbit/s circuit into a VC12, VC4 and thence into an STM-1, mentioned the existence of other sizes of VC. The complete family of VCs, together with their allowed multiplexing routes up to STM-1, are shown in Figure 1.14. So far mappings into these Synchronous Containers have been defined for all the common plesiochronous bit rates, together with few others, notably the 125Mbit/s FDDI signal. This latter mapping is somewhat wasteful of transmission bandwidth, as it loads the 125Mbit/s FDDI signal into a VC4 which has a payload capacity of around 149Mbit/s. It might be thought that this degree of inefficiency is more or less inevitable for any further type of signal whose bit rate does not correspond roughly with that of one of the existing Synchronous Containers. In fact, this is not necessarily so, because ITU-T G.708 and G.709 contain provision for the concatenation of both TU2s and AU3s and AU4s.

As a hypothetical example, to illustrate the use of concatenated TU2s, an incoming service signal at, say, 16Mbit/s is mapped into a group of three VC2s, known collectively as a VC2-3c. (See Figure 1.18.) These three VC2s are loaded into the VC4 with identical pointer values, and are subsequently transported, as a group, across the entire SDH network. The best current example of the use of this technique is in the area of video transmission, where a TV signal is digitally encoded at around 32Mbit/s, and subsequently loaded into a concatenated group of five VC2s (VC2-5c). This mapping allows up to four such video signals to be transported in a single VC4. If, instead, the normal mapping into a VC3 had been used, then only three video signals could have been accommodated within one VC4, hence a useful increase in efficiency by using concatenation.

So far, in this discussion, all the examples of a service rate signal being mapped into a Synchronous Container have assumed that the SDH network element makes no use of any structure that might be present in the service rate signal. In fact, this assumption is always

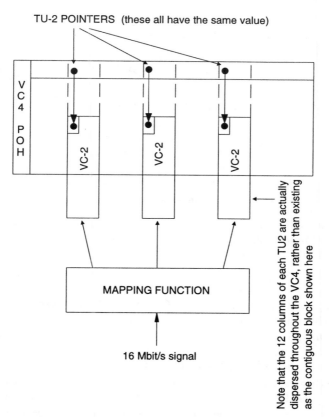

Figure 1.17   Loading of a hypothetical 16Mbit/s signal into 3 concatenated VC2s (VC2-3c) within a VC4

true when the service rate signal is plesiochronous, however, because of the way the PSTN service is usually operated, with all of the switches running synchronously with one another, it was decided to endow SDH with a second class of mapping, known as byte synchronous mapping. Currently, the only byte synchronous mapping defined is for a 2Mbit/s signal which has a G.704 frame structure (i.e. is byte orientated) and which is synchronous to the SDH network or, more precisely, synchronous with the network element which is

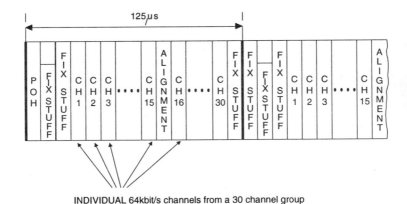

INDIANAL 64kbit/s channels from a 30 channel group

Figure 1.18   Byte synchronous mapping of a G.704 structured 2.048Mbit/s signal into a VC12, showing the fixed location of each of the 30 × 64kbit/s channels

mapping it into a Synchronous Container. In the course of a byte synchronous mapping, the SDH network element locks onto the incoming G.704 frame alignment word, and subsequently proceeds to load this, and every other byte in the G.704 frame, into predefined positions in the C12. (See Figure 1.19.)

This results in a situation whereby any channel of a 30 channel group can be easily located once the location of the VC12 POH has been established. The advantage of this mapping becomes apparent when considering two PSTN switches which are interconnected by several groups of 30 channels that are transported over an SDH network. (See Figure 1.20.) It is easy for such a PSTN switch to operate as part of the SDH network by generating and byte synchronously loading its own VC12s, because it already knows the location of all 30 channels. It obviously does not need to search for frame alignment, as this too is already known. At the receiving PSTN switch, because the VC12s were mapped byte synchronously, there is also no need for a frame alignment operation, because this follows automatically once the phase of the VC12 is known. The removal of the G.704 frame alignment process not only leads to a reduction in

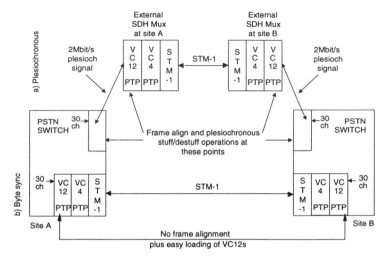

Figure 1.19   Comparison of plesiochronous and byte synchronous mappings of 30 channel groups between two PSTN switches

gate count (and hence cost), but also reduces the delay associated with this operation. These advantages apply not just to the PSTN example given above, but, in fact, to any network where visibility and routeing of individual 64 kbit/s channels is required, hence they could also apply to networks of PBXs or 64 kbit/s cross connects.

1.4.7 SONET and SDH

Several mentions have been made of SONET as being both the forerunner and the North American equivalent of SDH. The SONET standards were designed around the need for efficient transport of the existing North American PDH rates, the most important of which are the 1.5Mbit/s and 45Mbit/s rates. This leads to a standard where a 45Mbit/s signal is loaded into the equivalent of a VC3, which, in turn, is loaded into the SONET counterpart of an STM, known as a Synchronous Transport Signal-1 (STS-1), which runs at 51.84Mbit/s i.e. precisely one third of the STM-1 rate. As with SDH, there is also a concatenation mechanism for dealing with customer signals which do not easily fit inside any of the already defined VC payload areas. This mechanism is particularly useful for carrying rates such as 140Mbit/s, where the concatenation results in a SONET NNI signal known as an STS-3c, which has a bit rate that is identical to an STM-1, and an SOH and payload area of exactly the same size as well.

Other terminology within SONET is also different, in that SONET refers to Virtual Tributaries (VTs) rather than VCs, and the equivalent of the VC3, referred to above, is known as a Synchronous Payload Envelope (SPE). It also makes a distinction between the STS logical signal and its optical manifestation at an NNI, in which case it is referred to as an Optical Carrier (OC). North American transmission systems are usually referred to by their transmission rates in OCs e.g. OC3 or OC48.

1.4.8 NNI optical interface standardisation

Although recommendations G.707/8/9 have done an excellent job in standardising the logical signal presented at an NNI, this alone is not enough to ensure a Mid-Fibre Meet between equipment from two different manufacturers. G.957 recognises this problem and specifies the relevant physical parameters for a range of standard optical interfaces, at the preferred SDH rates of STM-1, STM-4 and STM-16. In addition, there is also an extension to the existing G.703 electrical interface specification to accommodate an electrical presentation of an STM-1 signal. Despite this, there is still no guarantee of anything beyond traffic path interworking, as the management channels that flow across the mid-fibre boundary may still be carrying information which is unintelligible to the network managers on the other side. This is an important area that the standards bodies are still addressing.

1.4.9 SDH network elements

Because traffic routeing flexibility is one of the reasons for the existence of SDH, the simplest way of considering any SDH network element is as a group of transport termination functions (TTFs)

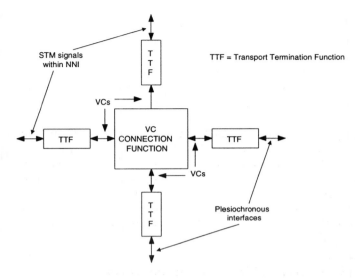

Figure 1.20   Generalised representation of the traffic paths through an SDH network element

surrounding a traffic path connectivity function (see Figure 1.21). The TTFs are essentially the conversion functions from the VC level to either the STM or plesiochronous signal levels, while the connectivity function allows VCs to be routed between the various TTFs. More than anything else, it is the size and flexibility of the connectivity function that distinguishes one type of network element from another. For example, a cross connect may have a large connectivity function, capable of simultaneously routeing a large number of VCs of a given type between a large number of TTFs, with very few restrictions on this connectivity. This, of course, is consistent with the normal role of a cross connect, as a major traffic routeing node in a transport network, where electronically controllable traffic routeing flexibility is its raison d'etre. At the other end of the scale come Line System Terminals (LTEs), which normally incorporate a multiplexer as well. The connectivity between tributaries and aggregate ports of such a multiplexer is normally hard wired, hence no flexibility whatsoever. Between these two extremes come drop and insert

(Add/Drop) multiplexers, which attempt to strike a balance that leads to adequate, rather than comprehensive, routeing flexibility, with an attendant reduction in equipment costs.

All of the above mentioned types of network element normally assume that any interconnection will be based on optical fibres. It is, however, also possible to use other interconnection media, in particular radio transmission. The problem in using radio interconnection is that, unlike optical fibres, the available spectrum is finite, and in short supply. The liberal use of overhead capacity in SDH only exacerbates the already difficult problem of squeezing the traffic information into the existing arrangement of radio channel bandwidths. These problems are by no means insuperable, but they do tend to restrict radio interconnection of NNI signals to the lower end of the SDH range e.g. up to STM-2 at present. This inability to match the transmission capacity of optical fibres will progressively force radio based systems out of the core areas of transmission networks, and into the more peripheral areas. In particular, it is likely that radio based SDH equipment will be heavily used for access duties.

The reduction in cost that accompanies a network element with restricted connectivity results not only from simpler hardware, but also from simpler control software. This is somewhat surprising at first sight, as it has often been said that SDH does not really make economic sense without a large measure of software control over all the network element functionality and, in particular, that of routeing flexibility. However, the complexity of even relatively simple SDH network elements leads to a situation where control of complete networks rapidly escalates unless some restrictions are put on the traffic routeing complexity. In short, every additional piece of traffic routeing flexibility is a potential network control headache.

The general problem of control of a whole SDH network, notwithstanding the traffic routeing problem, is almost impossible if it is composed of network elements from different manufacturers, which do not have some form of common control interface. Before we can arrive at such a universal interface, we must first standardise, to a large extent, on the functions which each of the network elements actually perform. This is where the network element functional standards, ITU-T G.781/2/3, come in. These are the recommendations

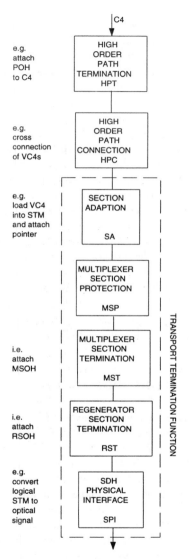

Figure 1.21   Fragment of an SDH network element broken down into atomic functions according to ITU-T G.783

which describe how the functionality of a network element can be decomposed into the basic 'atomic' elements of functionality, together with how such atomic functions may be combined and thereafter exchange both traffic and control information. (See Figure 1.22.)

The rules for combination of these atomic functions enable a variety of network elements to be synthesised, with differing traffic capacities and routeing capabilities. Indeed, one of the current problems is the potentially large number of different ways a comformant network element can be constructed. It is rather difficult for software based control systems to cope with this variety and hence there are efforts in several standards bodies (notably ETSI) to standardise on a more restricted range of network element functionalities. G.781/2/3 were created primarily to describe different types of drop and insert multiplexers; however, the general principles and indeed much of the detail are just as applicable to LTEs and large cross connects. Moreover, the formalism required to describe complete SDH networks was produced very much with this same functional decomposition in mind. We shall see, later, how these atomic functions may be paired between network elements on opposite sides of a network to produce a complete traffic path, that is sufficiently well defined for a computer to recognise.

1.5   Control and management

Control and management within any type of telecommunications network (not just an SDH one) can best be viewed in terms of a series of layers. (See Figure 1.23.) At the lowest level, there is internal control of an individual network element, which performs internal housekeeping functions and deals in alarm and control primitives. ITU-T G.783 has rigorously defined a minimum set of control and alarm primitives for each of the SDH atomic functions, and these are the basis of all SDH management. However, beyond this ITU-T G.784 describes how such primitive information should be processed and ordered to produce derived information such as error rates etc., which is stored in logs of defined duration, and reported at set intervals etc. At the lowest level, some of this information may look

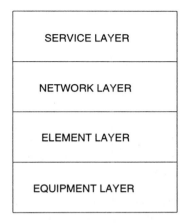

SERVICE LAYER	Management of a service e.g. 2Mbit/s leased lines, ISDN service
NETWORK LAYER	Management of paths across a complete network requires an understanding of network topology
ELEMENT LAYER	Management of individual network elements e.g. multiplexers and cross connects
EQUIPMENT LAYER	Internal management of the network elements

Figure 1.22   Network management layering for the control of telecoms networks and services

rather different to that specified in G.783/4 etc.; however, the internal network element control system takes these and from them synthesises the information that is required by the next level in the management hierarchy i.e. the element manager.

The element manager is a piece of software which can control many individual network elements (usually in the range 10–1000), but it can only control them as individual elements and does not have any view of the traffic relationships between them. Usually it is located remote from the elements it is controlling and more often than not it runs on some form of workstation. The interface between the element manager and the network elements is an obvious area for standardisation, as without this there is little chance of a single element manager controlling network elements from more than one manufacturer. Despite the progress that has been made in rigorously describing the network element atomic functions, it has still proved very difficult to agree on a software description of them. The approach adopted in ITU-T, ANSI, and ETSI has been to describe complete network elements as collections of 'objects' in line with the rules of 'object orientated' programming.

The idea is that an object is a software entity that has both attributes and behaviour. External stimuli (i.e. information, commands etc.) trigger an object to behave in a certain way e.g. change its attributes, transmit information, commands etc. The claim is that a standardised object could be looked upon as the software equivalent of a hardware integrated circuit. One of the biggest areas of disagreement in generating an agreed standard set of SDH objects is the questions of whether an object should represent a piece of functionality or whether an object should represent a (small) piece of hardware. Although ITU-T G.783 functionally decomposes SDH equipment, its says almost nothing on the way such atomic functions are split or combined in any real hardware implementation. The current view within both ITU-T and ETSI is that the set of objects (collectively known as the 'Information Model') should present both a functional and a physical view of the network element that they represent. ETSI, in particular, is making good progress in generating a model along these lines.

Not only is it necessary to have a standardised information model, so that the network element and element manager can understand one another, it is also necessary to have an agreed message set to go with it. Fortunately, this flows reasonably easily from the definition of the objects themselves. However, the existence of such a message set then leads to the requirement for an agreed information protocol stack with which to transport it. For information transferred between a network element direct to its element manager, ITU-T G.773 details several allowed protocol stacks, which split into two groups, those which have a full 7 layer structure and those which have a 'short stack', where layers 4, 5, and 6 are absent. Most observers favour the use of the heavier, but more flexible, seven layer protocol stacks for SDH networks, while the 'short' stacks are more appropriate for PDH equipment for which it is more difficult to justify the burden of the additional layers.

Not only are there defined protocol stacks for information transfer direct from element manager to network element, but there is also a defined protocol stack for information transfer between individual network elements. In general, the majority of information transfer between network elements is actually information arising from an

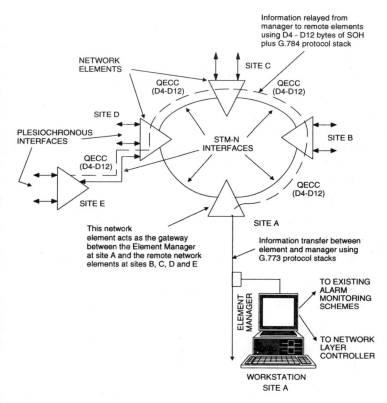

Figure 1.23 Control channels and protocols within an SDH network

element manager, which is being relayed by an intermediate network element to a more remote element. (See Figure 1.24.) This flow of management information amongst network elements, element managers and yet more managers at the network and service levels gives rise to the concept of a Telecommunications Management Network (TMN).

The main recommendation concerning the TMN is ITU-T M.30, which attempts to define a series of interfaces between different management entities in such a network. It is not confined purely to

SDH networks, but SDH networks will probably be the first to implement an M.30 style TMN.

1.6 SDH based networks

An SDH based network can be viewed as the transmission bedrock which supports all other terrestrial telecommunications services. (See Figure 1.25.) As already mentioned, the main advantages of such a network are the ease and precision with which the available network bandwidth can be partitioned amongst the higher layer services, together with accurate monitoring of the quality of the transmission links. Despite this, the control and management of complete networks of the size operated by BT, France Telecom, or DBP is a difficult problem, which requires some degree of standardisation in the way such networks are functionally decomposed, in much the same way as the individual network elements have already been functionally decomposed into their atomic elements by ITU-T G.783.

The basic idea behind the functional decomposition described in ITU-T G.sna1 is that a transport network can be stratified into a

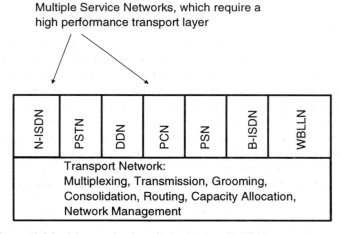

Figure 1.24   Managed transmission network; SDH network as a bearer for other services

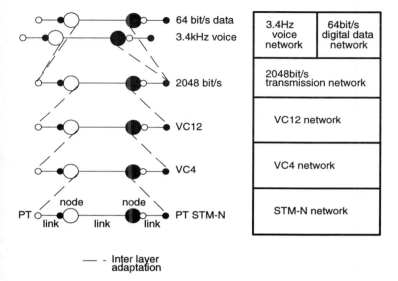

Figure 1.25 Layering and client server relationships between the layers of an SDH network

number of layers. Each layer provides a service to the layer above it, and is, in turn, a client of the layer below it, in much the same way as the ISO seven layer information transfer model consists of layers which participate in client-server relationships with their vertical nearest neighbours. (See Figure 1.26.) This layering within an SDH network could be viewed as a subdivision of ISO layer 1. As an example of a non-SDH client-server relationship in a transport network, consider Figure 1.27, which shows a 64kbit/s circuit being a client of the 2Mbit/service layer i.e. the 2Mbit/s layer, which can be viewed as a 2Mbit/s network, transports the 64kbit/s circuit between its desired end points. In order to do this, the 2Mbit/s layer will probably call upon the services of the 8Mbit/s layer, and so on up to the 140Mbit/s layer. The SDH counterpart of this simple PDH example is slightly more complicated in that the transport layers are divided between those concerned with end to end networking (i.e. the Path Layers) and those concerned with transport between each pair of

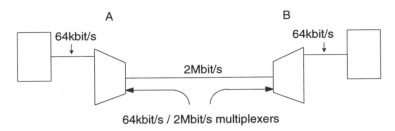

64kbit/s / 2Mbit/s multiplexers

Figure 1.26   64kbit/s circuit making use of a 2Mbit/s service in order to get from A to B

SDH network elements along the route (i.e. the STM section layer). As an additional complication, there are two path layers, the lower order paths consisting of VC1s, VC2s or VC3s, and the higher order paths, which are VC4s in CEPT countries, but could also be VC3s. (See Figure 1.28.)

Usually when a client layer makes use of a server, it is necessary to adapt the client signal to a form suitable for transport by the server layer. (See Figure 1.29.) Examples of this 'adaptation' function are the plesiochronous 'stuffing' which occurs when a 2Mbit/s channel is multiplexed into an 8Mbit/s one, or the progressive change in a VC12 pointer value to accommodate a small frequency mismatch with the VC4 into which it is being loaded. The adaptation function is only one of the network atomic functions that have been described in G.sna1, and it is indeed fortunate that G.sna1 has been developed in full recognition of the contents of G.782/783 because many of the equipment and network atomic functions are identical.

G.sna1 not only describes a series of vertical client-server relationships for an SDH transport network, it also gives a structure to each of the individual layers. Each layer can be viewed as a network in its own right, which can be partitioned into a series of subnetworks. (See Figure 1.30.) These subnetworks are connected together by 'link connections', and can, if necessary, be further subdivided into yet smaller subnetworks. The logical place to stop this process is where a whole subnetwork is completely contained within one network element. As an example consider a VC12 cross connect. The switching matrix (connectivity function) within this element could be con-

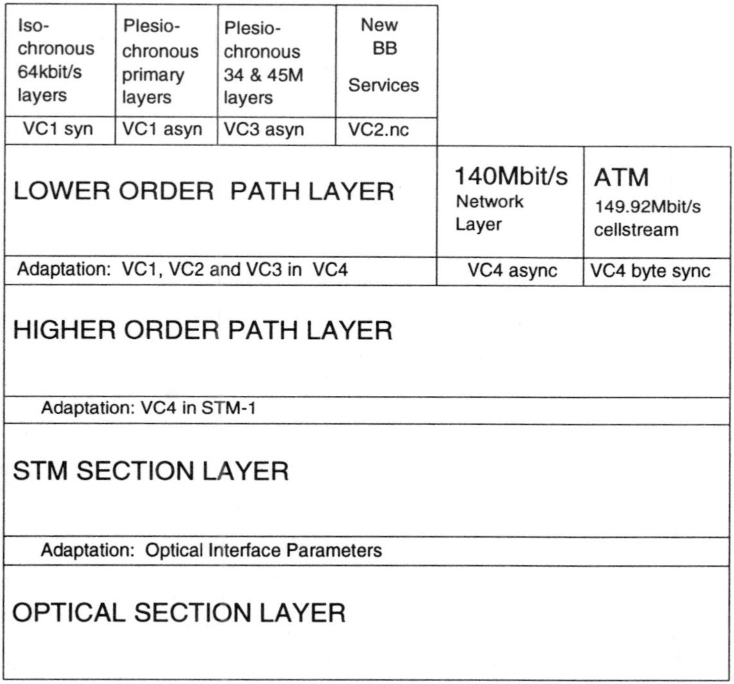

Iso-chronous 64kbit/s layers	Plesio-chronous primary layers	Plesio-chronous 34 & 45M layers	New BB Services		
VC1 syn	VC1 asyn	VC3 asyn	VC2.nc		
LOWER ORDER PATH LAYER				140Mbit/s Network Layer	ATM 149.92Mbit/s cellstream
Adaptation: VC1, VC2 and VC3 in VC4				VC4 async	VC4 byte sync
HIGHER ORDER PATH LAYER					
Adaptation: VC4 in STM-1					
STM SECTION LAYER					
Adaptation: Optical Interface Parameters					
OPTICAL SECTION LAYER					

Figure 1.27   Layering in an SDH transport network

sidered as a subnetwork, which is capable of making VC12 layer subnetwork connections from one port to another. (See Figure 1.31.)

To connect one of these VC12s to another cross connect, a link connection is now required, which will need to make use of the VC4 and STM layers. This concatenation of subnetwork and link connections across the VC12 path layer network begins and ends at the points where the VC12 is created and destroyed, namely the path termination points. It is at these points that the VC12 POH is added or removed, exposing only the C12 Synchronous Container. This same path termination function is recognised in both G.783 and G.sna1 and it is located immediately next to the adaptation function

Link connection in client layer

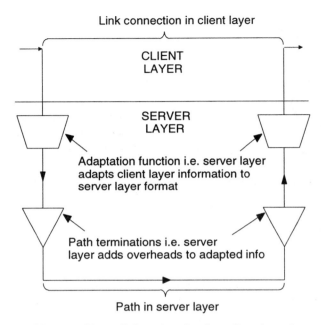

Figure 1.28   Handling a link connection in a client layer by a path in a server layer

described above. On the assumption that the C12 in question is carrying a 2Mbit/s circuit, then the combination of adaptation functions, termination functions and the chain of subnetwork and link connections in the VC12 layer have succeeded in transporting this 2Mbit/s circuit between the two end points of a single 2Mbit/s link connection. (See Figure 1.31.) From this point, the above analysis can now be repeated in the 2Mbit/s layer, where the particular 2Mbit/s circuit cited above will probably be found to be serving as part of a link connection for a number of 64kbit/s circuit. (See Figure 1.27.)

This formal description of an SDH network opens up the prospect of real control and management of large networks consisting of network elements from several manufacturers. The pairing of path termination functions on opposite sides of a network, together with a similar operation on the same functions in the STM layer, allows a

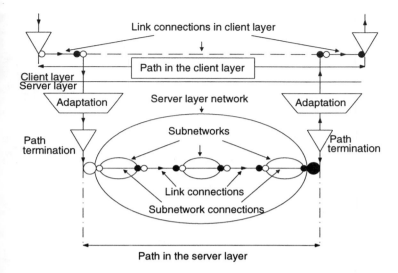

Figure 1.29   Partitioning of a transport layer network into a series of subnetworks

PTO to accurately monitor the service which the SDH network is delivering, and to pin-point those network elements responsible for any poor performance. Beyond that, the SDH network model greatly facilitates management of the all important traffic flexibility points i.e. those subnetworks which consist of an electronically controllable connectivity function.

1.6.1 SDH network topologies

Once again traffic routeing flexibility, its control and physical distribution within an SDH network, are the most important influences on the topologies proposed for the deployment of SDH equipment. The most obvious manifestations of this are the drop and insert ring topologies that are finding favour in the former junction areas of PTO networks. (See Figure 1.32.)

   The idea behind a drop and insert ring is that the ring structure can give a high degree of protection against cable cuts etc. due to its

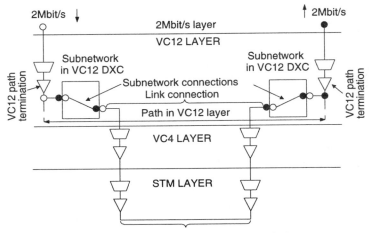

Figure 1.30 Use of two VC12 cross connects to produce a path within the VC12 layer

potential for routeing traffic either way round the ring. In fact, one of the biggest advantages, in control terms, of this topology is the limitation on the re-routeing possibilities for any traffic affected by a cable break. Anything more complicated than a simple clock-wise/counter-clockwise routeing decision requires up to date knowl-edge of a rather more extensive portion of an SDH network than just a simple ring. The nodes of such a ring are populated by drop and insert multiplexers which have a restricted traffic routeing flexibility that is tailored to the requirements of a ring. This gives a relatively low cost ring implementation, which nevertheless, when viewed as a single entity, appears as a restricted form of a cross connect. The versatility of drop and insert rings also extends to drop and insert chains, which can be considered as a 'flattened' version of a conven-tional ring. (See Figure 1.33.) Beyond this, a ring can also be made from a chain of drop and insert multiplexers, whose ends have been joined by an SDH line system. The main problem with implementing this type of ring, at least in the junction area, is that the existing layout of cables and ducts usually takes the form of a star, which formerly

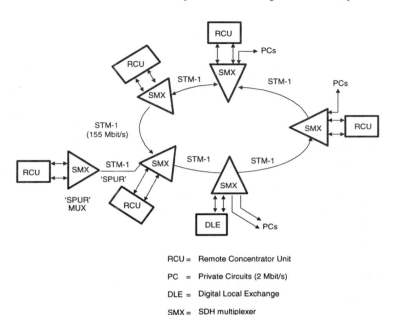

RCU = Remote Concentrator Unit

PC = Private Circuits (2 Mbit/s)

DLE = Digital Local Exchange

SMX = SDH multiplexer

Figure 1.31 SDH multiplexers deployed in a drop and insert ring

linked the old analogue local exchanges to their district switching centre. In many cases, a partial physical ring can be created by a small extension of the existing cable pattern. This can be supplemented by creating a logical ring when existing cables are laid in a star arrangement, although this obviously affords less protection against cable breaks. (See Figure 1.34.) Finally, it is sometimes possible to produce a physical ring by linking some of the ring nodes with microwave radio rather than optical fibre.

Outside of the former junction areas, i.e. within the transmission core of the average PTO network, the normal topology advocated is that of a mesh of cross connects, interconnected by point to point transmission systems. (See Figure 1.35.) For this application, the SDH transmission systems, like their PDH counterparts, require almost no routeing flexibility. This is more than compensated by the

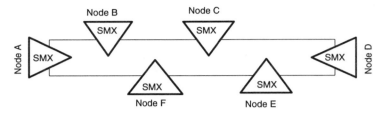

Figure 1.32   Drop and insert chain produced by 'flattening' a conventional drop and insert ring

cross connects, which provide complete traffic routeing flexibility at the VC4 and VC12 (and possibly other VCs as well), although not usually in the same network element. Used in this way, cross connects can be viewed as electronic replacements for the present day digital distribution frames. The benefits of this deployment of flexibility are alleged to be those of easier traffic path provisioning and a fast, efficient scheme for restoring failed paths which requires the absolute minimum of standby transmission capacity. This last benefit is heavily dependent on the control that is exercised over the cross connects, and here there are some potential problems.

The main problem is that of database integrity. With a network of meshed cross connects, when a transmission link fails, the path restoration action will usually involve re-routeing all the affected paths through several alternative cross connects. In order to do this efficiently the network control system must rapidly command simultaneous switching actions in all of these cross connects, which usually implies that the control system has a pre-determined plan of action which is based on the spare bandwidth that is thought to be available on the relevant transmission links and cross connects. Unfortunately the integrity of the control system's database may have been compromised because of other recent reconfiguration. This problem escalates rapidly as the number of cross connects in a network increases.

There are several potential solutions to this problem. One is simply not to use the cross connects for protection against transmission failures, and instead rely on transmission systems having 1+1 or 1:N protection. In this case the cross connects are used solely for off-line management of the network's transmission capacity. This is often

PLESIOCHRONOUS

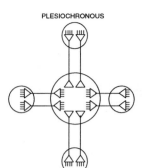

SDH DROP & INSERT
IMPLEMENTATION
PHYSICAL STAR - LOGICAL RING

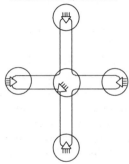

NEW LINKS PRODUCE
PHYSICAL RING

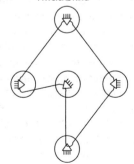

Figure 1.33 Comparison of topologies possible with PDH and SDH multiplexers

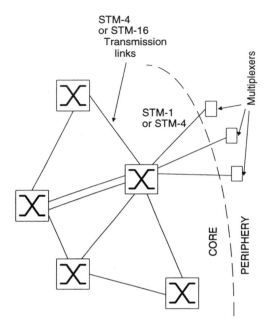

Figure 1.34   Example of core transmission network topology that relies on cross connects for flexibility

called 'Facilities Management' in North America. An alternative is to deploy the cross connects in a rather more bounded topology than the completely free mesh topology assumed above. A limiting case of this idea is to deploy them in a ring. The restriction on routeing choices imposed by such a topology greatly eases the control problem, albeit with some significant increase in the standby line transmission capacity that must be available to allow a traffic re-route. Although the present day cost of such standby capacity is considerable, it has already been observed that raw point to point transmission capacity is the one thing that will continue to become cheaper, in real terms, for some time to come, hence this option may look increasingly attractive.

   Finally, the most interesting possibility is to endow a network of cross connects with a signalling system that will allow it to dynamically set up and clear down paths, in much the same way as a PSTN sets up conventional 64kbit/s circuits. The idea is that the intelligence required for this type of operation resides, not in a single large network manager, but, like the PSTN, distributed throughout the whole network. This greatly reduces the database integrity problem, and should operate quickly enough to meet the criteria for fast restoration of failed paths, as well as facilitating other operations such as rapid provision of bandwidth (i.e. bandwidth 'on demand') in response to requests from the client services of the SDH network.

1.6.2 Deployment strategies

There are three main strategies for the deployment of SDH equipment:

1. Synchronous islands.
2. 'Thin' overlay networks.
3. Ad hoc deployment dictated by traffic growth etc.

Many PTOs are currently using the ad hoc approach and deploying the latest STM-16 (2.5Gbit/s) transmission systems, not so much because they conform to the SDH standards, but because they offer higher transmission capacities than any available PDH systems. Even so, most PTOs which are doing this are intending to eventually fill in the gaps between these ad hoc deployments so as to create an SDH overlay network.

The idea behind the 'thin overlay' strategy is to rapidly deploy a limited SDH capability across the whole of a PTO network so that a small nucleus of key business customers can be offered the benefits of SDH as soon as possible. This type of deployment is most appropriate to networks where the important communities of interest are geographically widely dispersed.

The synchronous 'island' deployment strategy assumes that the most important communities of interest are geographically concentrated, and that each one can start to benefit from SDH without necessarily having full SDH connectivity with similar communities of interest. The classic example here is that of the financial community in the City of London. With the passage of time, a synchronous island would normally increase in geographical size, so as to eventually coalesce with other islands. Long before this, they would probably be interconnected by an emerging SDH trunk network.

1.7 Impact of broadband standards

As an ISO layer 1 transport standard, intended for building the PTO's backbone transmission networks, SDH currently has no real rivals. The nearest thing to a competitor that has emerged so far is Asynchronous Transfer Mode (ATM), and its adoption was strongly favoured by several European PTOs. However, ATM, as with most of the other popular broadband standards, comes under the heading of 'Fast Packet' technologies.

As with all packet transfer techniques, it tends to be better at transporting bursts of traffic, rather than the largely constant traffic load presented by the PSTN. On top of this, ATM is a standard that is really aimed at the problem of rationalising the switching machines required for the complete range of telecom services, rather than producing a bedrock transport network. In theory, it is capable of doing this, but at present, commercial implementations of ATM switches are thought to be at least five years away. In the meantime, SDH equipment will be deployed to such an extent that it will be impossible to dislodge it from its position as the workhorse of all PTO transport networks.

ATM switches, when they are introduced, will appear to the SDH network as yet one more client service which needs SDH transmission bandwidth allocated to it. As the operational problems of running a cell based service are progressively overcome, we can expect an increasing proportion of the SDH transmission network capacity to be routed to these ATM switches.

Besides ATM, there are several other Fast Packet techniques that have been proposed, which are either already available, or promised soon. They are all aimed at satisfying the business communities' requirements for wide area data transmission, and, in particular, the burgeoning requirement for LAN interconnect. In view of what was said in Section 1.1 about the needs of business customers driving

PTOs to install SDH networks, it is essential to determine whether the introduction of these other techniques will render SDH superfluous.

1.7.1 Frame Relay

The current front runner in the Fast Packet standards is Frame Relay. This is actually a network access protocol which, like X.25, says nothing about the interfaces between internal nodes in the network i.e. it is only a UNI standard, and has no counterpart to the SDH NNI. The best way to view Frame Relay is as a supercharged version of X.25, which is designed to handle the high speed (i.e. up to 2Mbit/s and beyond) but bursty LAN interconnect traffic that X.25 is far too slow for.

The reason that a Frame Relay network can deliver much higher throughputs than an X.25 network is that it uses a very 'lightweight' protocol, which removes the majority of the X.25 processing burden from the network access nodes and, in all probability, in the internal nodes as well.

In particular Frame Relay provides no end to end error recovery, but instead leaves this function to the ISO transport layer protocols (layer 4), which are assumed to be installed in the customer's equipment, rather than the network access nodes. This makes a Frame Relay network heavily dependent on the quality, especially the error rate, of the underlying transport network, which is where SDH comes to the rescue. The high quality ISO layer 1 service provided by SDH is exactly what the lightweight layer 2 protocol of Frame Relay requires if it is to avoid excessive frame retransmissions from the CPE.

This symbiotic arrangement should, in theory, result in a peaceful coexistence; however, the issue is, as ever, clouded by that of tariffing. If a 2Mbit/s circuit, delivered by SDH, is tariffed sufficiently attractively, then, for many private networks, it may be cheaper to run multiple, point to point 2Mbit/s links, rather than obtain the same connectivity from a Frame Relay network. However, experience to date with quasi Frame Relay networks in North America indicates that this will not be the case, and that Frame Relay and SDH will not compete directly for business traffic.

1.7.2 Switched Multimegabit Data Service (SMDS)

Like Frame Relay, SMDS is another broadband wide area service aimed at achieving economies in transmission bandwidth by statistical multiplexing of bursty data traffic. Rather than being a standard in its own right, SMDS refers to a service which is delivered over a wide area network, which employs the DQDB standard for its access protocol. Originally it was targeted at rather higher bandwidths than Frame Relay i.e. 1.5Mbit/s to 45Mbit/s, but now it too is being repositioned to serve the LAN interconnect market. SMDS encapsulates the customer's data in trains of fixed sized cells, which are then relayed, via the SMDS switches, to their destinations. Like Frame Relay, SMDS needs a high quality layer 1 service, in order that the number of cell corruptions is kept to a minimum. Once again, there is a technical sybiosis between SMDS and SDH, and they will only be in direct conflict if there are inconsistencies in some tariff structures.

1.7.3 Fibre Distributed Data Interface (FDDI)

FDDI is a high speed LAN that was designed for private operators who were able to install their own cables. However, the extension of the original interface definitions to incorporate single mode, as well as multimode, optical fibre has increased the maximum ring circumference to 100km. This potentially brings it into conflict with PTO provided MANs e.g. SMDS. This is even more likely now that there are proposed mappings of the full FDDI 125Mbit/s signal into a VC4, so that PTO transmission facilities can be used to bridge those spans where the private operator cannot run his own fibre. Unfortunately, there are some problems relating to the maximum delay that an FDDI ring can withstand. As it is this minimum ring delay which limits the size of an FDDI ring, care must be taken in the routeing of the VC4 in order that this extra delay does not significantly reduce the maximum ring size. In short, because of the self-contained nature of the FDDI standard, together with its rather narrow targeting as a high-speed LAN, as opposed to MAN or WAN, we expect no competition at all between SDH and FDDI.

1.8 Future technologies

Equipment which implements the SDH standards will be strongly influenced by the capabilities and cost of the enabling technologies. This section reviews the impact on both equipment, and the standards themselves, of some of these developments.

1.8.1 Integrated circuits

The unrelenting trend to faster, smaller and cheaper traffic handling ICs (ASICs) obviously leads to cheaper network element hardware. This, in turn, will eventually lead to the introduction of SDH equipment onto the premises of business customers. The trend to higher functional integration will probably lead to changes in PTO premises design because of increased heat dissipation in a given volume of rack space.

1.8.2 Optical interfaces

Very low cost SDH optical interfaces are expected to produce the long awaited shift in PTO station cabling from coaxial copper to optical fibres. There are several advantages to optical interconnection e.g. relatively long range, no crosstalk, physically small calling volume. However, perhaps the biggest advantage is the future proofing which results from the fact that an optical interconnect cable can, within reasonable limits, carry any bit rate. Besides enabling the reuse of cables that would be difficult to reuse otherwise, it also reduces the problem of successive layers of interconnect cables physically preventing the withdrawal of the older, disused, cables that they are burying.

1.8.3 Optical amplifiers

Erbium doped fibre amplifier technology has made great strides in the last three years. By using such amplifiers at both ends of an optical link, it is possible to greatly increase the maximum distance between transmitter and receiver, with distances up to 300km being predicted for links that employ low loss optical fibre cables (e.g. present day optical links at 565Mbit/s which can typically span 40-70km). This great increase in span capability holds out the prospect of interconnecting the majority of large centres of population in Europe by unrepeatered line systems i.e. the line systems consist of two LTEs plus cable, without any intervening simple repeaters. (Drop and insert repeaters are a different case, as they are deployed to drop and insert traffic, rather than solely to boost the amplitude of the optical signals.) The resulting extinction of conventional line system repeaters means that the SDH RSOH in the STMs will eventually become redundant for terrestrial systems.

In addition to this, there is also the future proofing that results from replacing a conventional, electronically regenerating repeater with a repeater that merely amplifies the transiting optical signals. Optical amplifiers are largely bit rate independent, hence it should be possible to upgrade the capacity of a line system by merely changing the LTEs, and not the repeaters. This idea is particularly exciting for undersea line systems where a major part of the total system cost lies in the repeaters. Up till now, these have always been constrained to operate at a fixed bit rate.

1.8.4 Optical switching

The use of optical switching, together with various forms of Wavelength Division Multiplexing (WDM), will lead to a requirement for yet another layer in the SDH hierarchy beyond the STM section layer. Real high speed optical switching, together with wavelength conversion, is still some way in the future, hence there is no pressure to extend SDH at present.

1.8.5 Memory and processing power

As soon as it becomes economically feasible, more memory and processing power will be installed in individual SDH network elements. The use of this capability to support ever larger blocks of software will result in the average software download action transferring ever more bytes, thus putting a strain on the Embedded Communication Channels (ECCs) that are built into the STM SOHs. There is also the chance that larger quantities of more sophisticated element control software will result in more management traffic between network elements and between elements and their controllers, further increasing the load on the existing ECCs. Thus, at some point in the future it is very likely that the SDH standards will have to be altered to expand the capacity of the ECCs beyond their current rates of 192 and 576kbit/s.

1.9 Conclusion

SDH is here to stay as the dominant public network transmission standard of this decade. However, the effects of the full range of SDH standards will probably be felt over a much wider area of telecommunications, because of their general applicability. For example the mere existence of the SDH optical interface specifications will probably lead to their use in a variety of non-SDH applications, simply because there is a dearth of competing standards. Another example is that of the SDH network recommendations which, with relatively little modification, are applicable to a wide variety of non-SDH networks, in particular, plesiochronous networks.

1.10 References

Ash, J.D. and Von Schau, P. (1993) Introduction strategies for SDH, *Telecommunications*, August.

Barratt, M. (1995) Synchronous optical networks harmonise, *Lightwave*, May.

Bellamy, John (1991) *Digital Telephony*, 2nd Edition, Wiley, ISBN 0 471 62056 4.

Cook, T. (1994) SDH: Pointer problems, *Telecommunications*, August.

Ferguson, S. (1991) A common denominator for Broadband, *Telecommunications*, August.

58 References

Ferguson, S.P. (1994) Implications of Sonet and SDH, *Electronics & Communication Engineering Journal*, June.

Flood, J.E. and Cockrane, P. (eds.) (1991) *Transmission Systems,* Peter Peregrinus, ISBN 0 86341 148 7.

Gibbons, D. (1994) SDH: The changing face of transmission, *Telecommunications*, June.

Mathews, M.S. and Newcombe, P.J. (1991) The Synchronous Digital Hierarchy, *IEE Review*, May and June.

Pikkarainen, H. (1994) Strategies and network architecture, *Communications International*, June.

Ross, J.A. (1995) In search of Sonet interoperability, *Lightwave*, January.

Sexton, M.J. (1990) New directions in Transport Networks, *Telecommunications,* October.

Shetty, V. (1993) SDH scores as a powerful bit mover, *Communications International*, June.

Wilson, A. (1995) Quality of service in mixed PDH/SDH networks, *Telecommunications*, February.

Wilson, M.R. (1995) The evolution of synchronous optical networks, *Lightwave*, March.

Wolff, G.A. (1995) Network synchronisation: getting the best out of SDH, *Telecommunications*, January.

2. The Integrated Services Digital Network

2.1 Introduction

The main features of any network can be categorised into the transmission, switching, signalling and control capabilities of the network. All three of these areas in the Public Switched Telephone Network have evolved in different stages and at different rates. However, they have evolved in such a manner as to enable them to converge towards an Integrated Services Digital Network (ISDN) at minimal cost.

Until fairly recently the whole of the Public Switched Telephone Network (PSTN) was based upon analogue transmission and switching techniques. The telephone converts the acoustic waves of the speaker into an electrical signal occupying a bandwidth of the order of 4kHz (300Hz to 3400Hz). This is transmitted over the telephone network in this form to a remote telephone which then reconverts the electrical signals back to acoustic waves. The electrical signals are carried over a copper pair in the local network to a switching node.

Switching at the local exchange used space division techniques, originally Strowger and later crossbar and reed relay, on the baseband signal in order to concentrate traffic onto junction routes to main network switching centres which were again of the space switching type. Trunk routes then interconnected these main network switching centres and it is on these high capacity routes that we first saw the introduction of Frequency Division Multiplexing (FDM) techniques which required separate go and return channels.

During the late 60s and early 70s digital techniques began to emerge to replace the analogue techniques. First we saw the introduction of digital transmission to carry the analogue telephony signal. The 4kHz analogue signal is sampled at 8kHz and the resulting samples quantised into 256 levels according to the A law logarithmic code and encoded into 8 bit bytes to produce a rate of 64kbit/s. Thirty of these channels are then assembled, along with a 64kbit/s signalling channel and a 64kbit/s framing channel, into a 2048kbit/s system. Digital transmission has gradually become more cost effective to such an extent that a higher order TDM structure has been established at rates up to and above 565Mbit/s and it is now the normal method of provision.

In the same way that technology had made the use of digital techniques in the transmission field more attractive, so digital exchanges became cheaper to implement and maintain. These digital exchanges are designed to handle the 64kbit/s transmission channels transparently using both space and time division digital switches. These digital main network exchanges together with the digital transmission form what is known as the Integrated Digital Network (IDN). In the UK the first digital exchanges were put into the main network in 1980 and now all the main network exchanges are digital and fully interconnected by digital transmission routes and by the middle of 1991 half of the local exchanges were digital.

The introduction of digital transmission and digital exchanges was complemented by the introduction of common channel message based signalling systems, where messages relating to different connections are statistically interleaved on a common channel. CCITT (now ITU-T) signalling system No. 7 is the system defined for use between switching nodes.

The conversion from the analogue signal produced by the standard telephone to a digital signal occupying 64kbit/s is now occurring at the front of the local exchange. Therefore connections across the main network between local exchanges are able to provide:

1.   A completely transparent 64kbit/s channel.
2.   A powerful digital signalling capability.
3.   The flexibility provided by stored program control exchanges.

These facilities have been provided in order to support telephony in the most economical way possible. They have, however, set the scene for the development of what has become known as the ISDN, Integrated Services Digital Network.

2.2 International standards for ISDN

The principles guiding the evolution of the public telephone network from the analogue to the digital environment were established within ITU-T in the 1970s. However towards the end of this decade ITU-T recognised the high level of interest in evolving this network further to establish the concept of an Integrated Services Digital Network (ISDN). An initial series of recommendations, the I-Series, were first agreed and published at the end of the 1980–84 plenary period. These were further enhanced during the 1984–88 plenary period resulting in a full set of recommendations being published in the Blue Book and during this plenary period further enhancements have been made and published in 1992.

The ITU-T I series recommendations are structured so that new recommendations can easily be included in the appropriate sections. The structure is shown in Figure 2.1 and described in detail in Recommendation I.110. It comprises six main parts as follows:

1.   Part I - General Structure; I.100 series.
2.   Part II - Service Capabilities; I.200 series.
3.   Part III - Overall Network Aspects and Functions; I.300 series.
4.   Part IV - ISDN User/Network Interfaces; I.400 series.
5.   Part V - Internetwork Interfaces; I.500 series.
6.   Part VI - Maintenance Principles; I.600 series.

The recommendations state that ISDNs will be based on the concepts developed for telephony IDNs and may evolve by progressively incorporating additional functions and network features, including those of any other dedicated networks such as circuit switching and packet switching for data, so as to provide for existing and new services. As far as practicable, new services introduced into ISDN should be arranged to be compatible with the 64kbit/s switched digital connections, although later enhancements may include bit rates higher and lower than this, this also includes an element of packet switching. The network will contain intelligence for the purpose of providing service features, maintenance and network management functions. The I.100 series recommendations therefore

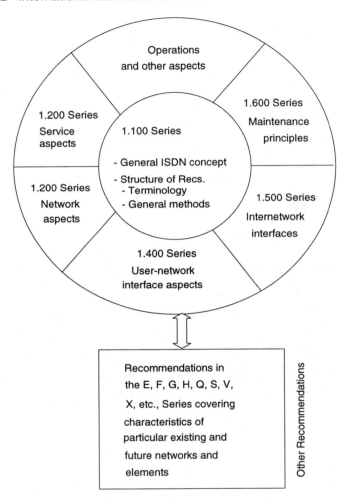

Figure 2.1 Structure of CCITT I. Series Recommendations

describes the general structure of the recommendations, a vocabulary and a description of ISDNs which include the framework for providing additional packet mode bearer services.

The majority of the current I series recommendations are on what is called narrowband ISDN based upon 64kbit/s rates; however during the last few years a lot attention has been given to what is called a Broadband ISDN. In Part I of the recommendations there is also a recommendation (I.121) which describes the Broadband aspects of an ISDN, giving significant details of the main parameters of such a network which will be based upon asynchronous transfer mode (ATM) techniques. These aspects will be discussed in more detail later.

2.3 ISDN services aspects

When we refer to services in the ISDN context what is meant are the telecommunication services offered by a network operator, or service provider, and which are accessed by users either at an ISDN interface or within a terminal connected to the ISDN. The telecommunication services are the products which are supported by the ISDN as such and there are various categories of telecommunication services supported by the ISDN.

The ITU-T Recommendations on telecommunication services to be offered by an ISDN appear in the I.200 series of Recommendations, and the first of these, Recommendation I.210, defines the general principles and categorisation of services. The ITU-T has developed a hierarchical structure for the definition of services in the ISDN because of the wide range of services likely to be offered. There are two main categories of telecommunication services, bearer and teleservices, to both of which can be added a third category of supplementary services.

2.3.1 Bearer services

Bearer services supported by an ISDN provide the capability for transferring information between ISDN user/network interfaces and involve only low-layer functions (layers 1 to 3 in the protocol stack).

Customers may choose any set of high-layer protocols for their communications and the ISDN does not necessarily ascertain compatibility at these layers between customers.

An example of a bearer service is a switched 64kbit/s circuit mode unrestricted service.

Bearer services are characterised by a set of low-layer attributes and these are classified into three categories:

1.   Information transfer attributes.
2.   Access attributes.
3.   General attributes, including operation and commercial attributes.

The following circuit-mode bearer services have been defined in the 1988 recommendations :

1.   64kbit/s unrestricted, 8kHz structured.
2.   64kbit/s, 8kHz structured, usable for speech information transfer.
3.   64kbit/s, 8kHz structured, usable for 3.1kHz audio information transfer.
4.   Alternate speech, 64kbit/s unrestricted, 8kHz structured.
5.   2 × 64kbit/s unrestricted, 8kHz structured.
6.   384kbit/s unrestricted, 8kHz structured.
7.   1536kbit/s unrestricted, 8kHz structured.
8.   1920kbit/s unrestricted, 8kHz structured.

The following packet-mode bearer services have been identified:

1.   Virtual call and permanent virtual circuit.
2.   Connectionless (for further study).
3.   User signalling (for further study).

2.3.2 Teleservices

Teleservices provide the full capability for communication by means of terminals, network functions and possibly functions provided by dedicated centres. They involve the standardisation of the higher layer function (layer 4 to 7 in the protocol stack). Examples of teleservices are telephony, teletex, videotex and message handling. Teleservices are characterised by a set of low layer attributes, a set of high layer attributes and operational and commercial attributes.

2.3.3 Supplementary services

The two categories of services that have been described above are referred to as 'basic services'. The basic service is what the customer gets when he asks for a communication capability.

A supplementary service modifies or supplements a basic telecommunication service, for example redirection of calls to another number. Consequently the supplementary service cannot be offered to a customer as a standalone service, and must be offered in association with a basic telecommunication service. It is possible for the same supplementary service to be common to a number of telecommunication services.

The technique for describing supplementary services also uses the attribute method. However, because of the complexity of these supplementary services, the description technique has now also been widened.

The following categories of supplementary service have currently been standardised:

1. Number identification supplementary services; (Recommendation I.251).
2. Call offering supplementary services; (Recommendation I.252).
3. Call completion supplementary services; (Recommendation I.253).
4. Multiparty supplementary services; (Recommendation I.254).
5. 'Community of interest' supplementary services; (Recommendation I.255).
6. Charging supplementary services; (Recommendation I.256).
7. Additional information transfer supplementary services; (Recommendation I.257).

2.4 Network aspects

2.4.1 Network capabilities

The ISDN functional description defines a set of network capabilities which enable bearer services and teleservices to be offered to customers. The services require two different levels of ISDN capabilities: low layer which relate to bearer services and high layer which, together with low layer capabilities, relate to teleservices. By the network capabilities it means all the technology and techniques which are available in the ISDN to support the telecommunication services. This involves the transmission, switching, signalling and control procedures which will exist in various parts of the network, or interconnected networks, involved in supporting a call end to end. These network capabilities are described by various 'connection types', which use the attribute method for this description and are described in Recommendation I.130.

An ISDN connection is a connection established between reference points; thus, it is the physical or logical realisation of an ISDN connection type. Each ISDN connection can be categorised as belonging to a connection type depending on its attributes of information transfer rate, signalling access protocol and performance which are all examples of ISDN connection type attributes. An ISDN connection is composed of connection elements as shown in Figure 2.2, and these concepts provide the basis of a very powerful tool for defining network capability in a rigorous manner to enable interworking, quality of service and performance and routing studies to continue.

Recommendation I.320 describes a protocol reference model for ISDN. It is based on the general principles of layering given in the X.200 series of Recommendations and has been developed to model the information flows, including user information and control information flows to and through an ISDN, and to take into account the separate channel signalling nature of the ISDN. In order to construct the ISDN protocol reference model, a fundamental generic protocol block has been identified and is shown in Figure 2.3.

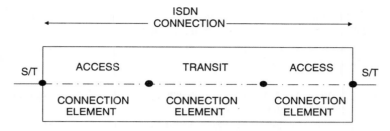

Figure 2.2   Example of connection elements forming an ISDN connection

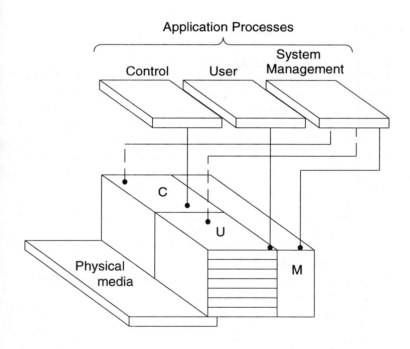

Figure 2.3   Generic protocol block

In particular, the model has been designed so that protocols in an ISDN can be studied in a structured and uniform way with account being taken of the wide range of communication modes and capabilities that can be achieved in the ISDN. For example:

1. Circuit-switched connection under the control of common-channel signalling.
2. Packet-switched communication via the circuit-switched or packet channel.
3. Signalling between users and network-based facilities.
4. End-to-end signalling
5. Combinations of the above in multimedia communications.

2.4.2 ISDN numbering

ISDN numbering and addressing principles are detailed in Recommendation I.330, and Recommendation I.331 (E.164) describes the numbering plan for the ISDN era. It has been agreed that the ISDN numbering plan should be based on and evolve from the existing telephony numbering plan, and therefore the telephony country code is used to identify a particular country. The principles relating to an ISDN number in relation to the user/network reference configuration are that an ISDN number shall be able unambiguously to identify a particular:

1. Physical or virtual interfaces at reference point T, including multiple interfaces.
2. Physical or virtual interfaces at reference point S, including multiple interfaces, for point-to-point configuration.
3. Interfaces at reference point S for multipoint configurations (for example, passive bus).

The ISDN numbering plan, Recommendation I.331, indicates that the international ISDN numbering shall consist of three parts: the country code, the national destination number and the subscriber's number. The country code is used to select the destination country (or geographical area) and varies in length as outlined in Recommendation E.163. The national (significant) number is used to select the destination subscriber. In selecting the destination subscriber, however, it may be necessary to select the destination network. To accomplish this selection, the national (significant) number code field can be seen as comprising a national destination code (NDC) followed by a subscriber's number. The NDC code field will be variable in length dependent upon the requirements of the destination address. It can be used to select a destination network serving the destination subscriber or used in a trunk code format to route the call over the destination network in the called country. The ISDN address can be further expanded by the addition of an ISDN sub-address but this is not part of the network numbering plan. The full structure of the ISDN address is shown in Figure 2.4.

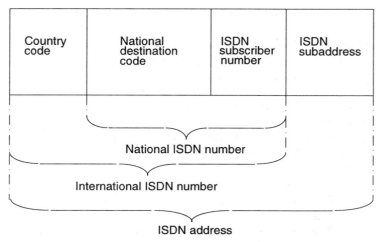

Figure 2.4   Structure of ISDN address

2.5 User/network interfaces

From a user's perspective, an ISDN is completely characterised by the attributes that can be observed at an ISDN user/network interface,

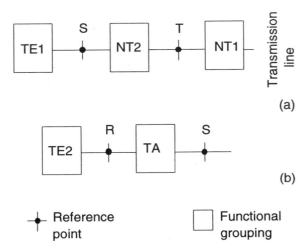

Figure 2.5 Reference configuration for the ISDN interfaces:
(a) S and T; (b) R and S

including physical, electromagnetic, protocol, service capability, maintenance and operation and performance characteristics. Recommendation I.410 lists the requirements of the user/network interface and outlines the scope to be covered in defining the interface characteristics and capabilities.

A key objective in the definition of ISDN has been that a small set of compatible user/network interfaces can economically support a wide range of user applications, equipment and configurations. To assist the definition of ISDN user/network interfaces, the ITU-T has produced a reference model for user/network terminal arrangements, shown in Figure 2.5, which is described in Recommendation I.411.

2.5.1 Reference model

The ISDN user/network interface Recommendations apply to physical interfaces at reference points S and T. At reference point R, physical interfaces in accordance with existing ITU-T Recommendations (for example, X-series and V-series) or physical interfaces not included in ITU-T Recommendations may be used. There is no reference point assigned to the transmission line to the local exchange since an ISDN user/network interface was not envisaged at this location.

In the reference model the NT1 functional grouping includes functions equivalent to layer 1 of the Open Systems Interconnection (OSI) Reference Model and are associated with the proper physical and electromagnetic termination of the network.

The NT2 functional group includes functions equivalent to layer 1 and higher layers of the OSI Reference Model. PABXs, local area networks and terminal controllers are examples of equipment or combinations of equipment that provide NT2 functions.

The terminal equipment (TE) functional grouping includes functions equivalent to layer 1 and higher layers of the OSI Reference Model. Digital telephones, data terminal equipment and integrated work stations are examples of equipment or combinations of equipment which provide TE functions.

Two types of TE have been categorised:

1.   TE1 is an ISDN terminal equipment with an interface that complies with the ISDN user/network interface.
2.   TE2 is a terminal equipment with an interface that complies with non-ISDN interface Recommendations (for example, the ITU-T X-series and V-series interfaces) or interfaces not included in ITU-T Recommendations.

The terminal adapter (TA) functional grouping includes functions equivalent to layer 1 and higher layers of the OSI Reference Model that allow a TE2 terminal to be served by an ISDN user/network interface.

2.5.2 Interface structures

Structures and access capabilities of the ISDN interface are described in Recommendation I.412. A set of channel types has been defined for the ISDN user/network interface.

The main types of channels which are recommended by ITU-T are as follows:

1. B channel. This is a 64kbit/s channel. It carries user information such as voice encoded at 64kbit/s (with 8kHz sampling), or wideband voice, or data information.

2. D channel. This is either 16kbit/s or 64kbit/s. It is primarily intended to carry signalling information for circuit switching by the ISDN. In addition to signalling it may also be used to carry packet-switched data. It uses a layered protocol in accordance with the ITU-T Recommendations I.440, I.441, I.450 and I.451.

3. H channel. This is currently defined at 384kbit/s (the H_0 channel), 1536kbit/s (the H_{11} channel) and 1920kbit/s (the H_{12} channel). The H channel is intended to carry user information for services requiring high information throughput (e.g. fast facsimile, videoconferencing).

Two main interface structures are currently defined at the T and S reference points, a basic rate interface and a primary rate interface. The basic interface structure is composed of two B channels and one D channel, 2B + D. The B channels can be used independently, that is, in different connections at the same time. With the basic interface structure, two B channels and one D channel are always present at the ISDN user/network interface, but one or both B channels, however, may not be supported by the network.

The primary rate interface structures correspond to the primary rate of 1544kbit/s and 2048kbit/s. At the 2048kbit/s primary rate, the interface structure is 30B + D, although one or more of the B channels may not be supported by the network. Channel types at rates higher than 64kbit/s have been defined such as 384kbit/s, 1536kbit/s and 1920kbit/s, and these will also be supported by this interface.

The ITU-T 'brand' name for the basic access interface is I.420 and for the primary rate interface I.421. These recommendations then call up I.430 and I.431 respectively for the layer 1 descriptions, and common recommendations for layer 2 in I.440/1 and layer 3 in I.450/1. The relationship between these recommendations is illustrated in Figure 2.6. The characteristics of these recommendations will now be described in a more detail since they represent an important aspect of the ISDN.

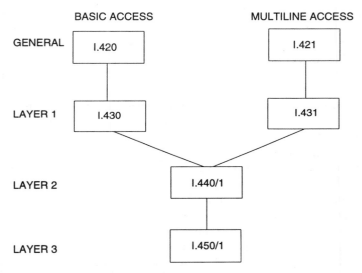

Figure 2.6   Relationship between CCITT Interface
Recommendations

2.5.3 Layer 1 — Basic rate access

The ISDN terminates in the Network Termination 1 (NT1) and the
socket in the NT1 is the regulatory boundary between the Public
Telephone Operator's (PTO) network and the liberalised customers'
premises environment in Europe. (In the United States the local loop
pair is the regulatory boundary and the NT1 is part of this customer's
premises equipment). It provides the layer 1 interface between the
local loop transmission system and the ISDN interface layer 1. Into
this socket is plugged the four wire bus often known as the S or T bus
because it is at the S and T reference points in the ITU-T reference
model. This bus can operate in 2 modes, point to point or point to
multipoint. In the point to point mode one Terminal Equipment (TE)
is connected at the end of up to about 1km of cable. In the point to
multipoint mode up to 8 terminals can be connected in parallel

anywhere along the bus, but the bus length is now limited to 200 metres.

Over this bus passes the two B channels, which are transparent 64kbit/s user channels, as well as the D channel, which is the 16kbit/s signalling channel, and other bits used for miscellaneous purposes such as frame synchronisation. The B channels contain the user data which is switched by the network to provide an end to end transmission service. B channel paths are established by signalling messages in the D channel.

In a multi-terminal situation all terminals have access to the D channel by the use of an access procedure, but each B channel is allocated to a particular terminal during call set-up and is not capable of being shared between terminals.

The line coding used is Alternate Mark Inversion (AMI), with the binary ones encoded as high impedance and the binary zeros as full width pulses. Violations of the coding mark the beginning and end of the layer 1 frames. The physical connection across the interface consists of eight wires, 2 balanced pairs being used for transmission of the layer 1 signals to and from the network and 2 pairs for power feeding which are optional.

Power feeding is also possible over the transmit and receive pairs via the phantom, and may be used to provide power from the network to the terminal in order, for example, to maintain a basic telephone service in the event of local power failure. However to save power fed from the local exchange, both in the local network and the NT1, an activation/deactivation procedure is defined. Deactivation is also provided to reduce electromagnetic radiation.

A connect/disconnect indication is used by layer 2 to determine if a terminal is plugged into the bus. This is necessary as each terminal is given a random, unique identity (its TEI value) by the network. If disconnected the terminal must forget its original identity to prevent duplication when reconnected. The connect/disconnect indication is achieved by monitoring the presence of DC power on the bus.

The layer 1 structure for supporting these functions is shown in Figure 2.7. The dots demarcate those parts of the frame that are independently d.c. balanced. The frame is 48 bits long and lasts for 250µs resulting in a bit rate of 192kbit/s with each bit approximately

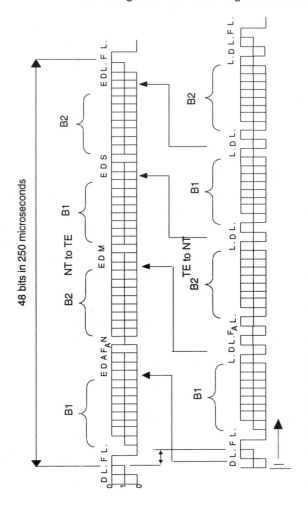

F   =   Framing bit
L   =   DC balancing bit
D   =   D channel bit
E   =   D echo - channel bit
F_A =   Auxiliary framing bit

N   =   Bit set to a binary value N = $\overline{F_A}$ (NT to TE)
B1 =   Bit within B channel 1
B2 =   Bit within B channel 2
A   =   Bit used for activation
S   =   Reserved for future standardisation
M   =   Multiframing bit

Figure 2.7   Basic access interface — layer 1 frame structure

FLAG 01111110	ADDRESS	CONTROL	VARIABLE LENGTH INFORMATION FIELD	FRAME CHECK SEQUENCE	FLAG 01111110
8 BITS	16 BITS	8/16 BITS	MULTIPLE OF 8 BITS	16 BITS	8 BITS

Figure 2.8   Layer 2 structure

5.2µs long. Figure 2.8 shows that there is a 2 bit offset between transmit and receive frames. This is the delay between a frame start at the receiver of a terminal and the frame start of the transmitted signal. It also shows a 10 bit offset between the D channel leaving a terminal, travelling to the NT and being echoed back in the E channel. This 10 bit delay is made up of bus and transmission delays in the NT. A frame contains several L bits, which are balanced bits to prevent a build up of DC on the line.

2.5.4 Layer 1 — Primary rate access

The primary rate access is contained in Recommendation I.431 and is based on existing primary rate PCM multiplex structures, and therefore reflects the two alternate standards of 1544kbit/s and 2048kbit/s. In Europe the 2048kbit/s standard contains 30 B channels, one D channel and a 64kbit/s synchronisation channel. The primary rate access is permanently activated and operates in a point to point manner and therefore does not require any activation/deactivation procedures. An HDB3 line code is used over coaxial or screened balanced pairs and it has a reach capability restricted to 6dB loss.

2.5.5 Layer 2

The layer 2 structure and features are based upon the High Level Data Link Control (HDLC) procedures shown in Figure 2.8 and has the following fields.

1.   The flag acts as a unique delimiter and additional circuitry ensures that the flag pattern never occurs in the bits in the rest of the frame.
2.   The address field is used to indicate whether the message is a command or a response, a signalling or maintenance message and to which channel it refers.
3.   The control field is one or two octets depending on the frame type and carries information that identifies the frame and the layer 2 sequence numbers used for link control.
4.   The information field contains the signalling or level 3 message.
5.   The Cyclic Redundancy Check (CRC) bits enable the receiver to determine whether any errors have been incurred during transmission.

In more detail the address field enables layer 2 multiplexing to be achieved by employing a separate layer 2 address for each LAP in the system. To carry the LAP identity the address field is two octets long and contains a service identifier (SAPI), a terminal identifier (TEI) and a command/response bit. This address identifies the intended receiver of a command frame and the transmitter of a response frame. The address has only local significance and is known only to the two end points using the LAP. No use can be made of the address by the network for routeing purposes and no information about its value will be held outside the layer 2 entity.

The Service Access Point Identifier (SAPI) is used to identify the service that the signalling frame is intended for. Consider the case of I.420 telephones sharing a passive bus with packet terminals. The two terminal types will be accessing different services and possibly different networks. It is possible to identify the service being invoked by using a different SAPI for each service. This gives the network the option of handling the signalling associated with different services in separate modules. In a multi-network ISDN it allows layer 2 routeing to the appropriate network. The value of the SAPI is therefore fixed for a given service.

The Terminal Endpoint Identifier (TEI) takes a range of values that are associated with terminals on the customer's line. In the simplest case each terminal will have a single unique TEI value. It is important that no two TEIs are the same and therefore the network has a special TEI management entity which allocates TEIs on request and ensures their correct use. The values that TEIs can take fall into the ranges:

1.   0–63 for automatic assignment TEIs which are selected by the user.
2.   64–126 for automatic assignment TEIs selected by the network on request.
3.   127 for a global TEI which is used to broadcast information to all terminals within a given SAPI.

The combination of TEI and SAPI identify the LAP and provide a unique layer 2 address. A terminal will use its layer 2 address in all transmitted frames and only frames received carrying the correct address will be processed.

In practice a frame originating from telephony call control has a SAPI that identifies the frame as 'telephony' and all telephone equipment will examine this frame. Only the terminal whose TEI agrees with that carried by the frame will pass it to the layer 2 and layer 3 entities for processing.

2.5.6 Layer 3

The general structure of the layer 3 signalling messages is shown in Figure 2.9. The first octet contains a protocol discriminator which gives the D channel the capability of simultaneously supporting additional communications protocols in the future.

The call reference value in the third octet is used to identify the call with which a particular message is to be associated. Thus a call can be identified independently of the communications channel on which it is supported. This feature is particularly important in connection with incoming call offering procedures on a passive bus arrangement since the channel is only allocated to the called terminal after answer.

The message type code in the fourth octet describes the intention of the message (e.g. a SETUP message to request call establishment). A number of other information elements may be included following

Bits

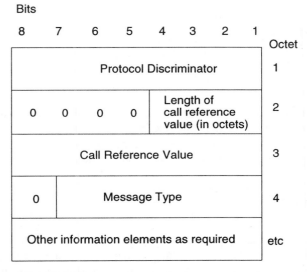

Figure 2.9 Signalling message structure

the message type code in the fourth octet. The exact contents of a message is dependent on the message type; however the coding rules are open ended and in principle it is a simple matter to include additional information elements to satisfy any requirement which may be identified in the future.

In order to make an outgoing call request, a user must send all of the necessary call information (i.e. called party number and supplementary service requests) to the network. Furthermore the user must specify the particular bearer service required for the call (i.e. speech, 64kbit/s unrestricted or 3.1kHz audio) and any terminal compatibility information which must be checked at the destination. This information element may also be used to specify low layer terminal characteristics such as data rate. Where applicable the non-voice application to be used on the call may be specified via the High Layer Compatibility information element (i.e. Group 4 FAX, teletex, videotex or slow scan video).

As well as bearer services and teleservices the ISDN is able to support a range of supplementary services similar to those that are available on PABXs and private networks today. Two generic layer 3 signalling protocols have been specified for the control of supplementary services, namely stimulus and functional signalling procedures.

In stimulus procedures, the terminal is not required to have knowledge of the supplementary service invoked. No records of the supplementary service call state are held by the terminal and layer 3 messages are generated as a result of human action (e.g. pressing a button on the keypad). The operation of the terminal (e.g. display of messages, lighting of lamps etc.) is controlled by the network via layer 3 messages.

The network response to facility requests will be generally in the form of a sequence of IA5 characters in a DISPLAY information element or an in-band tone or announcement. The arrangement of IA5 characters within a DISPLAY information element follows similar rules to the coding of facility requests. Use is made of the separators '*' and '#' so that sequences are machine readable and suitable for display to a human operator.

There are 2 types of stimulus procedures defined, the Keypad Protocol and the Feature Key Management Protocol. Both procedures use the basic call control layer 3 messages, particularly the INFORMATION message, as the transport mechanism for conveying the information between the terminals and the network.

In the Keypad Protocol the user invokes a service by keying in the appropriate sequence of digits delimited by "*" and "#". Only the generic procedure has been specified and the sequence and digits for any given supplementary service is network dependent.

The feature key management protocol requires the network to hold a terminal or service profile for a given terminal. A given terminal is allocated a feature number which is invoked by the terminal signalling that number to the network. This mechanism is very similar to that currently offered on PABXs where the PABX terminals have feature keys which can be programmed to correspond to a particular supplementary service.

In functional signalling, the terminal must have knowledge of the supplementary service being invoked and have the associated signalling protocol implemented. Both the terminal and the network then hold records of the supplementary service call state. The functional protocol is based on using the facility information element conveyed in the basic call control messages if the supplementary service is invoked during call establishment or call clearing and in the FACILITY message otherwise.

For the control of supplementary services which are independent of the active call, the REGISTER message is used. In addition, specific layer 3 messages have also been defined for the function of holding and retrieving a call.

2.6 ISDN applications

The extension of the 64kbit/s digital capability of the network together with the provision of a much more powerful signalling capability to the customer opens up the opportunity for new services and applications together with an improvement in the performance of some existing services.

2.6.1 Digital telephones

A complete digital transmission path will mean that voice quality transmission should be much better with little or no noise and interference from extraneous sources. 64kbit/s transmission will also give the opportunity for using different encoding techniques which provide a wider bandwidth, such as 7kHz speech transmission. Alternatively other techniques could be used to carry more than one voice channel provided they are all destined for the same remote customer. Customers will also see the benefits of digital signalling with fast call set-up and a range of advanced supplementary services. New digital telephones are therefore being developed which will take advantage of these features, in particular the supplementary features such as calling line identity.

2.6.2 Videophone

Video compression techniques now enable video and speech signals
to be compressed into 128kbit/s either using one 64kbit/s channel for
speech and one for video or other combinations that add up to
128kbit/s. Videophone terminals are currently becoming available
throughout the world. Although still expensive they are in their early
days as regard development and prices can be expected to fall in the
future.

2.6.3 Video conferencing terminals

Video conferencing units are already available which support this
service at a number of different rates. Originally developed for use at
2Mbit/s they are now in use at 384kbit/s and 128kbit/s and therefore
can be supported on a standard ISDN basic access interface.

2.6.4 Facsimile terminals

Current analogue facsimile terminals conforming to the Group 3
standard can take between 1 and 3 minutes to transmit an A4 size
page. A new Group 4 standard has been agreed that can exploit the
64kbit/s capability of the ISDN and these terminals are now coming
onto the market. They feature high definition pictures with various
options and are able to transmit an A4 size document in 4 to 5 seconds
over a 64kbit/s channel.

2.6.5 Terminal adapters

Terminals with non-ISDN standard interfaces will continue to exist
for some time. Terminal adapters which support the I.420 interface on
the network side and a range of non-ISDN standard interfaces on the
terminal side are therefore becoming widely available. They support
such interfaces as the standard analogue telephony interface, the V.24
asynchronous interface, various versions of the X.21 interface and the
V.35 leased line interface.

2.6.6 PC terminals

Personal Computers (PC) are currently being enhanced to support access to the ISDN via I.420 interface cards. These are seen as one of the main sources of ISDN terminals because of their ability to support a wide range of different software applications. Cards are therefore available for most makes of PC. Some of the applications that are available are:

1.   Telesurveillance, which is a slow scan TV (SSTV) surveill-ance application, often with the ability to display images from a number of remote cameras. The refresh time for a slow-scan TV frame on ISDN is 3 to 4 seconds. This speed of picture replenishment makes SSTV viable for remote security sur-veillance and for medical diagnostic purposes.
2.   Image database, which is a video image application which provides the means to store scanned and photographed colour images on a central database which can then be accessed via an ISDN link and PC. An initial application is for use by estate agents and travel agents for showing pictures of properties and resorts.
3.   File transfer, these applications allowing files to be transferred from one PC to another via ISDN. Conferencing can also take place between the two users on the file and updates provided to the files in virtually real time. Other conferencing applica-tions can involve speech, text, and or graphical information from a light pen.
4.   PC videophone, which is a future application that is becoming available on a PC similar to the standard videophone terminal. The picture is now displayed on a standard PC screen just as any other application in the windows environment.

2.7 Broadband ISDN

The specification of a Broadband Integrated Services Digital Net-work (B-ISDN) is actively being pursued in international standards bodies, such as ITU-T who adopted accelerated procedures for a number of recommendations in 1990. In Europe this activity is being led by the European Technical Standards Institute (ETSI) whilst in the USA, the American National Standards Institute (ANSI) is the driving force. (Similar standards bodies in Australia, Japan etc. are also contributing to the debate.) Also in Europe the European Commission are supporting a collaborative research programme called RACE (Research into Advanced Communications in Europe) to work towards an Integrated Broadband Communications Network.

The rationales in Europe and the USA in pressing for these standards have been fundamentally different. In the USA pressure has arisen for B-ISDN standards because of the perceived need for high speed local area network (LAN) interconnect to form wide area networks (WANs). As a consequence contributions to these standards are heavily influenced by LAN and WAN procedures. In Europe on the other hand, B-ISDN is seen as an integrated network capable of supporting all services from a few bit/s up to the bandwidths required for high definition TV.

2.7.1 Services

The main need for a broadband network capability comes from two main areas, those services requiring high quality video and those requiring the exchange of large amounts of data such as certain computer automated design applications and the interconnection of high-speed local area networks. In ITU-T two main service categories have been defined in recommendation I.211, interactive services and distributive services. The interactive services are subdivided into conversational services, message services, and retrieval services.

Conversational services are generally bi-directional, although in some circumstances they can be unidirectional and in real time between users, or between a user and a host. Examples include videotelephony, videoconferencing, and high speed data transmission. Message services will offer communication via storage units such as mailbox or message handling functions which not only include speech but also moving pictures and high resolution images. Retrieval services offer user access to information stored centrally and accessed on demand. Examples of these services include film and high resolution images together with audio.

The distributive services are differentiated between those services without individual user presentation control such as the broadcast services for TV and radio, and those with individual user control. The latter includes centrally based services which broadcast cyclical stored information and as a result the user is presented with the information at the beginning of a cycle.

The availability of high bandwidth will enable a number of different types of information to be supported by one service resulting in the development of multimedia services. For example, videotelephony will include audio and video, and also possibly text and graphics. Discussions are now being held to try and establish a limited set of information types and how they may be assembled to provide multimedia services, given that each information type will have different characteristics and require different network performance characteristics.

The emergence of multimedia terminals supporting a number of types of communicating information with a wide variety of bandwidths therefore makes it desirable that a switching and transmission technique (the transfer mode) is chosen that is able to carry all services efficiently and in a cost effective manner.

2.7.2 Transfer mode

In the 1988 ITU-T Recommendations it was agreed that the most effective technique for handling broadband services and yet still be capable of handling all the narrowband-ISDN services should be a network based upon Asynchronous Transfer Mode (ATM) techniques. This decision therefore influences the standardisation of not only switches and interfaces but of the digital hierarchies and multiplexing structures. The technique is relatively new and immature although research centres have been investigating it for the last decade in various forms. It can be thought of as a technique that is between the pure circuit switching technique used for the B channel of N-ISDN (which can be called a Synchronous Transfer Mode

(STM)) and the packet switching technique of a datagram packet network (conforming to X.25 Datagram Protocols).

In circuit switching a connection is established for the duration of the call between the two end users, usually providing a transparent path between the two, the connection being established by means of signalling messages at the start of the call. This is called a connection oriented service. Although information may not be sent all the time the connection is held and the user is paying for it until the connection is cleared (unless a leased line is being used). This happens in narrowband ISDN and the exact structure of the information carried over the connection is of little interest to the carrier. In the X.25 datagram protocol, information to be carried to the remote user is assembled into packets of varying length and the routeing information for each packet is contained within it. A connection is therefore not established, making it a connectionless service.

A series of packets to the same destination could therefore go over different routes. Since the routeing information is carried at layer 3, at each switch the layer 2 protocols have to be terminated and layer 3 interrogated. Potentially this can cause long and variable delays in the transmission of the signal, possibly making it unacceptable for real time services such as speech.

A technique was therefore needed that avoids the under utilisation of the circuit switch channel when carrying sporadic information and the time consuming processing of the X.25 type service. The chosen technique was the ATM technique. This requires the information to be assembled into fixed length packets or cells as they are now called. Each cell comprises a 5 byte header and a 48 byte information field as shown in Figure 2.10.

The main purpose of the header is to identify cells belonging to the same call, since calls are allocated virtual channels over the network when a number of them are multiplexed onto a single bearer. The technique is connection oriented since effectively a virtual connection across the network is established at the start of the call by the use of special signalling cells. Each cell in the call is then routed over this virtual channel by referring the information in the header to a look-up table in the exchange.

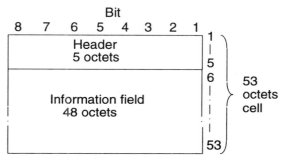

Figure 2.10   ATM cell structure

The advantage of the ATM technique is that it is able to multiplex services requiring different cell throughput rates from a few cells per second up to perhaps several hundred thousand cells per second in any combination on a 150Mbit/s circuit. The services don't have to produce information at a constant rate either, which will be more efficient when transmitting interactive data or using video coding techniques where only changes in picture content has to be transmitted.

It is for these reasons that ATM is seen as an ideal candidate for an integrated broadband network.

2.7.3 Reference models

For B-ISDN a reference model similar to that for the narrowband ISDN has been adopted in ITU-T with the reference points being labelled S_B and T_B instead of S and T as shown in Figure 2.5. As with N-ISDN the functions of B-NT1 are to terminate the transmission systems in the local line plant and support the interface to the B-NT2. In Europe this function is seen as part of the public network and also provides maintenance features for use by the network operator. The B-NT2 contains a local switching element equivalent to the narrowband PABX or LAN.

One of the issues currently being debated is the relationship between the interfaces at the T_B and S_B reference points and whether these interfaces should be point-to-point or point-to-multipoint. It is desirable that the two interfaces are compatible to ensure terminal portability between the large business customers and the small domestic customer who may not need an NT2. However it is imperative that the interface at S_B, which may be in the majority, is of minimum cost. The cost of any additional features required at the interface at T_B should therefore not have to be borne by the interface at S_B.

Another issue is centred on the number of interfaces that need to be defined, in particular at S_B. Since different terminals will support different services and applications, the throughput across the interface will vary considerably. This could be from the few bit/s of a telemetry service, through the tens of kbit/s required for telephony, to the hundreds of Mbit/s required for high definition visual services. However with the flexibility provided by an ATM interface, multi-service and multimedia terminals supporting various combinations of services and applications should emerge.

2.7.4 Customer's access connection

The customer's access connection between the B-NT1 and the first switching node in the network, often referred to as the 'U' reference point may take many forms. It may be a copper pair, coaxial cable, optical fibre cable, satellite or cellular radio. The transmission equipment may use existing plesiochronous multiplex or the new synchronous digital hierarchy standards. It could be a network employing passive optical devices with time-diversion multiple access (TDMA) equipment, or in the future a cellular radio network with a restricted throughput.

The B-NT1 will provide the interworking between this range of media, rates, transmission standards supported by the network operators and a common interface for all terminal equipment and customer premise networks. This will ensure portability of CPE across the whole range of satellite, cellular and terrestrial networks. The functions that therefore could be performed by the B-NT1 in addition to the standard transmission conversion may also include rate conversion from the standard interface rate to a wide range of rates supported by the access network, which would then identify a need for flow control across the interface.

2.7.5 The user/network interface

The narrowband ISDN presents two well defined network interfaces to the customer that are able to support a range of services up to 64kbit/s, in the same way B-ISDN must present a minimum set of well defined interfaces that supports all services up to 150Mbit/s. Well defined stable interfaces are necessary to enable customer premise equipment to evolve to support new applications inde-pendently of the public networks. In Europe the interface at the T_B reference point also provides the regulatory boundary between the liberalised customer premise equipment and the public network as for narrowband ISDN. Considerable effort has therefore gone into the definition of this interface.

2.7.5.1 *Physical layer*

Two interfaces are to be defined at both the reference points at T_B and S_B and the bit rates have been standardised at 155.52Mbit/s and 622.08Mbit/s by ITU-T (although the use of 622.08Mbit/s at the S_B reference point is for further study). These rates were chosen to align with the synchronous digital hierarchy (SDH) rates at levels 1 and 4 (STM-1 and $4 \times$ STM-1) and at the same time provide sufficient capacity for carrying encoded HDTV channels. However the whole of these bit rates are not available to the user; of the 155Mbit/s a maximum of only 135Mbit/s can be used due to the maintenance overheads and the ATM header.

Several different types of media can be considered for the physical layer, but only coaxial cable and optical fibres are serious contenders since they will both satisfy the performance requirements for both interfaces. In the short term it can be shown that two coaxial cables are more cost effective for the 155Mbit/s interface giving a reach of up to 100m. However the cost of optical transmission components is expected to fall and it is anticipated that an optical interface will become economic in the future if current cost trends continue and this could give a reach of up to 2km.

As well as the physical media the physical layer also includes the framing structure. Two alternatives have currently been identified, the cell based structure and the SDH based structure. The first consists of a continuous stream of cells each containing 53 octets; in the second the stream of cells are mapped into the payload of an STM-1 frame of the SDH as shown in Figure 2.11. Maintenance messages are contained within the section and path overheads of the SDH frame in the latter case, but special operation and maintenance cells have been defined for inclusion in the former such that they can easily be recognised at the physical layer from a unique pattern in the header.

2.7.5.2 *ATM layer*

This layer specifically addresses the ATM cell structure and coding. As shown in Figure 2.11 the cell is composed of a 5 octet header and a 48 octet information field. The primary role of the header is to identify cells belonging to the same virtual channel in the ATM stream. To do this the header contains a routeing field comprising a Virtual Channel Identifier (VCI) and a virtual path identifier (VPI). A virtual channel is fully defined at the interface by the combination of VCI and VPI, since two different virtual channels in different virtual paths may have the same VCI.

The header also contains a Generic Flow Control (GFC) field, which is used to control traffic flow during short term overload conditions, a Payload Type (PT) field, used to indicate whether the information field contains user or network information, a Cell Loss Priority (CLP) field to indicate whether the cell has a lower priority and therefore can be discarded during overload conditions and a Header Error Control (HEC) field which covers the entire header. The structure of the header is shown in Figure 2.12.

2.7.5.3 *ATM Adaptation Layer*

As the name implies this layer adapts or maps the functions or services supported by the higher layers onto a common ATM bearer

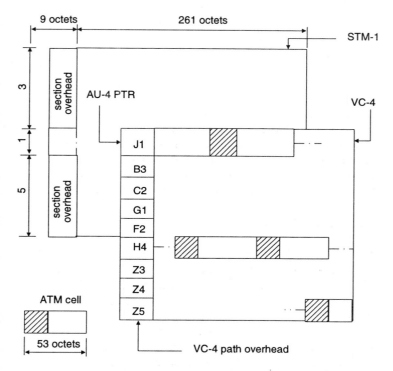

Figure 2.11 Mapping of ATM cells into the STM-1 frame

service. Different services therefore require different ATM Adaptation Layer (AAL) protocols if the carriage of each service is to be optimised. However it is hoped that a minimum of AAL protocols need be derived with only minimal degradation to some of the services.

Two sublayers have been defined in the adaptation layer, these are the Segmentation and Reassembly sublayer (SAR) and the Convergence Sublayer (CS). The SAR divides the information to be carried by the ATM layer into segments suitable for carrying in the 48 octet information field of the ATM cell and vice versa. Other functions

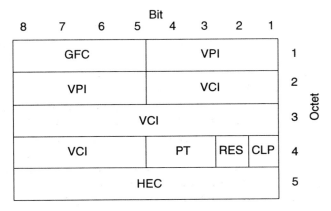

Figure 2.12   ATM header structure

such as handling cell delays variation, cell loss, timing and error
monitoring and control are handled by the service dependent CS.

2.7.5.4 *Higher layers*

The higher layers in the user, signalling and management information
are all supported on a common ATM bearer service with specific
service dependent adaptation layers adapting the features of the
higher layers of these services. Each service or application in the user
plane for example will have differently specified higher layers, whilst
the higher layers of the signalling in the control plane may be different again. For example signalling may be based upon the narrowband
ISDN signalling with layer 3 signalling messages and protocols
defined in I.450/1 (Q.930/1). In which case decisions will need to be
taken as to whether they should still be supported by the layer 2
specification (I.440/1) or whether these functions can be performed
by the adaptation layer.

Signalling is established via a signalling circuit which is implemented by assigning two virtual channels, one for each direction,
across the interfaces. Any number of signalling circuits can be established. These Signalling Virtual Channels (SVC) are identified by

Signalling Virtual Channel Identifiers (SVCI) and are only assigned when required. To assign, check and remove these SVCs a meta-signalling protocol has been defined which is carried in a meta-signalling virtual circuit with a predefined VCI and which is always present.

Discussions are still proceeding on the specification of the signalling protocols. A short term solution may be to base these on the narrowband ISDN signalling protocols defined in I.450/1 (Q.930/1); however a longer term solution may be to define new signalling protocols suitable for use both in the access network and main network.

2.8 Bibliography

Bonnati, Casali and Popple (1991) *Integrated Broadband Communications: Views from RACE* , North Holland.

CCITT (1988) *Blue Book – Fascicle III.7 to II.9*, CCITT/ITU.

Clark, M.P. (1991) *Networks and Telecoms*, Wiley.

Communicate (1995) Devising a strategy for ISDN, *Communicate*, February.

Frankel, D. (1995) ISDN reaches the market, *IEEE Spectrum*, June.

Galvin, M. and Hauf, A. (1994) The expanding US market for ISDN access, *Telecommunications*, November.

Griffiths, J.M. (1990) *ISDN Explained*, Wiley.

Griffiths, J.M. (1986) *Local Telecommunications 2 — Into the Digital Era*, Peter Peregrinus Ltd.

Marsden, B.W. (1988) *Communication Network Protocols*, Chartwell Bratt.

NCC (1983) *Handbook of Data Communications*, NCC Publications, England.

Nye, R. (1994) Lift off for ISDN, *Connexion*, 28 September.

Pettersson, G. (1995) ISDN: from customer to commodity service, *IEEE Spectrum*, June.

Purser, M. (1987) *Computers and Telecommunication Networks*, Blackwell Scientific Pub.

Redmill, F.J. and Valdar, A.R. (1990) *SPC Digital Telephone Exchanges*, Peter Peregrinus Ltd.

Rutkowski, A.M. (1985) *Integrated Services Digital Network*, Artech House Inc.

Tredinnick, I. (1995) X.25: a new lease of life with ISDN, *Telecommunications*, March.

Valiant, M. (1994) An application for ISDN, *Telecommunications*, November.

Vanclair, F. (1994) ISDN file transfer comes of age, *Communications International*, November.

Zeal, C. (1993) LAN/LAN technology with ISDN, *Telecommunications*, May.

3. Video transmission

3.1 Principles of video transmission

The development of electronic television in the mid 1930s, for the first time, presented communications engineers with the need to handle signals having a base bandwidth measured in MHz rather than the kHz required for the early multichannel telephony systems. For the original UK black and white television broadcast standard of 405 line, 2:1 interlace, 50 fields (25 frames) per second, the video bandwidth was of the order of zero to 3MHz in all sections of the programme chain from camera to transmitter, and similarly for the video amplifier in the receiver. This stimulated the development of broadband, linear circuitry and transmission systems which soon found application also for multiplexed telephony transmission.

Within the television broadcasting environment, communication links include the routeing systems within the studio complex, linking cameras with mixers (switchers) and between mixers and a central apparatus room etc., often involving hundreds of metres of cabling; contribution links from OB (remote) venues to the studio centre or for incoming 'live' programmes from distant studio centres or overseas broadcasters; distribution links from studio centres to transmitters, including the inter city links required for network operation, inter country, inter continental links for programme exchanges.

Short range microwave links may also be used for portable radio cameras used in ENG (electronic news gathering), sportscasting etc., linking the camera with a mobile control room or portable video recorder.

The original broadband video/sound links were concerned with analogue signals of black and white video; the later introduction of analogue composite (encoded) waveforms for colour television re-quired significantly more stringent performance standards in order to minimise picture degradations resulting primarily from differential gain and differential phase.

Over many years, radio relay links have used frequency modulated carriers to convey analogue video waveforms, but from the 1970s onwards increasing use is being made of digital video, digital audio and digital data signals within parts of the programme chain with a corresponding introduction of digitally modulated carriers for terrestrial radio relay and optical fibre links and also, to some degree, for satellite links in accordance with ISDN hierarchical levels.

Video signals conveyed over relatively short distances of coaxial cable in studio routeing systems are normally transmitted directly at video frequency. When the cable path exceeds about 100m the distribution amplifiers may provide passive equalisation to offset the distortions caused by the attenuation and delay characteristics of the cable.

For cable systems extending beyond about 500m, the video signal modulates a carrier frequency between about 20MHz to 70MHz, using either double sideband or vestigial sideband amplitude modulation, suitable for distances up to a few km without intermediate amplifiers.

A re-broadcasting link (RBL) is a commonly used method of feeding programme information from a main transmitter to its low power gap filling relay transmitters.

The key component of an RBL is a high grade re-broadcasting receiver (RBR). RBLs may also be used to link high power main transmitters forming a regional network. Incoming signals presented to the RBR are usually not demodulated at gap filling relays but converted to an intermediate frequency (e.g. 70MHz) and then reconverted to the required channel (frequency translation).

Signals coded in digital form are more resistant to the effects of noise and distortion in transmission links, although vulnerable to multipath distortion, and can be regenerated without loss of fidelity. The quality of the pictures and sound is determined primarily by the coding.

Telecommunications practice is tending towards digital links and networks designed to carry a flexible mixture of television, telephony and data services.

The European standard ISDN levels are: 64kbit/s, 2048kbit/s, 8448kbit/s, 34.368Mbit/s and 139.264Mbit/s. The last two of these levels are of particular interest in television broadcasting, and are usually referred to as 34Mbit/s and 140Mbit/s respectively.

Straightforward PCM coding of 625 line PAL generates a digital signal with a bit rate of about 100Mbit/s. The CCIR (now part of ITU-R) component digital standard (Rec. 601, 4:2:2) for YUV components generates a source signal of 216Mbit/s.

Recently developed video bit rate reduction techniques can reduce the bit rate by a factor of about 8 to 10 times; feasibility studies, using computer simulation, suggest that it may be possible to reduce video bit rates by a factor between about 20 and 40, permitting digital broadcasting to the home of 625 line composite or component video within the bandwidth of terrestrial TV channels.

An example of such studies is the Eureka 625 project VADIS (Video Audio Digital Interactive System) aimed at multiplexing video, audio and data information for transmission in high speed LANs and future broadband telecommunications networks.

Video bit rate reduction involves the use of such techniques as sample rate reduction, differential coding (DPCM), transform coding, variable length coding and vector quantisation, or a combination of these.

The channel bandwidth of a digital signal depends on both the bit rate and the modulation process. It should however be noted that where digital video has been subjected to appreciable bit rate reduction, or is in composite rather than component form, it cannot be further processed or manipulated within the production process; the requirements of a contribution link may thus differ from that of distribution links.

Direct to home digital broadcasting from terrestrial transmitters would permit a very significant reduction of transmitter power and might permit the use of the so called 'taboo channels' denied to terrestrial broadcasters on account of co-channel and/or adjacent channel interference.

Multipath leading to inter symbol distortion and consequent high bit error rates can be minimised by the use of special modulation techniques such as Orthogonal Frequency Digital Modulation (OFDM) of a large number of spaced carriers.

3.2 Television transmission

3.2.1 Fundamentals and standards

All television systems are based on translating a scene into a series of small points, termed picture elements (pixels), by methodically tracing out or scanning the picture, and then conveying the intensity (light value) of each picture element in an agreed sequence. At the receiver, a reproduction of the image is built up by means of an identical and synchronised scanning sequence (Figure 3.1). The display screen glows with an intensity dependent upon the light value of the pixels, with a degree of integration (memory) in both camera and display. This, combined with the persistence of vision of the eye, gives the viewer the impression that the display is presenting a complete series of pictures with a resolution depending on the total number of pixels in each frame; if subsequent frames follow sufficiently rapidly the illusion of natural movement, as in a cinematograph film, is provided.

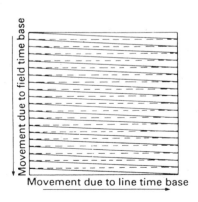

Figure 3.1   Simplified representation of sequential scanning

A series of images presented to the eye at a rate above about 10 per second (10Hz) gives an illusion of continuous motion but accompanied by a pronounced flicker. If the rate is increased to 25Hz or 30Hz the flicker is much reduced but still just noticeable, particularly when the images are bright. A repetition rate of 50Hz provides motion virtually without flicker although for some very bright pictures 60Hz or even higher may be desirable. The rate at which video images (frames) follow one another is called the frame rate.

To transmit a series of sequentially scanned pictures at a frame rate of 50Hz or 60Hz would require an excessively large bandwidth if the line resolution is more than about 300 lines. An alternative technique, universally adopted for broadcast transmission, is termed interlacing; instead of transmitting each adjacent horizontal line in sequence, alternate lines are scanned first, to form a field, with the missing lines traced out subsequently as a second field, the two fields forming one complete frame. Since the eye hardly perceives individual lines of a single frame, the effect is to provide 50 (60) 'images' per second, although transmitting only 25 (30) frames per second, at the cost only of introducing a small degree of interline flicker at the 25Hz (30Hz) rate. It has also been shown that with digital memory in the receiver, it is possible to display an interlaced picture with sequential (progressive) scanning. With interlaced scanning the final line of the first field and the first line of the second field are half lines, the line starting at the centre of the top line with a similar half line at the bottom of the picture, as in Figure 3.2.

Since the scanning process has to be carried out synchronously in the studio and in the receiver, it is necessary to provide synchronising signals that accurately define the start of the field scans and each line scan. Conventionally, this is achieved by transmitting two sets of timing pulses which are used by the receiver to lock its horizontal and frame timebases, although it is feasible, using digital technology, to provide only one set of pulses from which both rates can be derived by counting techniques.

The way in which 625 line video signals are combined with line sync pulses is shown in Figure 3.3.

Colour television requires the transmission of additional information which, in practice, takes the form of two chrominance signals,

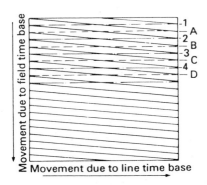

Figure 3.2 Simplified representation of double interlaced scanning

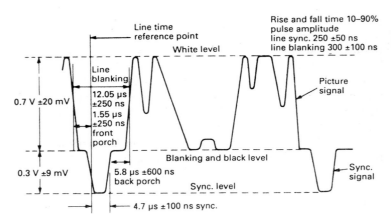

Figure 3.3 The waveform of a typical line showing synchronising signals

which together with the black and white (luminance) signal defines the picture in terms of the three primary colours, red (R), green (G) and blue (B).

Any colour can be defined by three characteristics: its brightness (luminance); its hue (dominant electromagnetic wavelength/frequency); and its intensity (saturation) which corresponds to its colourfulness.

In colour television systems, chrominance information defines the hue and saturation of the pixels independently of the luminance, so that theoretically any distortion of the chrominance information does not affect the detail of the picture. A system designed to satisfy this condition is termed a constant luminance system, although in practice some departure from this ideal is to be found in systems currently in use.

It was recognised that to achieve wide acceptability of colour in an era when black and white television had achieved popularity, a colour system needed to be compatible, that is the colour transmissions should be receivable as black and white pictures on a black and white only receiver, and should also have reverse compatibility whereby black and white transmissions should be receivable as black and white pictures on a colour receiver.

The standard adopted to define whiteness is the colour temperature (which determines the amount of blue or green in peak white). The standard adopted in Europe is Illuminant D corresponding to 6500K.

To define completely the luminance and chrominance information, a colour source, such as a camera, analyses the light from the scene in terms of its red (R), green (G) and blue (B) components by means of optical filters and then gamma corrects these to take into account differences between source and display tube characteristics. Gamma corrected signals are termed R', G', B' signals which are processed to provide the basic luminance signal (Y).

The green and red signals contribute more to luminance than blue and in practice a matrixing network is designed such that Equation 3.1 is satisfied.

$$Y' = 0.3\,R' + 0.6\,G' + 0.1\,B' \tag{3.1}$$

Table 3.1 International standards for television broadcasting. (*Amplitude modulated sound)

System	Line/ field	Chan- nel width (MHz)	Video width (MHz)	VSB width (MHz)	Polarity vision modula- tion	Sound/ vision carrier spacing (MHz)
B	625/50	7	5	0.75	Negative	5.5
D, K	625/50	8	6	0.75	Negative	6.5
G	625/50	8	5	0.75	Negative	5.5
H	625/50	8	5	1.25	Negative	5.5
I	625/50	8	5.5	1.25	Negative	6.0
K1	625/50	8	6	1.25	Negative	6.5
L	625/50	8	6	1.25	Positive	6.5*
M	525/60	6	4.2	0.75	Negative	4.5
N	625/50	6	4.2	0.75	Negative	4.5

Since the four signals Y', R', G' and B' are related mathematically it is unnecessary to transmit all four. Since for compatibility a Y' signal is needed, this is transmitted with two (chrominance) signals obtained by taking the red and blue signals and subtracting from them Y', that is (R' - Y') and (B' - Y'). (G' - Y') can be derived within the receiver by matrixing. The transmitted signals are thus Y', as in Equation 3.1 and (R' - Y') and (B' - Y'). These three signals allow Y', R', G' and B' to be recovered in the receiver.

Tables 3.1 to 3.3 provide an overview of the international standards and the countries using them. Detailed information on the international standards for television broadcasting is given in CCIR Report 624 (ITU Sales Service, Place des Nations, CH-1211, Geneva 20, Switzerland).

Table 3.2   Composite colour video signals in terrestrial systems (simplified)

System	Chromin- ance	Chromin- ance subcarrier (MHz)	Chrominance subcarrier modulation
PAL	E_U , E_V	Approx. 4.43 (3.58 for M/PAL)	Suppressed carrier AM of two subcarriers in quadrature
NTSC	E_I , E_Q	Approx. 3.58	Suppressed carrier AM of two subcarriers in quadrature
SECAM	D_R, D_B (line sequential)	Approx. 4.41(D_R) Approx. 4.25 (D_B)	Frequency modulation alternating one line D_R one line D_B

3.2.2 Bandwidth

The maximum upper frequency of a video signal is governed by the picture content and the scanning standard being used. For the UK System I this is normally taken as 5.5MHz.

Were conventional double sideband AM to be used, this would imply a maximum vision bandwidth of $2 \times 5.5 = 11$MHz. In addition, further bandwidth would be required for the sound signal. In view of the restricted frequency spectrum at v.h.f. and u.h.f., it has for many years been the practice to reduce the bandwidth of one of the two sidebands to produce vestigial sideband or asymmetric sideband vision transmission. In System I the full upper sidebands to 5.5MHz

Table 3.3 Television systems by country (*v.h.f. band only)

System	Country
I/PAL	Angola* Botswana Hong Kong Ireland Lesotho South Africa UK
B G/PAL	Albania Algeria Australia Austria Bahrain Bangladesh* Belgium Brunei Darussalam* Cameroon Denmark Equatorial Guinea* Ethiopia Finland Germany (FRG) Ghana Gibraltar Iceland India* Indonesia* Israel Italy Jordan Kenya Kuwait Liberia* Luxembourg Malawi Malaysia Maldives* Malta* Monaco Mozambique Netherlands New Zealand Nigeria* Norway Oman Pakistan Papua New Guinea Portugal Qatar Sierra Leone Singapore Spain Sri Lanka* Sudan* Sweden Switzerland Syria Tanzania* Thailand Tunisia Turkey Uganda* United Arab Emirates Yemen (AR)* Yemen (PDR)* Yugoslavia Zambia* Zimbabwe*
N/PAL	Argentina* Paraguay* Uruguay
D/PAL	China
M/PAL	Brazil
D K/PAL	Korea (DPR) Romania
B G/SECAM	Cyprus Egypt Germany Greece Iran Iraq* Lebanon Libya* Mali* Mauritania* Mauritius* Morocco Saudi Arabia Tunisia
D K/SECAM	Afghanistan* Bulgaria Czechoslovakia Hungary Mongolia* Poland USSR Viet Nam
K1/SECAM	Benin Burkina Faso Burundi Central African Republic Chad Congo Cote d'Ivoire (Ivory Coast) Djibouti* Gabon Guinea Madagascar Niger Senegal Togo Zaire
L/SECAM	France Luxembourg Monaco
M/NTSC	Bermuda* Bolivia British Virgin Islands* Burma* Canada Chile Colombia Costa Rica Cuba Dominican Republic* Ecuador* Guatemala* Haiti* Honduras* Jamaica* Japan Korea (Republic of) Mexico Montserrat* Netherlands Antilles* Nicaragua* Panama Peru Philippines* St. Christopher & Nevis* Suriname* USA Venezuela

are transmitted but the bandwidth of the lower sideband is restricted to 1.25MHz (in 625 line System G as used in many countries the lower sideband is restricted even more to 0.75MHz).

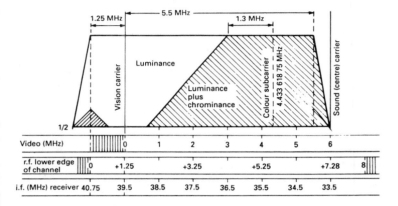

Figure 3.4   The frequency bands occupied by colour picture components and sound signal from an ideal 625 line System 1 transmitter as related to video, vision, and the i.f. of a receiver (BREMA standard i.f.)

This means that for System I the total vision bandwidth is 1.25 + 5.5 or 6.75MHz and a gap of 0.5MHz is left before the sound carrier, which is thus 6MHz above the vision carrier, as shown in Figure 3.4

For both Systems I and G in the European region the agreed international u.h.f. channels occupy 8MHz; in System I the vision carrier is always +1.25MHz from the lower end of the channel; the FM sound carrier +7.25MHz. Figure 3.4 shows the vision response curve of System I as related to the video signal, the r.f. channel, and the standard BREMA receiver i.f. channel. The FM sound is trans-

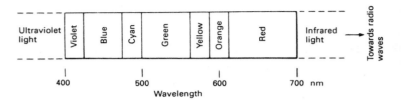

Figure 3.5 The electromagnetic spectrum of visible light. Short wavelengths such as these may be quoted in Angstrom units (10^{-10} m)

mitted with a maximum a.f. signal of 15kHz and with a peak carrier deviation (corresponding to a 400Hz tone at a level of +8dBm at the modulator input) of ±50kHz. The pre-emphasis time constant is 50μs.

The use of an asymmetric sideband vision signal results in a degree of quadrature distortion when the signal is envelope demodulated: this form of distortion (which can usually be detected only with some difficulty, even on a test card) can be eliminated by the use of synchronous demodulation.

Although the chrominance signals generated in the colour camera occupy the full range of video frequencies, it is only the luminance signal that requires to be transmitted to this degree of resolution. The ability to resolve fine detail depends on visual acuity, and our ability to resolve colour in small details of a picture is inferior to that for corresponding black and white or grey pictures. Since the human eye does not resolve colour in small areas there is no need to reproduce this, even for high quality television pictures (Figure 3.5). This influences many aspects of colour television, not least the ability to limit the bandwidth of chrominance information relative to that required for the luminance signal. In practice chrominance information in a 625 line system can begin to roll off at about 1.3MHz. The

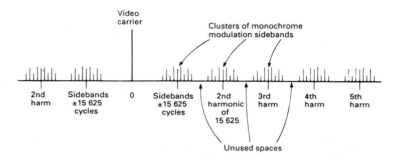

Figure 3.6 In a monochrome television transmission the sidebands are in groups around harmonics of 15625Hz, leaving spaces in which colour information may be inserted

restriction of chrominance bandwidth makes possible inband transmission of chrominance information, although this technique gives rise to some loss of compatibility (dots and crawl being seen on a monochrome display) and also cross colour effects on colour reproduction (flaring of patterned jackets is a common example), due to luminance signals appearing in the colour channels.

Basically the information in a monochrome signal is distributed in a series of packets separated by the line frequency, with only little spectrum energy in the gaps between as shown in Figure 3.6. By choosing a colour subcarrier frequency that is accurately placed between multiples of the line frequency, and noting that chrominance modulation energy is similarly in the form of packets, it is possible to interleave the basic energy spectra of the luminance and chrominance signals for 625 line transmission. The colour subcarrier frequency is maintained very precisely at 4433618.75Hz ±1Hz, with a maximum rate of change of subcarrier frequency not exceeding 0.1Hz/s.

The relationship between subcarrier and line frequency is given by Equation 3.2 where f_h is the line frequency and f_v is the field frequency.

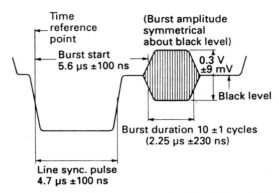

Figure 3.7 The colour burst on a standard level signal (700mV white level)

$$f_{sc} = \left(284 - \frac{1}{4} \right) f_h + \frac{1}{2} f_v \quad Hz \tag{3.2}$$

The way in which colour information is transmitted in the PAL System 1 standard is shown in Figures 3.7 to 3.10.

3.2.3 Analogue component hybrid systems

The picture impairments inherent where the colour information is encoded within the luminance signal ('mixed highs') for PAL, NTSC and SECAM can be eliminated by maintaining the three fundamental component signals representing red (R), green (G) and blue (B) or, more practically, by separation of the luminance (Y) and colour difference (U, V, or I, Q) chrominance signals. However, if the RGB or YUV signals are maintained within the studios, and as far as the transmitter, it is impractical to transmit a frequency multiplex of such component signals within the channels available in Bands I, III, IV, V or the 12GHz DBS/FM bands. Additionally, component signals would not be compatible with existing black and white, PAL, SECAM or NTSC receivers. There would also be great difficulty in retaining accurate timing (phasing) of separate analogue component signals during routeing or over distribution links.

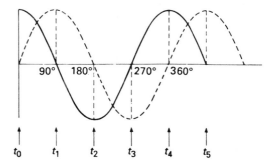

Figure 3.8 The principle of synchronous demodulation of quadrature modulated signals. Two carrier waves are shown of the same frequency but in quadrature. If each is amplitude modulated by different information and if two demodulators, one synchronised with each carrier, sample the waves only at the times when one is at a peak and the other at null, then the two sets of information can be separately retrieved at the receiver. The solid line waveform is sampled at times t_0, t_1, t_4, etc. and the dashed line curve at times t_1, t_3, t_5, etc.

A digitally based system that permits the time division multiplexing of YUV analogue signals into a form suitable for DBS/FM transmission within the 27MHz channels (19MHz carrier separation) was developed initially by the IBA and subsequently adopted for DBS in Europe in the early 1980s. This system (now comprising a family of systems) is termed Multiplexed Analogue Components (MAC), with the separate YUV signals digitally time compressed and

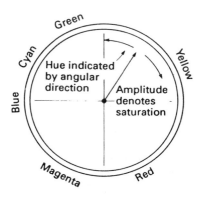

Figure 3.9 In the NTSC and PAL systems any hue can be
represented by a phasor having a specific phase angle and an
amplitude representing the degree of saturation

then time division multiplexed to occupy the active line periods of the
625 line standard. Digital sound/data signals are inserted into the
video channel during the line sync periods and then frequency modulated with the video signals on a single carrier. Although digitally
processed, the video signals are thus transmitted in analogue form.
The receiver decoder demultiplexes the signal, restoring the YUV
signals to their original parallel relationship, making them suitable for
display as conventional 625 line YUV signals.

A number of MAC systems have been developed not only for DBS
applications but also for use as a multiplexed signal within studios or
for OB contribution links, electronic/satellite news gathering etc.
There are also several different standards relating to the way in which
the digital audio/data signals are transmitted:

1. B-MAC. This system developed by Scientific-Atlanta for sat-
    ellite cable distribution links or DBS can carry six digital
    audio channels as baseband data symbols and is designed for
    minimum complexity in its data multiplex, requiring only
    15000 gates in the decoder IC. It is a fixed format system (i.e.
    not individually addressed 'packets').

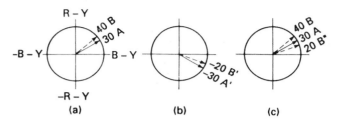

Figure 3.10   Principle of PAL automatic line correction by averaging: (a) hue A transmitted with a positive (R–Y) component; received as B because of a phase shift; (b) same hue transmitted with negative (R–Y) component A'; received as B' due to a phase error equivalent to that at (a); (c) after reversing the polarity of (b) the two received signals B and B' represent B and B'' which when averaged give the correct hue A

2.   C-MAC/packet transmits up to eight digital high quality audio channels directly modulated on to the carrier during the line blanking periods using binary phase shift keying. Data bit rate 20.25MHz.

3.   D-MAC/packet has the same data rate as C-MAC but with the data signal in duobinary form inserted on to the baseband signal as part of the multiplex rather than directly modulating the carrier.

4.   D2-MAC/packet has a format similar to D-MAC but the data rate is half that of D-MAC (i.e. 10.125Mbit/s). It can thus carry four high quality audio channels or eight medium quality channels.

The 625 line D-MAC/packet system was adopted as the UK DBS standard. The baseband video waveform of a D-MAC television line is shown in Figure 3.11.

Each line of luminance information is digitally compressed by a factor of 3:2 (52µs to about 35µs). The U and V colour difference

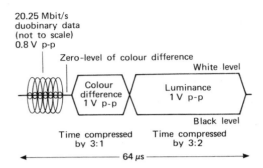

Figure 3.11 Baseband video waveform of D-MAC television line. The duobinary data burst conveys 206 bits and is followed by time compressed vision signals

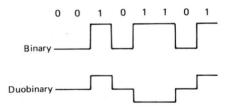

Figure 3.12 Comparison of binary and duobinary coding. After low pass filtering, the three level duobinary data signal is time division multiplexed with the time compressed vision signal

signals are reduced by a factor of 3:1 (52μs to about 17.5μs). This has the effect of increasing the maximum baseband video frequency from about 5.7MHz to about 8.5MHz. The remaining 10μs periods carry 20.25Mbit/s duobinary data, which take the form shown in Figure 3.12, inserted on to the baseband signal. Each line period thus has 206 data bits with a mean data capacity of about 3Mbit/s. Line 625 carries only data, with duobinary data inserted onto the baseband signal with

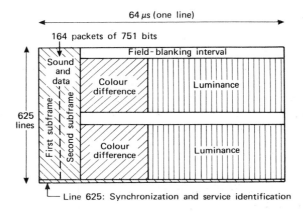

Figure 3.13   Simplified structure of D-MAC packet frame showing the distribution of vision and 20.25Mbit/s duobinary data. Organising the data into two sub-frames allows easy transcoding of one sub-frame into D2-MAC

a capacity of 1296 bits. The use of duobinary coding means that both vision and data signals are contained within a baseband of about 8.5MHz. The digital data are organized into 'packets' of 751 bits with 164 packets in each 625 line frame (4100 packets/s). The basic structure of a D-MAC packet frame is illustrated in Figure 3.13, having, for example, up to eight 15kHz audio channels with 32kHz sampling and NICAM companding of 14 bits/sample to 10 bits/sample, or up to sixteen 7kHz 'commentary' audio channels. The total data capacity is optionally available for any mix of teletext data, high quality stereo audio, mono/stereo 'commentary' channels, or for utilisation in part for the provision of analogue wide screen (16:9 aspect ratio) video information in various MAC enhanced modes or for the use of digitally assisted (DATV) vector motion enhancement.

All MAC systems facilitate the use of 'conditional access' encryption systems offering a high level of security for subscription television channels. One possibility is the use of 'double cut' component rotation, with the decoding key transmitted in the digital packets, addressed to individual receivers or groups of receivers.

The digital channel capacities of MAC/packet systems while analogue vision signals are present are: C-MAC and D-MAC 3.04Mbit/s; D2-MAC 1.52Mbit/s. In the absence of vision signals, the full channel capacity of a D-MAC channel can be used.

Within an analogue component area, MAC techniques can be used for routeing, contribution, ENG links etc. T-MAC for studio interconnection etc. retains the multiplexed analogue video component portion (4-2-0) of the MAC family of transmission formats, but dispenses with the packet data portion, substituting in its place a line repetitive sync pulse and sampling frequency reference burst. T-MAC signals are capable of conveying component originated video signals and an accompanying sound in sync audio signal over networks conforming to CCIR Recommendations 567 and 965. If the SNR set out in these Recommendations is exceeded, the subjective performance of T-MAC is better than PAL. Below this minimum SNR, the noise is more noticeable in T-MAC than in PAL, but the pictures may still appear better because cross colour effects are absent.

T-MAC was originally conceived as a means of transmitting the signals available from analogue component ENG equipment to studio centres, using existing transmission circuits. The following MAC luminance and chrominance compression ratios apply to routeing and contribution links etc.:

```
S-MAC    component 4:2:2 signals  Y 13:6 R-Y/B-Y  13:3
ACLE              component 4:1:1 signals  Y 14:9 R-Y/B-Y  56:9
T-MAC    component 4:2:0 signals  Y 3:2 R-Y/B-Y   3:1
—              component 3:1:0 signals  Y 4:3 R-Y/B-Y   4:1
```

3.2.4 Enhanced and high definition systems

During the past decade, much research and development work has been devoted to the study of electronic television systems capable of providing wide screen, flicker free pictures of a resolution comparable with that of 35mm cinematograph film. Such high definition TV systems (HDTV) are seen as being suitable for broadcast transmission, wideband cable distribution, electronic cinematography, for the production of master tapes for video cassettes and video discs, and for various applications in electronic graphics and printing. Efforts are being made to:

1. Establish worldwide production standards for 50Hz or 60Hz areas, or preferably for both.
2. Develop bandwidth compression techniques for broadcast, cable, contribution and distribution links and studio routeing systems capable of carrying HDTV signals with minimum loss of quality.
3. Develop display systems that could do justice to HDTV pictures at prices within consumer budgets.

Target areas for the development of HDTV and Advanced TV (ATV) systems include:

1. Image quality directly comparable with that of film.
2. Elimination of large area and interline flicker present with 50Hz and, to a lesser extent, 60Hz interfaced TV systems.
3. Elimination of the cross colour defects inherent in composite coded colour systems.
4. Wide screen displays with an aspect ratio of at least 16:9.
5. Economic conversion of material from tape to film and from film to tape, without noticeable degradation of picture quality.
6. Transmission systems compatible with existing receivers.
7. Sufficient flexibility for an HDTV standard to permit advantage to be taken of continuing improvements in display systems, digital signal processing etc.

While it is feasible that future fibre optic cables may permit, at least theoretically, the distribution direct to the home of HDTV RGB component signals with a bit rate of the order of 1Gbit/s, in practical terms an HDTV signal should be amenable to digital bandwidth compression (bit rate reduction) techniques to the ISDN level of 140Mbit/s.

It has been shown that, as in the cinema, a wide screen display, viewed at a distance of about three or four times picture height, has significantly more impact than pictures with the standard aspect ratio of 4:3 (width/height). For domestic viewing, market research tends to confirm that wide screen pictures, even of conventional resolution, are preferred by the great majority of viewers. This has led to increased interest in various techniques, including the MAC family, that can provide improved quality, wide screen pictures without increasing the basic scanning rates of conventional systems and are fully compatible with those systems. Some of these 'enhanced' or 'advanced' systems are suitable for transmission on terrestrial as well as satellite channels.

3.2.4.1 *HD-MAC*

A European Eureka EU-95 project in which a large number of organisations have co-operated is to develop a compatible HDTV satellite transmission and will make proposals to the CCIR for HDTV production and transmission standards. The project, initiated in 1986, concerns all aspects of HDTV, from programme production, recording and distribution to broadcasting, consumer equipment and display processing. The aim is to give a more realistic viewing experience by doubling the vertical and horizontal resolution, suitable for viewing on a 40 inch display that can be seen from the same distance as a conventional 625 line display but with an aspect ratio of 16:9.

The EU-95 project is proposing a production standard of 1250 lines, 50 frames/s in a sequential format, with 1920 pixels per line. Such a standard would permit high quality conversion to other standards, including both 625/50 and 525/60. A secondary production standard, for use within 50Hz areas, would use 1250 lines, 50 fields, 2:1 interlace.

HD-MAC transmission proposals are intended for broadcast DBS transmission within a standard 12GHz channel. Since the bandwidth of its HDTV material is about four times that available, the signals need to be compressed by about four times. It is a project requirement that the compressed HD-MAC signals should give an acceptable 4:3 aspect ratio picture when received on a DBS receiver with a standard MAC decoder. This requirement inhibits the use of all digital techniques, although it is recognised that a 12GHz channel could support digital transmission of HDTV pictures at bit rates of the order of

140Mbit/s, which has been shown to be a practical bit rate for the distribution of HDTV pictures/sound.

A complete HD-MAC system, shown in Figure 3.14, uses three basic techniques to reduce the bandwidth of the channels while retaining as much of the original image quality as possible.

1.   Diagonal filtering which can reduce the bandwidth by a factor of two with very little reduction in subjective picture quality.
2.   The exchange of spatial and temporal resolution.
3.   Motion compensated temporal resolution.

Technique (2) is used in conjunction with (3). A digital signal of about 1Mbit/s is added to the digital sound/data channel to provide the digitally assisted television (DATV) information needed to assist the receiver decoder. A bandwidth reduction of another factor of about two can be achieved by the exchange of spatial and temporal filtering with motion compensated information of the DATV channels used to minimise subjective effects.

For contribution links, where post production editing is required, the source bit rate of the active lines at roughly 1Gbit/s can be compressed to the 560Mbit/s ISDN level by the use of differential pulse code modulation (DPCM).

3.2.4.2 *Hi Vision*

The NHK broadcasting organisation, in collaboration with Japanese industry, has developed and widely demonstrated an HDTV system capable of excellent quality on closed circuit.

The system was originally proposed as a world studio production standard, for which purpose it has gained support primarily in 60Hz areas. It was not developed as a compatible system, but subsequently a number of bandwidth reduction systems – MUSE (Multiple Sub-Nyquist-Sampling Encoding) family – have been developed that permit the 1125 line material to be transmitted on terrestrial channels.

The original MUSE system permits the broadcasting of 1125/60/2:1 HDTV programmes in a single 12GHz DBS satellite channel, compressing the signal into a base bandwidth of 8.1MHz by

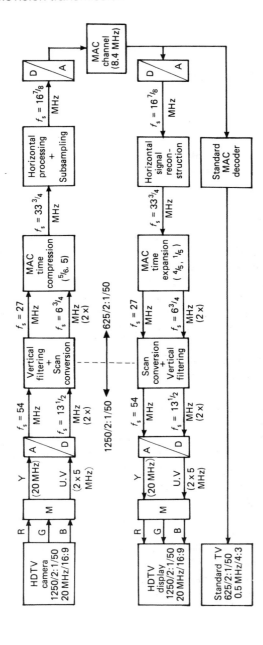

Figure 3.14 Complete HD-MAC system

multiple subsampling and includes techniques for motion compensation, quasi constant luminance principles and non-linear emphasis with a four field cycle. MUSE-T is a related system for the distribution of HDTV programmes to broadcasters via communication satellites, employing 2 field cycle subsampling for motion resolution improvement. It has a 16.2MHz signal bandwidth requiring an FM channel of approximately 50MHz. NHK has also proposed MUSE systems that would permit the transmission of NTSC compatible ADTV wide screen pictures on terrestrial AM channels: MUSE-9 in 9MHz channels; MUSE-6 in 6MHz channels.

3.2.4.3 *All digital systems*

In 1990, the USA began to investigate and compare a number of proposed all digital (transmission) systems capable of being introduced alongside ('simulcasting') the existing 525 line broadcasts and suitable for either terrestrial or satellite or cable distribution, using digital techniques for both source coding and channel coding. Proposed systems of bit rate production have been claimed to permit 525 line broadcast TV at bit rates from about 5Mbit/s to 10Mbit/s and HDTV at between 30Mbit/s and 50Mbit/s.

All the proposed digital systems use video bandwidth compression after basic analogue to digital conversion including interlace scanning, removal of source redundancy, making full use of human perception limitations, three dimensional processing (time as third dimension) and entropy coding.

Because a digital system could be transmitted at much lower transmitter power for equal coverage than conventional analogue AM systems, the possibility of using existing 'taboo' (adjacent channels etc.) terrestrial channels for additional 525/625 line channels is also under investigation.

Bit rate reduction for the distribution of digital TV (broadcast, and inter city/satellite distribution) is being investigated for both contribution and distribution circuits and possibly for broadcast distribution. Techniques include: sample rate reduction (reducing the sample rate to the minimum value possible within the quality objective); discrete cosine transform (DCT) which is similar to the discrete

Fourier transform with a block of N samples transformed to give N coefficients, representing the amplitude of specific patterns within the block and subsequently transformed back in the decoder to give the original N samples (effective because the majority of coefficients have an amplitude close to zero); variable length coding in which the number of bits assigned to a given quantised value depends on its probability; temporal prediction modes which take advantage of the similarity of one picture to another; video framing in which all the information relevant to the video signal is multiplexed together before being written into a buffer store.

Although DCT based coding techniques represent the most popular approach, it is possible that sub-band coding, based on splitting the picture into different two dimensional frequency bands (sub-bands) and encoding each one separately may give slightly better quality than equivalent DCT schemes, particularly for multi-resolution applications such as HDTV broadcasting.

3.2.4.4   *PAL plus*

The possibility of developing for terrestrial and satellite broadcasting an enhanced, compatible wide screen (16:9 aspect ratio) version of 625 line PAL came under investigation in Europe in the early 1990s by a consortium of major receiver manufacturers and a number of broadcaster research organisations.

Objectives include: 16:9 aspect ratio; freedom from PAL cross effects; improved resolution; compatibility with normal PAL and recordable on standard VCRs; a display compatible with HD-MAC/HDTV.

Various methods of meeting all these targets are considered technically feasible, although it is recognised that 'compatibility' must be a relative term since reception of PAL plus in either 'letter box' or 'side panel' formats would involve some loss to viewers with standard PAL receivers.

Cross effects could be removed or minimised by degrees of band segregation or phase segregation; increased resolution by the use of spectral folding. System specification (based on letter-box format) was agreed in late 1991.

3.2.5 Digital and component systems

Since the early 1970s, digital techniques in video/audio processing and transmission have been under intensive investigation and implementation. This work has led to the first worldwide production standard (CCIR Recommendation 601 of 1982), the implementation of a few experimental and operational all digital studios, the widespread use of 'stand alone' digital studio equipment for special effects, noise reduction, standards conversion etc. and the Nicam 728 dual channel digital system for television sound.

Initially, the introduction of digital processing was applied to encoded 'composite' waveforms with input and output from each unit in analogue form. However, it was soon appreciated that digital processing offered an opportunity to improve picture quality by eliminating the degradations inherent in the PAL, NTSC and SECAM colour encoding systems due to 'mixed highs' (frequency multiplex) insertion of chrominance information within the luminance baseband. Attention was therefore turned to use of 'component' signals with luminance and chrominance signals kept separate, although this involves an extension of the baseband of the analogue signals and consequently higher digital bit rates.

Advantages of handling signals in digital form include the more rugged nature of a digital signal, which requires a much lower signal to noise ratio, and its greater immunity to many forms of phase and amplitude distortion and interference. The ability to make use of picture redundancy and complex coding strategies can provide very large degrees of bit rate reduction without excessively increasing the harmful effects of bit errors. However, once large bit rate reduction has been applied, it becomes impracticable to use such production techniques as chroma keying 'downstream' of the bit rate reduction.

By 1987 digital cassette broadcast videotape recorders, based on the EBU/SMPTE D1 digital component format, had reached the market place, making possible all digital production centres. Such machines can produce more than 20 generations of tape without noticeable degradation, but represent a relatively high cost system applicable primarily to studios converted for component working. Digital cassette recorders for use on composite signals (D2 format) have also appeared. The increased packing density of metal particle videotapes has led to the successful development of lower cost analogue component cassette recorders using half inch tape formats (M.II and Betacam-SP) suitable for both studio and field operation.

During 1989, a further digital composite digital tape format (D3) was announced by Panasonic Broadcast (Matsushita) based on a half inch wide metal particle tape with a tape thickness of 10μm using M.II (VHS) type cassettes but with thinner tape. The cassettes are substantially smaller than those of D1 or D2 for equal running time. In all three formats there are four digital (PCM) audio channels plus analogue tracks for cueing and time code.

An analogue signal can be converted to digital form, processed and then reconverted to analogue form several times in tandem with little visible degradation. However, if this tandem chain is extended too far it will tend to lead to a marked increase in the quantisation noise caused by the use of a restricted number of amplitude levels. Other impairments in digital video may be due to aliasing, clock jitter, error rates and the impossibility of transmitting perfect pulses. Digital video signals may also call for added complexity for monitoring and measuring the impairments, and some still uncertain cost factors in equipment and maintenance.

The advantages of digital transmission include freedom from the ill effects of differential phase and differential gain and the ability to regenerate an exact replica of the input data stream at any point in the chain, thus avoiding cumulative signal to noise degradation. It was Shannon's communication theory that first underlined mathematically the outstanding efficiency of digitally encoded transmission systems.

However it is important to realise that digits do not eliminate all problems. From the earliest days of manual and machine cable telegraphy it has been recognised that the transmission of high speed pulses within a channel of restricted bandwidth can present severe practical problems, including inter symbol interference and susceptibility of the error rate to all forms of 'echoes' and multipath propagation.

Digital systems are inevitably subject to quantising noise, which depends upon the number and arrangement of the levels at which the original analogue signal is digitised, and also to aliasing foldover distortion. Aliasing represents spectral components, arising from the process of sampling, not in the original signal; when these fall within the spectrum of the sampled signal they result in foldover distortion. Aliasing can be minimised by effective filtering, although the ease and cost with which such filtering can be accomplished is very much a factor of the sampling rate.

The increasing use of digital equipment based on the CCIR Recommendation 601 (1982) as given in Table 3.4 created the need to interconnect equipments with outputs in either digital or analogue form. With the introduction of digital equipment it is easier to build a completely new centre rather than modify an existing complex.

CCIR Recommendation 656 (1986) provides interface standards for digital parallel working at 27Mbit/s and serial working at 243Mbit/s in fully digital areas.

Experience with digital video processing has shown that 8 bit PCM is not considered by some manufacturers as adequate for all intermediate interconnections within a processing chain. One result is that a de facto standard of 10 bits exists, which makes use of the spare contacts in the 656 (parallel) interface. A studio standard for GBR component working, rather than the colour difference (Y, Cb, Cr) of the 4:2:2 standard has been proposed.

The introduction of the D2-PAL/625 and D2-NTSC/525 digital composite standard into existing or new composite areas has led to operational VTR cassettes, VTRs and computer controlled 'cart' machines. Additionally, equipment for conversion between D1 and D2 digital formats, conversion from analogue composite, and between various combinations of digital interface has been developed. For D2, sampling frequencies, phased to the colour subcarrier reference burst and at four times the subcarrier frequency, are approximately 17.73MHz for 625/PAL and 14.32MHz for 525/NTSC. Digital composite recording is not practical for SECAM working, and in SECAM environments the signal must first be decoded back into Y, D_R, D_B and then re-encoded into PAL or else processed in component form.

In converting an RGB signal to digital YUV (see Figure 3.15) the signal is matrixed, filtered, clamped and digitised.

Table 3.4 Major parameters of the digital component standard
CCIR Recommendation 601 (1982):4:2:2

	Luminance (Y)	*Colour difference signals*	
		(R-Y)	*(B-Y)*
Sampling frequency (MHz)	13.5	6.75	6.75
Bandwidth (analogue) (MHz)	5.75 (±0.1 depending on sampling filters)	2.75 (+0, −1 depending on sampling filters)	2.75
Form of coding	Uniformly quantised PCM	8 bits per sample for Y, R−Y and B−Y	
Coded signals representing	Y	R−Y	B−Y
Samples per total line:			
625-50 systems	864	432	432
525-60 systems	858	429	429
Samples per active line:			
625-50 systems	720	360	360
525-60 systems	720	360	360
Quantized signal levels:			
Lowest level	16 (black)	16	16
Highest level	235 (white)	240	240
Zero chrominance level		128	128
SNR peak to peak r.m.s. unweighted (dB)	56	56	56
Sample structure	Orthogonal, line, field and picture repetitive. R−Y and B−Y samples co-sited with odd (1st, 3rd, 5th, etc.) Y samples in each line		

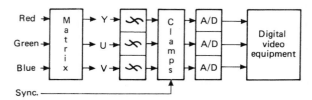

Figure 3.15   RGB to digital YUV interface

It has been noted that this may introduce a number of possible signal impairments including:

1. Lift errors (clamp, low frequency or digitising problems).
2. Delay inequalities (filter or path length differences).
3. Phase response differences (filter differences).
4. Non-linearities (digitising problems).
5. Quantization noise (digitising effect).

Such impairments can affect component more than composite signals, since the effects on the separate paths of the interconnections can be differential, and relatively small defects can significantly affect the colour balance of a picture. Differential delays within or without analogue component equipment can produce significantly more visible impairments than with a single composite signal. The visibility of some effects depends on the actual luminance and colour values of the picture.

CCIR Recommendation 656 (1986): 'Interfaces for digital component video signals in 525 line and 625 line television systems', Part I, covers common signal format of the interfaces and Part II covers bit parallel interfaces, including a table of contact assignments, as in Table 3.5.

Any spare pairs connected to contacts 11,24 or 12,25 are reserved for bits of lower significance than those carried on contacts 10,23. Parallel interfaces comprise 8×27Mbit/s pairs.

Table 3.5   ITU-T Recommendation 656 table contact assignments

Contact	Signal line	Contact	Signal line
1	Clock A	14	Clock B
2	System ground	15	System ground
3	Data 7A(MSB)	16	Data 7B
4	Data 6A	17	Data 6B
5	Data 5A	18	Data 5B
6	Data 4A	19	Data 4B
7	Data 3A	20	Data 3B
8	Data 2A	21	Data 2B
9	Data 1A	22	Data 1B
10	Data OA	23	Data OB
11	Spare A–A	24	Spare A–B
12	Spare B–A	25	Spare B–B
13	Cable shield		

Part III covers bit serial interface, including the recommendation that the 8 bit data words are encoded for transmission in 9 bit words in a specified form, set out in a detailed encoding table. The least significant bit of each 9 bit word should be transmitted first. The signal should be conveyed in NRZ (non-return to zero) form with the bit stream carried on either coaxial cable or fibre optic bearer. Peak to peak signal amplitude should lie between 400mV and 700mV measured across a 75Ω resistive load connected directly to the output terminals without any transmission line.

3.2.6 Digital transmission (links)

Digital transmission of video and/or audio programme channels over well engineered links is capable of offering a performance that is virtually independent of distance or of the number of regenerating, multiplexing or switching stages involved. Overall, quality is determined by the parameters chosen for the encoding of the signal and the performance of the encoders/decoders (codecs). Multiplexed digital signals can be transmitted without significant mutual interference (crosstalk). Digital links offer flexibility in their ability to carry video, audio, data facsimile and telephony signals with equal facility, and to carry such services without requiring a long 'lead time' to set up. Digital transmission is well suited to the use of optical fibre links with widely spaced regenerators.

It is foreseen that eventually inter city links for both television and sound radio will use digital transmission within the ISDN hierarchy.

The economics of digital distribution and contribution circuits is less certain. The introduction by telecommunications carriers of, for example, digital stereo links for outside broadcasts has tended to be accompanied by higher costs, leading to increasing use of satellite links for outside broadcast of sound radio.

The serial bit rate of digital video to the CCIR Recommendation 601 (4:2:2) standard within studio centres is 243Mbit/s (216Mbit/s of video data). However, once the requirement for editorial processing has been completed, the bit rate can be significantly reduced without noticeable loss of quality.

For inter city links, the bit rate will normally be reduced to meet the 140 or 70Mbit/s ISDN hierarchy levels. For international transmission via satellite or for satellite news gathering bit rate reduction can be to the 35Mbit/s level. A rate of 30Mbit/s to 45Mbit/s is practical for international TV links since two TV programmes, of better quality than with FM transmission, can be transmitted through a 36MHz transponder.

If necessary, for satellite distribution to cable networks, it is possible that four programmes at 15Mbit/s of NTSC/525 can be transmitted through a single transponder, although picture quality will be significantly degraded unless sophisticated bit-reduction systems are used.

Where the highest quality digital transmission of CCIR Recommendation 601 (4:2:2) digital signals is required, 140Mbit/s (or more precisely 139.264Mbit/s) represents the European standard fourth order digital transmission level chosen to provide $30 \times 4 \times 4 \times 4 = 1920$ telephone channels each of 64kbit/s, after taking into account the necessary housekeeping overheads incurred at each multiplexing stage.

For a typical 140Mbit/s system, 5Mbit/s are allotted for audio, asynchronous multiplexing and other system housekeeping, leaving about 134Mbit/s for the coded video signal. Removal of the line blanking periods from 4:2:2 digital component video results in 175.5Mbit/s representing the active line periods. This provides a theoretical bit rate reduction of 18% at the cost of some buffer storage and digital line sync data.

A further 8% reduction could be achieved by the removal of the field blanking intervals, although this would require significantly more buffer storage. With about 134Mbit/s available for digital video, the effective average data word length must still be reduced from its initial 8 bits to an average of not more than 6.11 bits. There are a number of ways in which this modest degree of reduction can be implemented. For example, an experimental system developed by the IBA investigated two main approaches. The first involved discarding alternate samples with sub-Nyquist sampling and the second used differential pulse code modulation (DPCM). Variations and combinations of these two basic techniques were simulated.

In sub-Nyquist sampling, advantage is taken of the two dimensional sampling nature of the digitised video signal to maintain horizontal and vertical spatial frequency response at the expense of some small loss of resolution and the introduction of some aliasing in diagonal frequencies. DPCM removes some of the redundancy in a typical TV signal by transmitting only difference information between samples within some areas of the picture.

Excellent results were achieved with hybrid (H) DPCM, in which every fourth word in a line quincunx structure remained in an un-modified 8 bit linear PCM sample. The pattern of these data words was then used as the basis of two dimensional predictor/interpolators for the intervening words, which were non-linearly coded 5 bit differences. This HDPCM 8-5-5-5 mode results in an average word length of 5.75bits, reducing the 175.5Mbit/s data to just over 126Mbit/s with virtually no perceptible loss of quality.

3.2.7 Teletext transmission

During the 1970s, a data transmission system riding 'piggy-back' on conventional television transmission was developed in the UK and introduced under the service designations Ceefax (BBC) and Oracle (IBA-ITV). An agreed technical specification was introduced in 1974. Teletext transmission systems have since been introduced in a number of countries, and basically similar systems but with rather different technical specifications have also been developed in some countries. Teletext (Figure 3.16) uses the broadcast television signal to carry extra information. These extra signals do not interfere with the transmission and reception of normal programmes. A teletext receiver, a television receiver with additional circuits, is capable of reconstructing written information and displaying it on the screen. The system allows the transmission of very many bulletins of information, and the viewer can choose any one by selecting a three figure

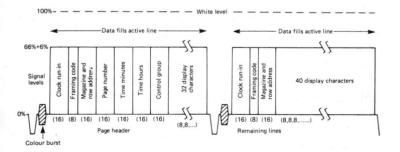

Figure 3.16   Teletext data organisation. (The figures in brackets are the number of binary digits)

number on a set of controls, usually push buttons. After a short interval the information appears and remains for as long as it is needed.

A major use of teletext is as an information service, but it can also supplement normal television programmes with subtitles or linked pages. The entire signal is accommodated within the existing 625 line television allocation, and so costs nothing in terms of radio frequency spectrum space. It was, effectively, the first broadcasting system to transmit information in digital form.

Teletext pages look rather like pages of typescript, except that they can also include large sized letters and sinple drawings. The standard sized words can use upper or lower case, and be in any one of six colours, red, green, blue, yellow, cyan and magenta or white. The shape of the characters is usually based on a 7×5 dot matrix, with a refinement known as character rounding. As many as 24 rows of the standard sized characters can be fitted on a page, and each row can have up to 40 characters. Each page can carry about 150 to 200 words.

The specification also allows the option of characters of twice the height of standard characters. Larger sized characters and also drawings are made by assembling small illuminated rectangles, each one sixth the size of the space occupied by a standard character, and these too can be in any of the six colours or in white. Part or all of each page can be made to flash on and off (usually once per second), to emphasise any particular item.

The page background is usually black, although the specification allows the editor to define different background colours for part or all of the screen. Also, at the teletext editor's discretion, text can be enclosed in a black window and cut into the normal picture. Furthermore, certain receiver designs allow the whole page (sometimes in white only) to be superimposed upon the picture.

It is potentially possible for the system to carry up to 800 single pages but, because of the way the pages are transmitted, this could mean an appreciable waiting time between page selections. So for the moment not all 800 pages are used at any one time.

Additional circuits are needed in a television receiver to decode teletext. First, data extraction and recognition circuits examine the incoming 'conveyer belt' of teletext data lines, and extract those signals which make up the page which has been selected. The data from these lines is then stored, usually in a semiconductor memory, so that the page can be displayed at the same rate as a normal picture. The binary number codes are then translated to their corresponding characters or graphics patterns. Finally a video raster scan representation of the page is switched onto the screen.

3.2.8 Digital audio standards

A number of different sampling rates have emerged for digital audio systems:

1. Broadcast audio distribution is based on a sampling rate of 32kHz to provide a 15kHz audio bandwidth, with 14 bit linear (uniform) coding.
2. Professional recording studios use a sampling rate of 48kHz equivalent to 1920 audio samples per video frame (625 line, 25Hz frames) or 2000 audio samples per frame for 24fps film, with 16 or 20 bit coding.
3. Compact disc records (masters) have a sampling rate of 44.1kHz (CD/EIAJ/RDAT replay only, 14 or 16 bits).

It is generally accepted that 16 bit/sample coding offers satisfactory quality, but for signals prior to level control, or combined signals having a very wide dynamic range, longer data words are required of 20 bits or more per sample.

Interface units permit conversion between sampling rates of 32kHz, 44.1kHz and 48kHz. Rate conversion between 44.1kHz and 48kHz is rather more difficult than 32kHz to 48kHz. Cascading a number of sample rate converters (SRCs) tends to degrade the signal. Mixing consumer and professional digital audio equipment can result in balance, level and impedance differences in routeing. Amplitude levels rather than reflections tend to cause the most problems. Digital audio synchronisation at mixing (switching) points represents a new requirement.

For the distribution of 48kHz digital audio, the EBU/AES/IEC system (see Figure 3.17) uses bi-phase Mark coding which has the

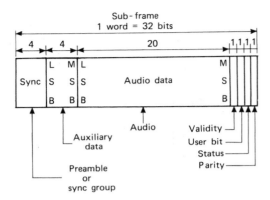

Figure 3.17 AES/EBU audio interface

effect of shifting the required frequency spectrum to between 1.5MHz and 3MHz rather than to 1.5MHz.

This system has 32 bit data words, 24 bits for audio data, sandwiched between a 4 bit sync/preamble and 4 bit parity and selection messages. Since this standard is not error corrected, it needs clean distribution (low bit error rate). With a 48kHz sampling frequency, the audio bandwidth is 20Hz to 20kHz (±0.5dB, depending on sampling filters) and quantisation provides 16 bits/sample linear (standard mode) and up to 20 bits/sample (high fidelity mode), giving a dynamic range of more than 90dB.

3.2.9 Audio digital companding

For the distribution of high quality (15kHz) audio signals in digital form, a sampling rate of 32kHz and a quantising level signal to noise ratio of about 75dB is desirable. The required SNR can be achieved in the initial digitisation with 13 bit linear PCM. This has a theoretical SNR of 83dB and is reduced to 81.5dB by the addition of a dither signal to remove 'granular' distortion on critical low level material. The dither signal can be at half sampling frequency and have an

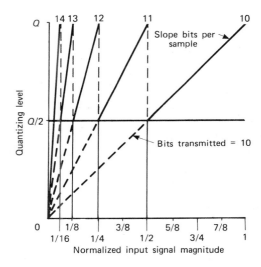

Figure 3.18   NICAM-3 near instantaneous companding law

amplitude equal to half a quantising step together with white noise at a level of 4dB below the inherent quantising noise. In practice for point to point links, a single parity check digit is added to each 13 bit sample word.

A 13 channel PCM sound distribution system introduced by BBC Radio in 1972 had a transmission bit rate of 6.336Mbit/s. This has been progressively superseded by a 6 channel system with near instantaneous companding (NICAM-3) (see Figure 3.18) with a total transmission bit rate of 2.048Mbit/s (676Kbit/s for each stereo pair).

High quality audio links are more vulnerable to bit errors than digital video. Without error protection, 'just perceptible' impairment can be detected with a BER of the order of $1:10^7$. With protection of the five most significant bits (MSBs), an equivalent impairment would need a BER of $1:10^5$.

With instantaneous companding, a limited number of digits are transmitted per sample word together with a scale factor indicating the significance (weight) of the transmitted word. For near instanta-neous companding, the scale factor is transmitted less frequency (for example, once every 32 samples), its value being determined by the peak signal level during the complete group of 32 samples.

NICAM-3 encodes the audio samples to 14 bits, placing each block of 32 samples (one millisecond) into one of five ranges, deter-mined by the largest value sample within the block. By discarding leading zeros and MSBs according to the range, this compresses the samples to 10 bits for transmission. This has the effect that the lowest level samples are encoded to 14 bit accuracy with the highest level samples to 10 bit accuracy. The range codes for three blocks of 32 samples are combined into a 7 bit code and four Hamming code protection bits are added. The five MSBs in each sample word are protected by parity checks, enabling error concealment by interpola-tion at the decoder.

3.2.10 Multichannel sound systems

Although the monaural sound channel of conventional television broadcasting is capable of providing high fidelity (15kHz) audio, this has seldom been reflected in the design of domestic receivers. In-creasing consumer awareness of the fidelity provided by other media, including FM stereo radio, stereo cassette tapes and digital CD records, has led to the development of systems for dual channel and multichannel audio for television capable of providing sufficient separation to permit simultaneous dual language broadcasting.

The desirable requirements include: general improvement of sound quality; possibility of receiving stereo sound programmes in mono (direct compatibility); possibility of receiving mono pro-grammes on stereo receivers (reverse compatibility); no discernible interference between picture and audio channels; possibility of trans-mitting either a stereo or two or more separate high quality mono channels; maximum possible technological compatibility with exist-ing systems and equipment, and receiver decoder costs compatible with perceived benefits to the viewer. For $(L + R)/(L - R)$ stereo a separation of 25dB to 30dB is considered sufficient. For bilingual transmission, separation of the order of at least 55dB is required.

3.2.10.1 *One carrier systems (with FM subcarriers)*

In the Japanese FM/FM system (1978) the subcarrier is locked to the second harmonic of the line frequency (31.5kHz for 525 line systems) with a switching (AM) subcarrier at 55kHz.

The American BTSC/MTS system (Broadcast Television Systems Committee/Multichannel Television Sound) is derived from the pilot tone FM stereo system used in radio broadcasting but with a pilot frequency (15.734kHz) locked to the video line frequency and with 'dBx' noise reduction. There is provision for a 15kHz stereo quadrature channel plus a 10kHz monophonic 'second audio channel' (sap) on a low level subcarrier at five times the vision line frequency and, where required, an engineer's order wire ('professional channel') on a subcarrier at six times the vision line frequency.

3.2.10.2 *Two carrier systems*

The German dual channel system for stereo or bilingual sound transmission has (for System G) a separate carrier located 5.742MHz above the vision carrier at −20dB in addition to the normal sound carrier at 5.5MHz above the vision carrier at −13dB. The 242kHz difference between the sound carrier is an odd harmonic of the vision line frequency. The usual sound FM carrier is modulated with (L + R)/2, and the second carrier with only the R signal (or with a second language or separate audio signal) with a deviation of ±2.5kHz. A mode identification signal is provided on a tone modulated 54.6875kHz subcarrier (unmodulated for mono, 117.5Hz AM for stereo, 274.1Hz AM for separate audio).

The Nicam 728 system uses digital quadrature phase shift keying to digitally modulate the second carrier located (for System 1) 6.552MHz above the vision carrier with a carrier level of −20dB with respect to peak vision. The two audio channels (stereo or bilingual) are combined in time division multiplex as a digital bit stream comprising 728 bit frames each of 1ms duration, giving a bit rate of 728kbit/s. The audio signals are sampled at 32kHz with an initial resolution of 14 bits/sample and near instantaneous compression to 10 bits/sample in 32 sample blocks. Error protection comprises one

Table 3.6 Main characteristics of NICAM-728

Item	Characteristic
Number of sound channels with 15kHz bandwidth	2
Pre-emphasis of sound signals	According to CCIT Recommendation J17
Sampling frequency	32kHz
Initial coding of sound signals	14 bits/sample linear PCM
Companding	Quasi instantaneous with compression to 10 bits/sample in 32 sample blocks
Error protection	Parity check of six most significant bits by adding a parity check to every 10-bit sample
Frame format	Frame length is 728 bits/millisecond (frame sync word 8 bits, control word 5 bits, additional data 11 bits, sound data 704 bits)
Bit rate of sound and data	728kbit/s
Transmission method of digital audio information and data in a composite video signal	Frequency multiplex by introducing an additional sound carrier at 5.85MHz (Systems B, G) or 6.552MHz (System 1) from vision carrier
Type of modulation of additional sound carrier	Four positional phase shift keying (DQPSK) i.e. differentially encoded QPSK
Spectrum shaping	100% cosine roll off split equally between transmitter and receiver (overall bandwidth of digital signal approximately 728kHz)
Scale factor signalling	By modification of 9 parity bits per scale factor bit, detected by majority decision logic (3 bits per sound coding block, two blocks per frame)
Bit interleaving (sound data)	44 x 16 (frame alignment word not interleaved)
Energy dispersal scrambling	By modulo two addition of a pseudo-random sequence of length 2^9-1 bits synchronously with the multiplex frame. Frame alignment word not scrambled

parity bit added to each 10 bit sample to check the six most significant bits. The transmission of the conventional mono channel is unaffected.

The characteristics of NICAM-728 for television standards B, G, 1 are shown in Table 3.6.

3.3 Cable distribution systems

Since the early days of television broadcasting, cable distribution systems have been around. They arose because of the difficulty of achieving good quality reception; this often required the aerial to be placed in an advantageous position, probably on high ground. It became natural then to share this facility by cabling to local households.

From the early local enterprises, perhaps initiated by electrical goods shops wishing to increase the sales of receivers, there arose specific cable TV firms. The first heyday of cable distribution systems in the 1950s and 1960s was as an off air TV, and radio, relay system. Though far from universal, it was a significant business in many countries covering areas of poor reception, hotels, appartment blocks, and sometimes towns where external aerials were not allowed for aesthetic reasons.

As over the air broadcast transmissions improved their coverage, the relay systems fell into disuse and cable TV had to look to providing additional services to prove its worth. Systems using coaxial cable were replacing the original multi-line twisted pair systems, and enabling more TV channels to be carried, so 'out of area' broadcasts, satellite receptions and tape based channels could be added. Coaxial systems carry 50 or more channels per cable, and fibre optics is starting to find a foothold, especially in hybrid fibre-coax systems.

Cable TV remains very variable in terms of its impact in different countries. From the 1970s it began to increase rapidly in North America and certain European countries, such that by the end of the 1980s some very high penetrations of the service (up to 90%) had been achieved. However in other places it remains in its infancy, or at least confined to certain special areas. Its spread has been influenced by broadcast TV quality, local terrain, prosperity, commercial pressures, and government regulations. The last of these became increasingly important when additional services were introduced, all the more now that carriage of non-TV services like telephony and data is under consideration in some countries.

3.3.1 Terminology

It is useful to establish at the outset some of the general terms used about cable distribution systems. The technical terms will be explained later as they arise.

CATV. Community Antenna TV; although still widely used in a general sense, it has connotations of a limited relay service. The term 'Cable TV' is superseding it for modern systems (those in the industry often just contract this to 'Cable').

MATV. Mast Antenna TV; a local system for a hotel or appartment block. Where a satellite dish supplements the off-air reception the term SMATV is used.

Homes Passed. The number of residences which could be connected to a cable TV system, given the existing extent of its build i.e. those needing just a final cable drop into the home.

Penetration. The number of homes connected as a percentage of the homes passed.

Churn. The proportion of customers ceasing and taking up the service.

Spin.   The changing of customers between levels of services (tiers of channels).

Head end. The source point for service on a cable TV network. This is where the video channels, radio, and any other service are formulated into a multiplex to be launched out on the network. Typically it might be fed itself by links from remote aerial sites and a studio (where the cable operator may generate tape based programming and process other channels).

Hub site. Further site(s) after the head end where sufficient processing occurs to warrant internal housing of equipment.

Figures 3.19 and 3.20 illustrate somes of these terms.

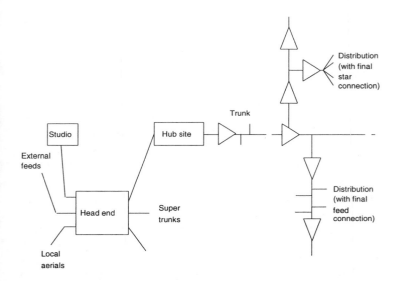

Figure 3.19   Tree and branch cable TV network

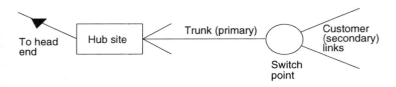

Figure 3.20   Switched star cable TV network

3.3.2 Services

Until recently the cable TV service package had been straightforward — multichannel TV and, probably, FM radio. National regulations may define a 'must carry' set of channels, probably those available locally off air and the radio. The operator would then normally for marketing reasons wish to segment the channels into tiers, a low cost basic tier incorporating the must carry set, and a number of premium tiers culminating in the recent film channel. This market need for varying the channel selection delivered to different customers, so called 'conditional access', has important technical implications; the pursuit of a cost effective and safe (from programme theft) means of doing this has been a major preoccupation of the cable TV industry.

Generally the video format to the customer has conformed to the standard TV receiver input, namely vestigial sideband amplitude modulation (VSB-AM) of the national standard format (NTSC, PAL, SECAM) in a frequency division multiplex (FDM) as illustrated in

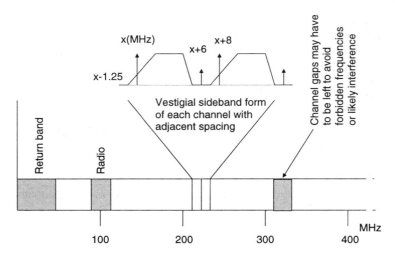

Figure 3.21 Typical spectrum on a tree and branch network. (8MHz spacing for PAL-1 shown; 6MHz and 7MHz spacing also used)

Figure 3.21. Because of the large channel capacity of cable TV systems there are three major differences from receiving off air signals. Firstly the frequency range covered is larger, meaning conventional TV set tuners may not cover it fully; secondly channel spacing may be closer and tuner selectivity may be inadequate; thirdly the number of presettable tuning buttons may be inadequate to give convenient viewing. In countries with high penetration so called 'cable ready' TV sets are available to which a network can directly input. Otherwise set top units may be required to select out the required channel and offer it to the set at an appropriate frequency.

In recent years further service types have come under consideration, the most prominent being pay per view. Whereas the tiers received by a customer will be determined by the monthly subscription paid, pay per view gives the opportunity for access to a specific premium programme at short notice. Technically this implies interaction from the customer; though achievable by a telephone call, more automated techniques are preferable to deal with a potentially large volume response in a short time window.

The term video on demand can encompass both pay per view and the video library concept. Whereas pay per view remains a broadcast service, offered to all prepared to pay the premium at the time, video library introduces narrowcasting, whereby a customer (or a limited group of them) accesses a particular item from a centralised source. This concept has had only limited trials to date, but continues to excite interest.

Radio relay has been a long term service provided by networks, with it being relatively easy to transmit the FM band at good quality on a coaxial cable. Recently there is interest in providing additional hi-fi audio services, including the possibility of an audio library.

Cable TV networks are starting to look beyond their traditional services into the following types of area:

1.   Audience interactive; voting, home shopping, home banking etc.
2.   Information services; data to the home or as text on a screen.
3.   Low speed data.
4.   Telephony.

3.3.3 Network types

3.3.3.1 *H.f. multipair*

In this old type of system individual channels were modulated at high
frequency (h.f. 3MHz to 30MHz region) onto individual twisted
pairs. Selection in the home was via a simple switch linking the
required pair to the input of a special h.f. TV set. TV sound could be
modulated with the video, but was often sent at baseband on its own
pair in company with other audio services.

The system was straightforward, there being low loss at h.f.,
capable of good quality, but of course limited in channel capacity
such that it is now obsolete.

3.3.3.2 *Tree and branch coaxial*

The obvious successor to multipair operation was coaxial cable carrying a multiplex of TV channels in the v.h.f. band (30MHz to
300MHz). As this signal spreads out from the originating head end
the structure resembles a tree trunk with branches arising as it is both
amplified and split (Figure 3.19). Originally systems were truly
confined to the v.h.f. region, but have in recent years spread into the
u.h.f. region to accommodate greater channel numbers.

By the end of the 1980s 550MHz systems were being installed
with 860MHz ones in the pipeline. With a 550MHz system channel
capacity can be from between 40 and 80 channels, the exact number
depending on factors such as channel bandwidth and spacing, forbid-
den frequency bands, and compatibility with TV receivers and over
the air broadcasts, all of which vary between and perhaps within
countries.

The network is of a broadcast nature with all channels reaching all
connected customers, unless special measures are taken. Conditional
access is achieved in two main ways. A frequency trap external to the
premises can remove blocks of channels. It is cheap but very inflexible; changes in tiers wanted (spin) mean a physical change of trap,
and more general rearrangement of channels into different tiers is
awkward for the cable operator.

A more flexible technique is to scramble all but the basic tier of channels, and provide a set top unit to descramble those that the customer has paid extra to watch. A simple unit would have fixed capability, but it then needs changing out if the customer needs a different service. Addressable units change their capability on commands from codes sent in a data stream over the network from the head end. The disadvantages of scrambling are that it involves a relatively expensive unit in the home, that it affects video quality, and that it is liable to programme theft from pirate versions of the set top unit.

There is a strong desire nowadays that at least the basic programme tier should be deliverable without the need for a unit in the home. Hence it should be placed in the spectrum so as to be able to feed directly into the TV set.

The dominant feature of the network design is the amplification need. Loss for a coaxial cable is proportional to the square root of frequency, so it is an increasing problem with modern systems. Amplifiers are required for two reasons, however, to allow for splitting as well as cable loss. For the trunk portion larger cross section cable and more sophisticated amplifiers can be afforded compared to the distribution area.

3.3.3.3 *Switched star*

From the late 1970s an alternative structure was being considered with a dedicated cable feed to each customer (Figure 3.20). This offered a number of potential advantages, most obviously easier interactivity. Control of the service selection via a video switch gave secure control (no need for scrambling to achieve tiering) and allowed a tailored service package to be delivered to the customer not constrained by the capacity of the final coaxial link (since only the wanted channels have to be transmitted along it). Technology was also a driver, since this network type was seen as an application for fibre.

In Europe a limited number of these systems have been installed, some all coxial, some part fibre, and some all fibre. Matching the low cost of the tree and branch networks for basic TV delivery has proved the expected problem. It was clear that the dedicated link would have to be kept short to reduce per customer cost; how short depended on technical solution, for u.h.f. delivery 200m and for v.h.f. delivery 500m maximum to avoid amplification on a coaxial link; for fibre 1km or more. In nearly all cases the switch was therefore street sited.

3.3.4 Transmission

3.3.4.1 *Modulation techniques*

For video there are the following main techniques employed:

1.   Amplitude modulation, the standard method matching the TV receiver input format. To reduce bandwidth (to between 6MHz and 8MHz) vestigial sideband (VSB) is normally used on cable networks, as done over the air. Although simplest and cheapest, it is not a robust technique, being prone to noise as it builds up through amplifier stages and to interfering signals (external or internal from intermodulation). Until recently it was not considered appropriate for fibre transmission, because of the intrinsic noise and non-linearity of optical sources; technology advances have dramatically changed this recently.
2.   Frequency modulation. The FM improvement factor gives greatly improved noise and interference immunity at the expense of bandwidth (30MHz per channel typically). It has been used quite extensively on longer super trunk links over both coaxial cable and fibre.
3.   Digital modulation. This similarly gives improved noise and interference immunity, but with the additional advantage of no degradation with repeatering. It is more suited to fibre than coaxial cable (the latter having considerable equalisation problems). It has had limited use to date because of cost, but there are signs now of it making a bigger impact.

For audio service the standard FM radio band (88MHz to 108MHz) has been relayed over the cable, perhaps repositioning the carriers and adding channels in on new carriers. However the FM improvement is very low for a stereo broadcast. This then presents almost as severe a problem for fibre as mentioned above for AM transmission of video. Digital audio transmission is now receiving interest because of its impact in the domestic equipment area; it promises very high quality over both coaxial cable and fibre within reasonable bandwidths.

3.3.4.2 *Coaxial*

The essence of designing a coaxial tree and branch system is the balancing of the cable and splitter loss incurred in delivery to the customers by the use of appropriate amplifiers, placed before signal degradation has gone too far. Because street sited amplifiers must be placed regularly at quite short distances (every few hundred metres), and with relatively little tolerance on the distance, design can only proceed with a detailed knowledge of the area to be cabled.

Cable loss varies according to the square root of frequency, and hence equalisation must occur in the amplifiers to boost the higher frequencies compared to the lower. This can be done by both compensation to the received signal, and deliberate tilt to the launched signal. Given that this is done, the basic loss balancing exercise can be done by considering one frequency (usually the highest). Thus a trunk cable might have a loss of 50dB per km at 450MHz. A cable run of 500m therefore needs an amplifier of 25dB gain at this frequency to restore the signal. A splitter in the run would add further loss, around 3.5dB to 4dB for each two way stage in an even split; an asymmetric split can be used to tap off a line at a high loss leaving the through loss relatively low.

As the network spreads out cost and convenience means that cable dimensions get smaller and losses higher. Thus at 450MHz a super trunk cable of diameter 39mm might have a loss of 25dB/km, whereas the final short underground feed might be only 8mm diameter and 170dB/km loss (overhead feeds being smaller and even higher loss).

Amplifiers are imperfect devices and introduce noise and non-linearity. Thus each time one is used the noise performance will deteriorate and cross modulation between the channels will occur; hence the 'run' of amplifiers is limited. The manufacturer's specification will indicate a noise figure and cross modulation performance, which enables the effects to be calculated. Given that the equalisation process is also imperfect, and there are other impairments, the run may be less than this basic calculation indicates.

There are different designs of amplifiers (Slater, 1988), push-pull, feed forward, and power doubling are three main types, each of which has different features in terms of noise, distortion, and of course cost. They are designed to match different parts of the network, there being trunk, distribution and line extender versions as the network progresses outwards. Some are also combinations of amplifier(s) and splitter(s) e.g. a mainline bridger combination giving amplification in both the trunk and branch line.

In modern systems impairment has been reduced by having for each channel incrementally related carriers (IRC, equal spacing between each channel) or harmonically related carriers (HRC, each carrier an exact multiple of the spacing). This ensures that carrier intermodulation products fall exactly on other carrier frequencies (2nd and 3rd order for HRC, just 3rd order for IRC) rather than within the actual video signal, where they would give subjectively annoying interference.

Another important feature to bear in mind is signal level. Amplifier inputs and outputs are designed for specific levels (though with some tolerance); differences may affect the gain and certainly could increase impairments. Additionally coaxial networks, particularly joints, are not perfectly immune from the outside world. Too low a level signal could be subject to external interference; too high a level could cause radiation beyond national regulations.

It is useful to define a zero reference level in dB terms, rather than voltage or wattage terms, since cable loss and amplifier gain are in this form. Thus 0dBmV is defined as the level corresponding to 1mV across 75 ohms (the characteristic impedance of all coaxial cable used in cable TV).

3.3.4.3 *Optical*

Except for super trunk links, optical transmission is in its infancy for cable TV application, but is rapidly becoming a major issue. In terms of network design the task is relatively straightforward because the long range of an optical link often means an external repeater can be avoided. The essential features in selecting an optical system are:

1.   Channel capacity per fibre.
2.   The video performance requirement, which will obviously influence the quality and cost of a link's components, but may also limit the channel capacity and the type of modulation method that can be used.
3.   The input and output interface requirements. For example, are the signals baseband or already modulated in a form suitable for optical transmission? Also how is TV sound to be carried?
4.   The length of link, and hence optical loss to be incurred.
5.   Optical power output, and whether there are any safety implications.

The designer may not need to know optical technicalities in any detail, but some aspects worth being aware of are:

1.   Fibre type, only single mode fibre will be relevant nowadays for video links. Multi mode is appropriate for shorter, lower capacity links. Single mode (core diameter $< 10\mu$) is a little more difficult to joint and connectorise than multi mode (core diameter $> 50\mu$).
2.   Wavelength 1300nm (1.3μ) or 1550nm optical devices could be used with single mode fibre. 1550nm offers slightly lower loss, but possible bandwidth limitation (caused by 'dispersion') which increases with transmission distance.
3.   Source output level, measured in milliwatts, or fractions thereof, for lasers, or microwatts for lower power LEDs. Alternatively dBm is used, which is the power relative to 1mW; thus for example −3dBm is 0.5mW, and +6dBm is 4mW.
4.   Receiver sensitivity, the minimum optical power that can be received whilst maintaining the required performance.
5.   Relative intensity noise (RIN), the noise within the optical source itself, which could degrade the signal prior to launching onto the fibre. It is measured as dB/Hz; better than −

120dB/Hz might be all right for a digital or FM link, but for AM better than −150dB/Hz is required.

6.   Optical budget, the difference in dBs between source output level and receiver sensitivity. It shows what is available for fibre loss, splice and connector loss, splitter (if used) loss, and a margin for temperature, ageing etc.

3.3.5 Switching

Most existing cable TV systems do not apparently incorporate switching. In fact the effective switch is the TV set tuner, selecting a channel by filtering it out from the incoming multiplex, demodulating it and routeing it to the set's output stages. A similar function will also be done within a set top unit, ending up with frequency translation of the selected channel to a convenient position in the spectrum (there may be intermediate demodulation to carry out descrambling),

Video switching within the network is of course a central feature of switched star systems. Two basic techniques are used, space switching and frequency agile switching.

3.3.5.1 *Space switching*

This is essentially the familiar crosspoint matrix (Figure 3.22) where an input is physically linked to an output line when a crosspoint is made. For a cable TV application a broadcast switch is needed i.e. one where one input might be connected to several outputs. Thus the loading of an input signal is variable from 1 to n outputs; hence there are buffer amplifiers needed as shown in Figure 3.22.

A number of devices can be used as the crosspoints. Relays make a direct wire connection, and coaxial versions are capable of very high performance and bandwidths; even miniature versions are relatively large and mainly suited to head end or studio uses. Semiconductors, such as the CMOS and DMOS FET devices, can provide analogue switches with a good degree of integration on a chip. Although 'on' resistances are at least a few tens of ohms and capacitive signal leakage occurs in the 'off' state, good quality compact matrices for cable TV use can be constructed able to switch baseband

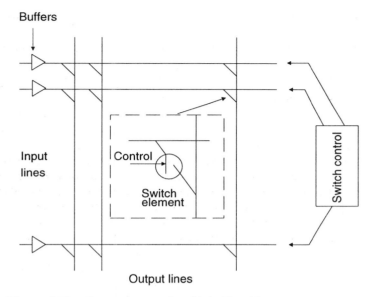

Figure 3.22 Crosspoint matrix with buffered inputs

video signals. Higher frequency switching is quite possible, but crosstalk problems will imply very careful board design and probably lower integration.

Digital crosspoints are relatively straightforward; a simple AND gate performs this function with one input as signal and one as control. Both ECL and CMOS technologies are used, the latter in particular being capable of high integration and high speeds (16 in/16 out chips working at 200Mbit/s have been produced). Their use for cable TV has been limited because nearly all transmission has been analogue.

3.3.5.2 *Frequency agile switching*

The second approach used has been frequency agile switching (Figure 3.23), utilising the tuner function described above. This is popular where the incoming feed is a frequency division multiplex of many

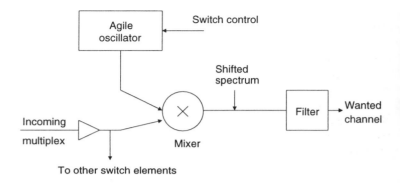

Figure 3.23   Frequency agile switch

channels, as on tree and branch systems. A frequency agile oscillator
is mixed with the multiplex, such that the desired channel is translated
to a specific frequency slot, where it is then filtered out from the rest
of the channels. Varying the oscillator frequency will therefore select
different channels. The attraction of the technique is that it deals
directly with the available signal without demultiplexing; its limitation is the relatively large size of equipment.

Other approaches not yet used in cable TV but of potential interest
in the future are:

1.   Time switching (i.e. moving from one time slot to another
     within a digital multiplex).
2.   Packet switching (useful if variable bit rate coding is applied
     taking account of the fact that changes in picture content vary
     from time to time).
3.   Optical switching, which can itself take the form of space
     switches, frequency (wavelength) switches, or time switches.

3.3.6 Performance standards

National standards for cable TV are set in many countries, though
they may only be guidelines rather than mandatory. Although broadly

in agreement on acceptable levels, there are some variations between countries, in particular due to the different TV standards (NTSC, PAL, SECAM). Further it may be possible to trade one parameter off against another, as explained below.

Compared to audio, there is for the uninitiated a bewildering array of video performance parameters, and it is a major topic in its own right. There are in fact two ways that a measured impairment may be quoted, in objective or subjective terms. The objective version is the physical measurement taken (e.g. in dBs, % etc.); sometimes it is converted into its subjective equivalent (using standard formulae) measured in 'imps'. This latter was derived originally from real viewing assessments made of different levels of each parameter for their annoyance value, and allows one to compare the impairment from different parameters in the same terms.

It is not sensible here to explain each type of parameter, but Table 3.7 does classify them into types and lists the objective value equivalent to 1/8th imp. In this table a weighting filter is used to allow for the eye's varying sensitivity to noise according to its position in the video signal's spectrum. Also the equivalent carrier/noise figure for VSB-AM signal is 45.6dB. Within reason imps can be added up, and the total for a good network might be no more than 1/2 imp. Most parameters must therefore fall well below the 1/8th imp value, but according to the nature of the network it may be sensible to let some produce more impairment than others e.g. K-rating and single frequency interference might be allowed to be relatively high.

The signal inputting to the network, perhaps received off air, will itself be already impaired, and this will contribute to the ultimate impairment at the end of the network. For concatenated links like this some parameters will add up predictably (e.g. signal/noise ratio), whilst others will not and indeed could even improve if opposite trends occur on the links.

Individual measurement techniques exist for each parameter, but nowadays automatic measurement equipment is available, which, though not cheap, will provide a read out of a large range of these. An associated test signal generator provides the source to input to the network or equipment under test. However most broadcast channels

Table 3.7 Video performance parameters and their equivalent to an impairment of one-eight imp, measured at baseband for PAL-1 signals

	Parameter	*Value*
Linear distortions	K ratings	5%
	Echoes	4.5%
	Chrominance/luminance gain inequality	27%
	Chrominance/luminance delay inequality	150ns
Non-linear distortions	Differential gain	21%
	Differential phase	24 degrees
	Luminance line-time non-linearity	21%
	Chrominance/luminance crosstalk	24%
Noise/ interference	Signal/noise (unified weighting)	45dB
	Single frequency interference	57dB at < 1MHz
	Crosstalk (undistorted)	50dB

also include the test signals in their vertical blanking period, allowing the total degradation to that channel to be assessed.

The above measurements relate to the baseband video signal, on which a full analysis of impairments can be carried out. However on coaxial tree and branch networks in particular, only signals in their r.f. multiplex are directly accessible; demodulation to baseband must be performed by high quality equipment to avoid this process adding significant impairment itself. Everyday analysis is often better carried out directly at r.f. for those parameters where it is possible; carrier to noise (C/N) is one such measurement (with a target of 43dB upwards for a full cable TV network), and to cover second and third order intermodulation performance composite second order (CSO) and composite triple beat (CTB) are parameters commonly used.

3.3.7 Future trends

This area is well served by papers in journals and conferences, and references are given later to which the reader should turn for detailed information. Service possibilities have been indicated earlier, and how these are taken up will affect the technical evolution significantly. The major areas of activity are likely to be as below.

3.3.7.1 *More channels*

Proposals for pushing the coaxial network technology to beyond 1GHz means 100+ channels becoming possible. Some of these may be available then for narrowcasting to one or a few individuals.

3.3.7.2 *Enhanced TV formats*

A number of higher quality formats for the video signal have been proposed round the world, and cable TV is having to start to think about catering for them. One basic point is that a channel may have to be transmitted in both the present standard (NTSC, PAL, SECAM) and the enhanced form. Thus it is another driver towards the need for more channel capacity.

True high definition TV (HDTV) with a base bandwidth of circa 30MHz would present a real problem, except for advanced fibre systems. More modest enhancements, and hence bandwidth requirements, arise from systems like the Japanese MUSE, the American advanced TV (probably now compatible with 6MHz spacing), and the European MAC family (ranging from 7MHz to 16MHz spacing needed according to type and implementation).

The main problem for the cable operator is to know which new format will be widely implemented, and when to plan for the extra capability.

3.3.7.3 *Conditional access*

Improved techniques will be sought here, particularly with pay per view in mind. Switching is one answer; another is interdiction (spoiling all but the wanted signal) rather than scrambling.

3.3.7.4 *Fibre optic enhancement*

This made some impact a few years ago with multichannel FM links in the super trunk, and now with significant interest in digital operation there. More recently the practicality of AM multiplexes over fibre has excited enormous interest. The prospect of replacing the large chains of coaxial cable amplifiers allows both improved performance (which in many existing systems has been decidely substandard) and more channel capacity. This now seems a major trend with perhaps a final feed of just 3 or 4 amplifiers left.

The AM fibre optic links in particular have not to date been cheap; as they reduce in cost this will help their application to become wider. The advent of the optical amplifier may help here, enhancing their modest optical budget and allowing optical splitting.

3.3.7.5 *New architectures*

The tree and branch structure has remained remarkably resilient and has itself made advances in increased capacity. The fibre optic enhancement above will be a major change, itself creating other openings. It will naturally zone a system into areas of a few hundred or thousands of people depending on its depth of penetration into the network. This may then favour associating with the zone, switches and multiplexers for data and telephony. A hybrid network may grow up mixing switched star and tree and branch concepts.

Instead of the point to point optical links now being installed, splitters will be introduced to share the capacity more economically (but will of course be combiners for any reverse traffic up the network). Whether fibre will ever sensibly be taken through to the home is a matter of fierce debate. Many see coaxial cable surviving for the final feed, both because optical equipment costs will not be

low enough on a per customer basis and to avoid powering and
housing it in the home. Another alternative to remember is the
possibility of radio as that final feed, probably at high microwave
frequencies.

3.4 Digital video coding

3.4.1 PCM

Pulse Code Modulation (PCM) encoding of a video signal comprises
the steps of sampling, quantisation and allocation of code words.
Sampling converts the continuous analogue representation into a
series of picture elements though this term and its short forms, pixel
and pel, are also used to refer to the digital versions. The Nyquist
criterion of the sampling rate being at least twice that of the highest
frequency present leads to minimum rates in the region of 10MHz to
12MHz for conventional 525 and 625 line television signals. Though
these values are satisfactory for monochrome or colour component
signals, it is common practice when sampling composite colour
signals to increase the sampling rate to an exact integer multiple of
the colour subcarrier frequency f_{sc}. This minimises the visibility of
beat frequencies between harmonics of the subcarrier and the sampling clock arising from non-linearities in the digital to analogue and
analogue to digital converters. Sampling rates of $3 \times f_{sc}$ have been used
in transmission equipments, where the emphasis is on minimising the
bit rate and $4 \times f_{sc}$, with its 90 degree subcarrier phase shift between
samples, has attractions when subsequent digital signal processing
will be employed to modify the input signal in certain ways.

Because of the scanning process, the energy spectrum of video
signals tends to be concentrated in the vicinities of harmonics of the
line scanning rate. By careful choice of a sub-Nyquist sampling
frequency it is possible to arrange for the alias spectrum to interleave
with the original and yet be separable at the decoder using comb filter
techniques. Some loss of diagonal resolution is introduced but using
this technique, composite colour signals have been sampled at $2 \times f_{sc}$
(Ratliff, 1983).

For 525 and 625 colour signals in component form, CCIR Recommendation 601 specifies a family of related sampling frequencies (CCIR, 1990a). The most widely used is the 4:2:2 version in which the luminance component is sampled at 13.5MHz and each of the two colour difference components at 6.75MHz. The latter lower rate reflects the reduced acuity of the human eye to colour detail. Unlike f_{sc} based ones, the CCIR 601 sampling frequencies result in orthogonal arrays of sampling points and they remain stationary from one picture to the next. Conversion of the analogue samples to digital form is normally performed with a uniform quantisation law and 8 bits of resolution. For the highest quality applications where multiple tandem encoding and decoding or subsequent processing will be encountered an extra 1 or 2 bits may be used. Some images, a notable example being medical scans, have a wide dynamic range and require significantly more bits.

CCIR 601 calls for uniformly spaced quantisation levels and 8 bit code words. The nominal black and white levels are represented by 16 and 235 respectively. The nominal range of the colour differences is from 16 to 240 with 128 representing a zero difference.

The resulting bit rate of the 4:2:2 version of CCIR 601 is 216Mbit/s. CCIR Recommendation 656 covers serial and parallel interface arrangements (CCIR, 1986). Some reduction of the bit rate of PCM encoded video can be obtained by omitting the blanking intervals and synchronising pulses as these can be regenerated at the decoder. CCIR 601 4:2:2 specifies a digital active line as containing 720 luminance samples. Taking into account the vertical blanking period, the net rate representing visible picture information is of the order of 166Mbit/s.

A PCM representation is invariably a prerequisite for video compression coding.

3.4.2 Bit rate reduction

Video signals contain several sources of redundancy which can be used to reduce the bit rate. Some techniques operate on the statistical redundancy and are fully reversible i.e. the original can be recovered exactly. Other techniques exploit the characteristics of the human visual system to conceal the distortion they introduce or minimise its visibility. Practical coders often incorporate both techniques.

3.4.3 DPCM

Differential Pulse Code Modulation (DPCM) exploits the facts that adjacent pels are likely to have similar values and that the human eye is more tolerant of distortion in areas containing higher spatial frequencies i.e. edges and detail. As shown in Figure 3.24, a PCM input sample is applied to one input of a subtractor. A prediction value, in this case a previously coded pel, is applied to the other input and the resulting difference, the prediction error, is requantised with fewer bits and with a non-linear law. The non-linearity is such that small differences, which occur in low detail regions, are coded accurately whereas more distortion is allocated to large differences generated in high detail areas.

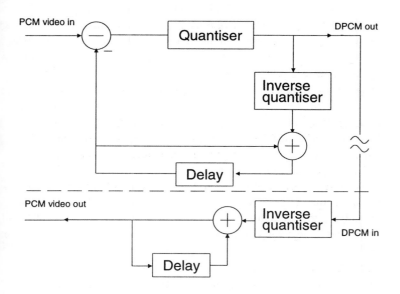

Figure 3.24   DPCM coder (top) and decoder (bottom)

The DPCM output is thus a sequence of short code words which index the quantiser levels. The decoder converts each index to the relevant representation level and adds it to the prediction to reconstruct each output sample. So that the encoder and decoder remain in track it is essential that the encoder uses only information also available at the decoder. Hence the encoder contains the essential parts of a decoder so that it uses a reconstructed version of the previous pel rather than its original input value.

The prediction can be the pel immediately to the left on the same scan line in which case the delay is one sample period. The delay can be one TV line in which case the pel immediately above is used. The pel in the same spatial position in the previous picture is the result of making the delay equal one picture period. The optimum delay depends on the localised picture content.

Simple DPCM coders utilise a fixed delay or a weighted combination of pels from fixed delays. More sophisticated versions dynamically select the optimum prediction and either explicitly indicate the choice in the coded bit stream or use rules applied to previously coded information. For composite colour signals sampled at $N \times f_{sc}$, setting the delay element to N samples reduces the occurrence of large outputs from the subtractor. Although the subcarrier is a high frequency it must be coded accurately as it is carrying low frequency colour information.

DPCM coding with 5 to 6 bits per pel is considered to offer the subjective quality of 8 bit PCM. The disadvantage is the increased susceptibility to transmission errors which affect all subsequent samples until a reset can be performed, for example at the end of a scan line or bottom of the picture. One way to mitigate against, but not eliminate, this is to introduce a leak factor in the feedback loop by multiplying the prediction by slightly less than unity. The error then diminishes over a number of pels which depends on the leak factor. Leak factors further from unity give faster recovery but at the expense of coding efficiency.

CCIR Recommendation G.721 describes a DPCM codec for use at 140Mbit/s (CCIR, 1990b). The input video is in 4:2:2 component form according to Recommendation 601. The predictor is two dimen-

sional using the average of the pel immediately above in the same
field and the pel immediately to the left on the same line.

3.4.4 Variable length coding

The use of variable length codes (VLCs), also referred to as Huffman
coding, or entropy coding, offers compression when the input data
does not have a uniform probability distribution (Huffman, 1952).
Short code words are allocated to frequently occurring events and
longer codes to infrequent ones.

The indexes from a DPCM coder typically have a peaked distribution centred on zero magnitude prediction errors and worthwhile
compression can be obtained from variable length coding. This coding is completely reversible in that the original input to the VLC coder
can be reconstructed exactly in error free conditions. Errors can cause
significant problems as the boundaries between code words can only
be found from inspection of the received bit stream.

A single bit in error can make one transmitted code appear to be
two shorter ones at the decoder or vice versa. Not only does this
corrupt the corresponding data but the following code words, even if
decoded to the correct values, will have a positional error. To limit
this error extension effect it is prudent to include some resynchroni-
sation code words.

3.4.5 Transform coding

Transform coding is another method to exploit the similarities of pels
which are in the same neighbourhood of space or time. The most
commonly used transform is the two dimensional Discrete Cosine
Transform (DCT), applied to a rectangular spatial block of m by n
pels.

The forward transformation is computed according to Equation 3.3
and the inverse (IDCT) by Equation 3.4, where x,y are spatial coordinates in the pel domain and u,v are coordinates in the transform
domain. C(u) and C(v) are given by Equations 3.5 and 3.6.

$$F(u,v) = \frac{1}{4} C(u) C(v) \sum_{x=0}^{m-1} \sum_{y=0}^{n-1} f(x,y)$$

$$\times \cos\left[\frac{(2x+1)u\pi}{2m}\right] \cos\left[\frac{(2y+1)v\pi}{2n}\right] \quad (3.3)$$

$$f(x,y) = \frac{1}{4} \sum_{u=0}^{m-1} \sum_{v=0}^{n-1} C(u) C(v) F(u,v)$$

$$\times \cos\left[\frac{(2x+1)u\pi}{2m}\right] \cos\left[\frac{(2y+1)v\pi}{2n}\right] \quad (3.4)$$

$$C(u) = \frac{1}{\sqrt{2}} \quad \text{for } u=0, \text{ otherwise } 1$$

$$\quad (3.5)$$
$$\quad (3.6)$$
$$C(v) = \frac{1}{\sqrt{2}} \quad \text{for } v=0, \text{ otherwise } 1$$

Blocks are commonly 8 by 8 or 16 by 16 though the horizontal and vertical dimensions are not required to be equal, nor to be a power of 2. Small blocks can fail to take maximum advantage of correlations from low spatial frequencies and may also incur a higher proportion of overhead data to address and describe them. Large transform blocks have a higher implementation difficulty. The transformation does not of itself produce data compression as the number of output values, termed coefficients, is the same as the input. However, the process tends to concentrate the energy into a few coefficients, usually those representing lower spatial frequencies, and the others can be omitted or coarsely quantised. The (0,0) component contains the average level of the block and is called the d.c. component. The others are a.c. components.

The DCT is the basis of the JPEG standard (ISO, 1991) for coding of continuous-tone still images. The basic coder structure is shown in Figure 3.25. After rearranging the input pels into 8 by 8 blocks they are transformed. The resulting coefficients are quantised, each with a

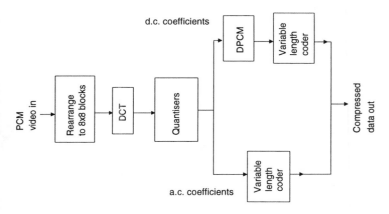

Figure 3.25 JPEG encoder

different uniform law; the stepsize reflects the visibility of the quantising errors in that coefficient after inverse transformation. The
quantised d.c. coefficients are DPCM coded from block to block with
variable length codes. The quantised a.c. coefficients are rearranged
into a zigzag order, $F(0,1)$, $F(1,0)$, $F(2,0)$, $F(1,1)$, $F(0,2)$, ... $F(7,6)$,
$F(7,7)$. Each non-zero a.c. coefficient is coded in combination with
the run length of the preceding zero value coefficients using variable
length codes.

The coefficient weighting matrix and the VLC tables for the d.c.
and a.c. coefficients are downloadable to the decoder and so can be
optimised for each picture by the coder to obtain maximum bit
efficiency. An additional parameter allows scaling of all the quanti-
sers thus providing flexibility of quality and hence compression ratio.

3.4.6 Sub-band coding

Sub-band coding (SBC) has similarities to transform coding in that
the video input is split into frequency bands. Because each sub-band
contains a limited range of frequencies it can be reversibly subsam-
pled so that the total number of pels in all the subpictures equals the
number in the original. The resulting subpictures are individually

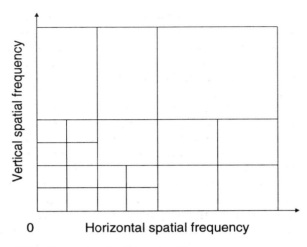

Figure 3.26 Example of sub-band split

coded, e.g. by DPCM, each with quantisation distortion appropriate to its visibility (Gharavi, 1988). The splitting is performed by filters, usually two dimensional (spatial only) but sometimes three dimensional including the temporal axis. The technique has more flexibility than the DCT in its partitioning of the input energy. In particular, the frequency bands are not constrained to be of equal extent as illustrated in Figure 3.26.

3.4.7 Vector quantisation

Vector quantisation (VQ) is the assignment of one code word to a group of two or more picture elements. Compression is achieved through the number of available code words being less than the number of permutations of the possible values of the input pels in the group. Thus several input patterns are mapped to one output code. This again exploits the likely similarities between pels in the same neighbourhood of space or time or both and the masking of distortion in highly detailed areas.

Although conceptually simple, the coding process is complex as the number of input permutations increases very rapidly with the number of pels in the group. For example, to implement a VQ encoder operating on a 2 by 2 block of 8 bit pels by means of a direct lookup table would need 32 address bits, which is significantly in excess of current integrated circuit technology. A 64 kbyte ROM has just 16 address lines; 65536 such devices would be required. For this reason it is common to employ a multi-stage approach though this may be suboptimal. A variation is to extract the mean level and scale the remainder before applying VQ to its shape. The index then consists of three portions.

Because of its complexity, VQ encoding is sometimes performed as an off line process at less than real time speed. By contrast, the decoding is simple as the lookup table required is of modest size.

A form of VQ is the encoding of the three digitised colour components of one pel by a code word having fewer bits than the three together. This technique is used in VGA colour display adapters for personal computers. By means of a colour palette, which is a programmable lookup table containing 256 entries each of 18 bits, a store size of only 8 bits per pel can provide any 256 colours from 262 144. The initial choice of which 256 colours for a particular image is the key step to producing good rendition.

3.4.8 Hybrid coding

Many of the above techniques can be applied together to yield additional compression. An example for moving pictures is shown in Figure 3.27. Spatial correlation is exploited by the DCT and temporal redundancy is reduced by DPCM coding of the transform coefficients from one frame to the next. Variable length encoding then provides further compression.

3.4.9 Motion compensation

DPCM inter-frame coding can be augmented by motion compensation. The moving areas generate the majority of bits in an inter-frame coder. However, if the motion is of a nature that it can be described

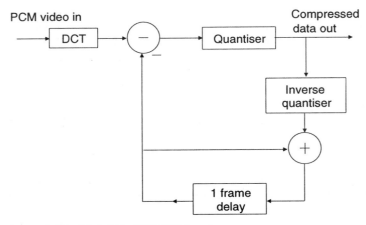

Figure 3.27 Hybrid DCT/DPCM coder

by a few parameters then more efficient coding can be obtained by suitably modifying the previous picture before using it as the prediction. For objects undergoing purely translational motion, a horizontal displacement and a vertical displacement are sufficient. The two components give rise to the term 'motion vector'. The overhead of transmitting a vector for individual pels would more than offset the savings elsewhere so the technique is applied to blocks of pels. In reality, motion is rarely purely translational but includes rotation and deformation and the edges of moving objects rarely coincide exactly with block boundaries. Inter-frame differences also result from uncovered background areas and from illumination variations. Nevertheless motion compensation substantially reduces the energy of inter-frame differences and can yield a halving of bit consumption.

Because the motion compensation is applied to pictures in their pel domain representation, it cannot be inserted directly in the scheme of Figure 3.27. Instead the DCT is positioned inside the loop along with an inverse transform (IDCT) as shown in Figure 3.28 to give a motion compensated hybrid DPCM/DCT codec. This generic structure has attracted a great deal of attention by standardisation bodies and is the basis of the algorithms from CCITT (now part of ITU-T), ISO and

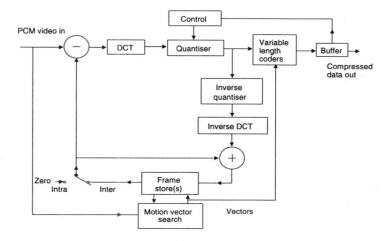

Figure 3.28   Generic diagram of motion compensation hybrid DPCM/DCT

CCIR described in the following sections. All three utilise an 8 by 8 DCT.

The incorporation of motion compensation in a decoder has only a small effect on its complexity; the main change is that the store in the loop ceases to be a purely serial delay but needs a degree of random access capability. The impact on an encoder is very large, the basic process being one of pattern matching. For the ITU-T coder, which is the least demanding of the three in this respect, an exhaustive search for the optimum vector requires over 5×10^9 additions or subtractions of 8 bit numbers per second. Fortunately, because the decoder needs to know only the vector value and not how it was determined, the search method need not be standardised. This permits simplified search methods to be implemented in encoders, though with some loss of performance.

3.4.10 ITU-T Recommendation H.261

This Recommendation is for a video codec for audio visual services at multiples of 64kbit/s up to 2Mbit/s (CCITT, 1990a). The primary application is videotelephone and videoconference. The first stage of bit rate reduction is achieved by reducing the sampling rates to below those required by CCIR 601. ITU-T sought an international standard for world-wide application which would permit users to converse without having to concern themselves over the existence of the two different television scanning standards, namely 625/50 and 525/60.

To meet this goal, the coding kernel operates on a single format known as the Common Intermediate Format (CIF) or its simply related, downsized version called Quarter CIF (QCIF). The luminance component of CIF has 288 lines of 352 coded pels, repeated 29.97 times per second. The two colour components each have half these numbers of pels and lines. QCIF has half the corresponding spatial sampling densities of CIF and is more suitable for the lower bit rates especially when the decoded images are for display on small screens. CIF and QCIF are a technical compromise between 625/50 and 525/60, the number of lines being simply related to the visible portion of the 625 system and the picture repetition rate being exactly half the field rate of the 60Hz format.

At bit rates below about 1Mbit/s it may be subjectively preferable to reduce the coded picture rate and introduce motion jerkiness rather than accept the full amount of spatial quantisation noise.

The motion compensation range is ±15 pels and ±15 lines. Weighting of transform coefficients is not incorporated.

3.4.11 ISO/MPEG Draft International Standard 11172

The mandate of the ISO Working Group is the coding of video and associated audio for storage applications. The first item in the workplan is for bit rates up to about 1.5Mbit/s and is addressed by the Draft International Standard 11172 (ISO, 1992). The algorithm has much in common with ITU-T Recommendation H.261 but also some significant differences. A very wide range of picture formats is possible to suit television and computer applications. The full CCIR 601 source quality cannot be maintained at the target bit rates and downsampling is usually employed before the coding kernel. Typical sampling rates are 288 non-interlaced lines of 352 luminance pels repeated 25 times

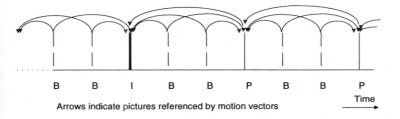

B   B   I   B   B   P   B   B   P

Time

Arrows indicate pictures referenced by motion vectors

Figure 3.29   Example of combination of predictive and interpolative coding in MPEG algorithm

per second and 240/352/29.97, these being simply related to 625 and 525 line television respectively.

To support random access, some pictures are coded entirely in intra mode, i.e. without reference to any information outside that individual picture. These are termed I-pictures. Two forms of motion compensated prediction are employed as shown in Figure 3.29. P-pictures are coded with respect to a previous picture but not necessarily the immediately previous one. The intervening B-pictures use the previous picture or the next picture or an average of the two as a prediction, the selection being possible for each 16 pel by 16 block. The latter mode uses two motion vectors for the block. The motion compensation resolution is half pel and half line, but the permitted range is many times larger than ITU-T H.261 or CCIR Rec.723.

The use of prediction from future pictures means that they must be rearranged in time order before entering the coding loop. This modified order is retained in the coded bit stream so that the decoder can process it directly. Restoration to the original time sequencing is carried out after the decoding loop and before display. These processes incur delay, depending on the number of contiguous B-pictures and so the delay through this MPEG algorithm can be significantly more than the ITU-T and CCIR ones. For storage applications this is unlikely to be a problem. Although 1 or 2 contiguous B-pictures have been found to work well, the standard permits more or less, including none.

Weighting matrices are applied to the transform coefficients and these are downloaded to the decoder, enabling the encoder to optimise them to the source material. B-pictures are not used as the basis for constructing any others and it has been found possible to quantise them more coarsely than the others. This can yield a small saving in bits.

3.4.12 CCIR Recommendation 723

This Recommendation covers coding of television signals for broadcast contribution quality at bit rates of the order of 30Mbit/s to 45Mbit/s (CCIR, 1990c). The algorithm handles CCIR 601 4:2:2 input video without any internal subsampling.

In addition to intra coding there are an inter-frame mode and an inter-field mode. The inter-frame one uses the field of the previous frame with the same parity as the field being coded. Motion compensation is performed with half pel resolution within the range 15 pels horizontally and 7.5 lines vertically.

The inter-field mode uses the immediately previous field and without motion compensation. Because of interlace, the previous field has a vertical spatial offset. This is compensated for by taking the average of two pels in the previous field, one directly above and one directly below, as the prediction.

Weighting matrices are applied to the transform coefficients in the quantisation process. The matrix for the two colour difference signals is different from the luminance one.

3.4.13 Buffering and coder control

Video coders utilising compression techniques inherently produce coded data at a non-uniform rate because the effectiveness of these methods is dependent upon the spatial and temporal activity of the input pictures and these are not constant. Transmission channels currently operate at fixed bit rates, though variable rate video coding is being studied (Morrison, 1991) for use on future networks which could support this mode (CCITT, 1990b). Buffers in the coder and decoder provide short term smoothing, up to around a few hundred milliseconds. Adjustment of the longer term average rate of bit generation must be accomplished by controlling the coder where, typically, the state of fill of its buffer is fed back to control the quantisation process.

The control strategy need not be known to the decoder. Consequently this and other items which do not affect compatibility between coder and decoder may be left open in standards. These then essentially contain only the syntax and semantics of the coded bit stream such that the decoder can reconstruct the pictures that the encoder intended.

Thus, product differentiation between coders is possible and may well result in two coders fed with identical input material giving different coded bit streams and subjectively different decoded qualities. This is more likely with the above ITU-T and ISO codecs where the relatively low bit rates mean that coding distortion is larger and more often visible than in the CCIR case.

3.4.14 Inverse DCT specification

In the above schemes it is important that the loops at coder and decoder track each other. Any divergences manifest themselves as noise and because of the recirculating nature of the loop this noise will steadily increase if there is a continual though small source of error. All the mathematical operations except the IDCT can be precisely specified and implemented. The IDCT, however, contains cosine terms and some of these are transcendental numbers which can never be represented exactly with the finite precision inherent in practical implementations.

Rather than define a unique fixed precision approximation to the IDCT which would have translated to a single architecture with specified accuracy and rounding at every intermediate step, the ITU-T chose in Recommendation H.261 to allow some flexibility to manufacturers.

The IDCT is specified with an error limit and the accumulation of mismatch between different implementations at coder and decoder is controlled by stipulating the minimum rate at which intra coding must be selected. This action of temporarily breaking the loop clears out any accumulated errors before they become too large. This approach and the same IDCT specification were adopted for the above CCIR and ISO algorithms and supported elsewhere (IEEE, 1990b).

3.4.15 HDTV coding

All the methods outlined above are directly applicable to High Definition Television (HDTV) coding. The higher sampling rates needed, in the region of 70MHz for luminance, currently present some technological challenges in the implementation of the more complex algorithms. The economic balance between the saving in transmission or storage cost gained by more efficient coding and the increased cost of the coding and decoding equipment must be considered. There is some interest in compatible coding schemes for HDTV which simultaneously provide decoded pictures for viewing on conventional displays.

3.4.16 New approaches

Though the techniques mentioned thus far have only recently been incorporated in standards, they have been known for many years, well investigated and further improvements in their compression factors are likely to be small. The attentions of researchers are thus being directed in other directions such as fractal based coding (Jacquin, 1990) and wavelet coding (Rioul, 1991).

An approach which shows promise for some applications such as videophone at very low bit rates is model based or knowledge based coding (Pearson, 1989). From a limited number of still images and knowledge of the generic shape of a human head and shoulders, the encoder and decoder construct a model of the subject. The encoder then transmits parameters to the receiver to move the model in some way e.g. to nod the head or open the mouth.

An extension is to ally this to more conventional methods which are brought into action when the model fails. Encouraging results have been shown for the synthesis part which is carried out by decoders. The analysis task which must be performed by encoders is more difficult.

3.5 Videophony and videoconferencing

Videophony and videoconferencing are companion audio visual services which are, at the present time, generally distinguishable by the factors given in Table 3.8.

However, for some applications at least, the boundaries between the two services are becoming less distinct; for example, desktop videoconferencing terminals operating over switched 56kbit/s and 64kbit/s networks are becoming available. The ITU-T, which is responsible for the video coding, audio coding and protocol standards for audiovisual services, has appreciated the future need for both types of service to interwork. As a result, the relevant standards ensure that any audio visual terminal adhering to the standards will automatically interwork with any other standard terminal with the same or lesser capabilities. The standards are discussed further in later sections.

Table 3.8 Comparison between videophony and videoconferencing

Videophony	Videoconferencing
Primarily person-to-person	Primarily group-to-group
Office environment	Studio or specially equipped room environment
Compact desk top terminals	Large floor standing terminals
On demand service via customer switched digital networks	Bookable service via digital leased lines
Picture quality consistent with low bit rate transmission (e.g. 64kbit/s or 128kbit/s)	Picture quality consistent with high bit rate transmission (e.g. 384kbit/s up to 2Mbit/s)
Telephony quality speech	Wideband speech quality

3.5.1 General design considerations

This section deals with the general design considerations for videophone and videoconferencing systems and terminals, but since a
number of the considerations are a consequence of the ITU-T Rec.
H.261 video coding algorithm used (CCITT, 1990a), the reader
should be familiar with the earlier section on digital video coding
before proceeding further.

3.5.1.1 *Display performance*

The optimum size of the display screen in a videophone terminal is a
function of a number of factors including the picture scanning standard, picture resolution (signal bandwidth), viewing distance and, if a
data compression scheme is implemented, the visibility of coding
artefacts. The 625 line television scanning standard in Europe (525
line in the USA and Japan) was chosen so that the line structure would
be imperceptible to the majority of people when viewed at a distance
greater than 6 times the picture height (a viewing ratio of 6H).

For videoconferencing terminals in a meeting room equipped with
large (65cm diagonal) CRT displays, a viewing distance of at least
2.5m is recommended. Videophone or desk top videoconferencing
terminals are usually positioned from 70cm to 1.5m from a single
user; for easy reach of controls which are integral with the terminal,
70cm is the more appropriate. At this distance, the display size should
be about 20cm diagonal to preserve a viewing ratio of 6H.

In practice, designers of wideband terminals may opt for a larger
display (25cm to 35cm diagonal), preferring the greater impact of the
bigger picture despite some visibility of the line structure. Equally,
where low bit rate coding algorithms are used, usually accompanied
by a deliberate reduction of the available picture resolution, designers
may prefer a smaller size (10cm to 15cm) to mask the loss of picture
quality incurred. Larger (30cm to 35cm diagonal) displays are normally used when positioned at the back of the desk, some 1.5m from
the user.

The brightness of the displays should be adjustable up to at least $100cd/m^2$, measured on a white rectangle occupying 50% of the screen area.

The most important advance in display technology over the past few years has been the development of colour liquid crystal displays (LCD) with the grey scale resolution required for television (White, 1988). At the time of writing, production LCDs for real time television applications are available in sizes up to 15cm diagonal (larger panels up to 35cm exist as development samples) and virtually all employ an active matrix of thin film transistors to control the transmittance of each cell. Colour is provided by having 3 cells per picture element and an overlay colour filter. A light source must be provided behind the LCD, usually by means of a colour matched cold cathode fluorescent tube.

The main attraction of the LCD is that there is much more freedom to design an attractive, compact unit than would be the case with conventional cathode ray tube displays. One limitation of LCDs is that they have a much more limited angle of view than CRTs, being typically ±20 deg. vertically and ±40 deg. horizontally.

Integrated videophone terminals tend to use LCDs up to 15cm diagonal, but a personal computer (PC) is an attractive alternative videophone terminal implementation, particularly where the potential user already has such a unit on his desk. In this case, where low bit rate coding is utilised, a reasonable implementation is to 'window' the small videophone picture into one of the top corners of the PC screen. For wideband videophone terminals, the whole PC screen can be used for the displayed picture if required.

For single viewer use, the normal 4:3 aspect ratio is near optimum for head and shoulders pictures. Although there have been experimental videophone terminals in the past with aspect ratios of 1 and less, to better match the shape of a human face, these were less than satisfactory because the natural sideways movement of a seated user caused difficulty in remaining in the field of view of the camera.

For videoconferences involving groups of people at each location, a 4:3 aspect ratio display is non-optimum, resulting in the pictures of say 6 participants in a central band occupying less than 20% of the picture area. This situation can be significantly improved, at the

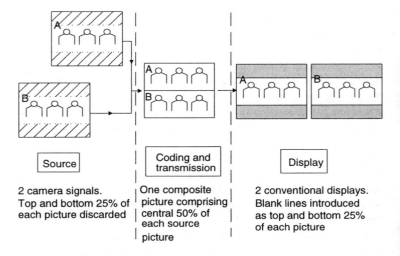

Figure 3.30   Split screen technique

expense of a second camera, display and some processing, by using the 'split-screen' technique (CCITT, 1988a) illustrated in Figure 3.30. Effectively, the aspect ratio of the display has been changed to 16:3 which is close to the optimum value for 6 participants.

3.5.1.2 *Camera performance*

For both videophone and 'split-screen' videoconferencing terminals, the camera should have a fixed field of view of about 44 deg. horizontally and 33 deg. vertically, which corresponds to a lens focal length of between 7.5mm and 8.5mm when used with an industry standard 0.5 inch format CCD camera sensor (active area about 6.4mm by 4.8mm). The width of the field of view will therefore be about 54cm at a subject distance of 70cm and about 2m at a subject distance of 2.5m. One third inch CCD sensors, already used in consumer video camcorders, are increasingly likely to be used for videophone applications; for the same field of view, the focal length of the lens is reduced to 5mm to 5.5mm.

Fixed focus lenses are to be preferred since, particularly in video-phone applications, auto focus lens operation in following small movements will result in picture changes which then have to be coded for transmission, thereby reducing the efficiency of the coding oper-ation. Even for the most critical fixed focus application, e.g. a video-phone terminal 70cm from the user and a 0.5 inch CCD camera with 8mm focal length lens and the aperture open at f2.0, the subject will be in focus over the range 40cm to over 3m for a QCIF resolution picture (176 picture elements per line), and over the range 50cm to over 1m for a CIF resolution picture (352 picture elements per line).

Videophone and videoconference terminals in a standard office environment need to operate satisfactorily in lighting conditions which range from bright sunlight to poor artificial lighting. It is the illumination of the user's face that is important, and the camera sensitivity, auto iris lens performance and electronic automatic gain control must be such that satisfactory pictures are obtained over a range of illumination from 200 to 4000 lux. In addition, the colour temperature varies among different types of artificial lights and the colour temperature of daylight also varies with time of day and prevailing weather conditions.

Therefore the camera needs an automatic or semi-automatic means of controlling the colour balance in the television pictures so that, for example, white objects always appear white and even more import-antly, facial flesh tones are well reproduced. The range of colour temperature over which such colour balance must be maintained is typically from 3000 to 6000 degrees Kelvin. In the more stable environment of a custom designed videoconference room, the need to automatically compensate for the range of lighting conditions described above is drastically reduced.

The signal/weighted noise ratio of the cameras should be at least 45dB, measured in lighting conditions of at least 400 lux (and the appropriate aperture setting) and using the unified noise weighting network specified in Rec. 567 (CCIR, 1990e). For videoconferenc-ing, the face camera should have a limiting resolution of at least 300 lines per picture height in the centre of the sensor area; for video-phone applications, this specification can be relaxed but graphics cameras need to be of higher resolution.

Another important aspect of the camera specification is that the field rate of the camera should be the same as the local mains frequency; when cameras are operated in artificial lighting, particularly from fluorescent tubes, the video signal is modulated by the illumination frequency (twice mains frequency). If, for example, a 60 field/s camera is operated in 50Hz lighting, there is 20Hz modulation flicker running through the displayed picture and 20Hz is close to the most visible temporal input frequency for the human eye-brain system.

Another disadvantage of such a system is that the ITU-T Rec. H.261 algorithm encodes differences between the current and previous pictures. The modulation flicker is interpreted as a difference signal and valuable transmission capacity will be used unnecessarily to encode the flicker. Means for removing or at least reducing the flicker exist (for example, use of an electronic shutter) but the expense and complexity involved may outweigh the advantage of having a universal camera and display standard.

To provide the most natural conditions for a videophone conversation, good eye contact with the displayed image of the remote user is essential and this implies that the ideal position for the camera is near the centre of the display screen. Systems using a semi-silvered mirror to achieve this apparent position do exist, although there is an inevitable consequential light loss to the camera and from the display. When the camera is mounted in the plane of the display, the options are to position the camera centrally above the display or on one side of the display on the anticipated eyeline of the displayed head and shoulders picture i.e. slightly above the centre line.

For a fixed viewing distance, the eye contact angle is minimised by positioning the camera above, and as close as possible to, the display, and by using the smallest acceptable display size. However, despite being a less than optimum arrangement, there are a number of videophone terminals (usually the smaller ones) with the camera positioned at the side. One of the reasons the industrial designers concerned give for preferring this arrangement is that a camera at the side is less obtrusive and dominant than one positioned centrally above the display. Further work is required to determine user preference.

A European standard (ETSI, 1991) is in preparation which addresses these and many other design aspects of videophone terminals.

3.5.1.3 *Audio performance*

For people to be able to converse freely via a telecommunications medium the transmission delay should be less than a few tens of milliseconds. However, with the video coding algorithm specified in ITU-T Rec. H.261, the processing delay can vary from 200ms to 500ms depending on the skill of the codec designer and the transmission bit rate available. To ensure acceptable lip synchronisation, the timing of the sound relative to the picture should be in the range −40ms to +20ms (CCIR, 1990f), and although the video delay can vary with the amount of movement to be coded, a fixed compensating audio delay for a given bit rate, if carefully chosen, may be acceptable. With compensating delay in each direction of transmission, the ease of conducting an interactive conversation is adversely affected, rather like telephony via one or two satellite hops, but the presence of a picture may help to avoid the tendency for both parties to speak at the same time as is often experienced by telephone users when the connection is via satellite.

Virtually all videoconferencing terminals use an 'open' audio system in which monophonic sound is transmitted and received on separate channels (4 wire operation). The positioning and relationships between microphones and loudspeakers should be based on the guidelines given in ITU-T Supplement No. 25 (CCITT, 1985). The echo return loss between loudspeakers and microphones should be greater than 6dB over the frequency range 0.1kHz to 8kHz to preserve stability. However, even in well designed studios with suitable acoustic treatment, it is difficult to avoid completely the possibility of the received sound being reflected into the microphones and being re-transmitted as a delayed echo (the total delay is room delay plus the processing compensation delay mentioned above) and the use of echo cancellation is advisable. The effect of echo cancellation is to enhance the echo return loss to a value of 40dB.

For videophone and desk top videoconferencing terminals having hands free operation, echo cancellation may not at present be a viable economical solution, and voice switched echo suppression, although inferior, may be the preferred solution. Further study is required to confirm satisfactory voice switched suppression when the audio signal has been delayed by a few hundred milliseconds. Where a telephone handset is used, the problem of room echo disappears and the only requirement is that the side tone attenuation should be at least 45dB, a figure that is achievable with a well designed handset.

3.5.2   Standards for audio visual communications

As interest has grown in a whole range of audio visual services supported by terminals with different capabilities, the ITU-T anticipated the need for a framework of interrelated standards to ensure satisfactory interworking at the highest level of compatibility existing in the different terminals. There are a number of Questions in ITU-T Study Groups addressing different aspects requiring standardisation for audio visual services, and the Rapporteurs for each Question co-operated in the production of a framework (CCITT, 1988b) of target Recommendations, which were designated the AV series. The AV designation is used while the Recommendation is being drafted, but once finalised and formally adopted by the ITU-T, the standard is allocated a number in the appropriate series of published ITU-T Recommendations.

Only the most significant members of the framework series can be summarised here.

3.5.2.1 *Audio coding*

Telephony quality speech, with a bandwidth of 300Hz to 3.4kHz, can be encoded using PCM into 64kbit/s or 56kbit/s as specified in Rec. G.711 (CCITT, 1984c). The Recommendation specifies different companding laws (A-law for Europe, μ-law for North America and Japan) and different rules as to whether the most significant bit is transmitted first or last. As a result of this incompatibility, there is a need for A-law/μ-law conversion when international digital telephone traffic is exchanged between incompatible regions.

Better quality speech, with a bandwidth of 7kHz, can be encoded into 64, 56 or 48kbit/s using the ADPCM algorithm of Rec. G.722 (CCITT, 1988c). The systems aspect of wideband audio are covered in Rec. G.725 (CCITT, 1988d). A draft Recommendation, AV 254, for 16kbit/s speech using a codebook excited linear prediction (CELP) algorithm is close to completion and is expected to be formally ratified by the ITU-T in 1992 as new Recommendation G.728.

Although other audio coding standards exist, the above are the only ones applicable to audio visual services at the present time.

3.5.2.2 *Video coding*

Rec. H.261 specifies the video coding algorithm for audiovisual services at rates from 64kbit/s to 1920kbit/s (video bit rate in the range 46.4kbit/s to 1856kbit/s).

3.5.2.3 *Audiovisual systems*

Rec. H.320 (CCITT, 1990c) covers the technical requirements for audio visual services at channel rates between 64kbit/s and 1920kbit/s. This Recommendation is the 'high level' document that calls all the other relevant Recommendations for audio visual services. It defines the allowable types of terminal and allowable transmission modes, and where interworking among different terminal types must be supported.

The standards to be adopted for subdividing a transmission channel (again in the range 64kbit/s to 1920kbit/s) into subchannels for the transmission of video, audio and ancillary data are embodied in Rec. H.221 (CCITT, 1990d). The framing structure defined in Rec. H.221 is octet based, with 80 octets per frame; the eighth bit is called the service channel. Each frame has an 8 bit Frame Alignment Signal (FAS) and an 8 bit Bit Allocation Signal (BAS) occupying the first 16 bits of the service channel and corresponding to a framing overhead of 1.6kbit/s; all the remaining bits of the service channel and the remainder of the frame can be used for a mix of video, audio and ancillary data. Hence, in a 64kbit/s videophone service, the maximum available video rate is 46.4kbit/s with 16kbit/s audio data and 1.6kbit/s framing overhead.

The protocols to be used to establish communications between audio visual terminals using channels up to 1920kbit/s are embodied in Rec. H.242 (CCITT, 1990e). By defining how the capabilities of different types of terminal are to be exchanged in an unambiguous manner in the BAS codes, each terminal can determine the highest level of common capabilities for interworking. The BAS codes also provide a number of other controls and indications (C&I) such as audio mute, camera identification and various multipoint controls. These are defined in Rec. H.230 (CCITT, 1990f).

3.5.3 Network aspects

3.5.3.1 *Background*

The early videoconference systems in the 1970s consisted in the main of public studios with analogue transmission of monochrome 525 line or 625 line television signals over dedicated leased circuits.

During the 1980s, the trend was towards private studios or rooms and the digital transmission of colour television signals, encoded according to Rec. H.120 (CCITT, 1988e) at the primary digital hierarchical rates (2048kbit/s in Europe, 1544kbit/s in North America and Japan). Again, digital leased circuits were almost universally used although some network operators introduced a limited switched capability (under their control, not the users') to provide some flexibility in connecting pre-booked calls.

In the 1990s, the trend will be towards user switched (dial up) videophone and videoconferencing services at bit rates in the range 64kbit/s to 384kbit/s using the coding algorithm specified in Rec. H.261, although premium services at rates up to 1920kbit/s will still be a user option.

3.5.3.2 *ISDN*

The new Integrated Services Digital Network (ISDN), the standards for which have been generated and refined by the ITU-T over the past decade and more, is the customer switched public digital network most likely to be used for videophone and videoconferencing services. Basic rate access to the ISDN (CCITT, 1984a) provides two full duplex 64bit/s digital connections (the bearer or B-channels) and a full duplex 16kbit/s signalling channel (the data or D-channel), and is commonly referred to by the shortform notation 2B+D. Initially, the marketing of the ISDN will concentrate on business customers as having the most likely need to transmit speech and a mix of data (fax, video, computer files etc.) over the same network.

Videophony and desk top videoconferencing are likely to utilise basic rate access, either 2B (video at 108.8kbit/s, speech at 16kbit/s and framing data at 2×1.6kbit/s; if a higher bit rate is used for speech as per Recs. G.711 or G.722, the video bit rate is reduced) or 1B only (video at 46.4kbit/s, speech at 16kbit/s and 1.6kbit/s framing data). It should be noted that in 2B operation, since video data is always present in both channels, the terminal has to synchronise the incoming B-channels to remove any differences in transmission delay before the video data can be correctly demultiplexed; the network does not guarantee this 'time slot integrity' for 2B operation.

Rec. H.320 stipulates that any 2B terminal must be capable of operating as a 1B terminal and this has the additional advantages that a videophone call can still be established if one of the B-channels is busy and the user can, during a 2B call, free one of the B-channels for other purposes. It is a designer option whether the video codec associated with the terminal supports CIF or QCIF picture resolution. User preferences vary as to the optimum trade off between spatial and temporal resolution, some preferring less sharp pictures with smoother movement to sharper but jerkier pictures. Again, however, CIF terminals must be capable of falling back to quarter CIF operation.

For videoconferencing between specially equipped rooms, the preference is likely to be for full CIF pictures with transmission at a rate of 384kbit/s emerging as a popular optimum compromise between picture quality and transmission cost. Switched 384kbit/s access to the ISDN is likely to be provided in the future in one of two ways; either by setting up six independent 64kbit/s connections (with again the need to synchronise all six incoming data streams for satisfactory operation) or by providing an overlay switch to allow direct 384kbit/s access and switching (with guaranteed time slot integrity) within primary rate ISDN access (CCITT, 1984b).

For premium service at rates greater than 384kbit/s, switched access at multiples of 384kbit/s and at the two primary rates of the existing digital transmission hierarchies (2048kbit/s and 1544kbit/s) are likely to be available in the future.

Although the ISDN is considered the most suitable available network to support videophone and videoconferencing services over the next 5 years, it is worth considering the ability of other existing and future networks to support such services, and the consequential effects on the services.

3.5.3.3 *Broadband networks*

If customer switched digital broadband networks were widely available, and call charges were acceptably low, the main advantages for videophone and videoconferencing services would be that the picture quality would be higher, the processing delay would be small and the video codec would be much simpler. There is currently much activity in the ITU-T defining the broadband ISDN (CCITT, 1990b) with a broadband user network interface rate of about 155Mbit/s, of which up to about 130Mbit/s is available for customer data. The optimum rate for videophony and videoconferencing will depend on the tariffing structure adopted for B-ISDN, but in any case, given the long lead time to plan the introduction of such a major change to the access network, it seems unlikely that B-ISDN will become widely available for some years to come.

3.5.3.4 *LANs*

A Local Area Network, principally used for interconnecting PCs and workstations, is one type of customer premises digital network that may be capable of supporting audio visual service. The data to be transmitted over a LAN is assembled into packets for transmission, and the ability of a terminal to transmit a particular packet depends on a number of factors, including how many other terminals are trying to do likewise at the same time; the transmission is therefore essentially asynchronous with an unspecified transmission delay. While it does not normally matter whether a computer file is transferred in a few seconds or a few tenths of a second, the quality of real time services such as speech and videophony would be severely affected unless an almost fairly steady throughput and bounded delay could be guaranteed. For this reason, LANs such as Ethernet in common use today are not suitable for real time services; however, the next generation of LANs will be based on the token exchange principle and are likely to be much faster and more intelligent (able to prioritise data), and so could well support videophone services of an acceptable quality.

3.5.3.5 *PSTN*

It is of interest to consider whether the public switched telephone network (PSTN), the most widespread telecommunications network available, could support a videophone service. Currently available full duplex PSTN modems can operate at a rate of 14.4kbit/s, and designers are confident that 19.2kbit/s will be possible in the near future; 19.2kbit/s modems for use on 4 wire circuits are already available commercially.

For 14.4kbit/s operation, the speech data would need to be encoded to about 4.8kbit/s and the picture data encoded to about 9.6kbit/s. To achieve the same picture quality as a 1B ISDN videophone, the video coding algorithm needs to be at least 5 times more powerful, but there is little international activity in standardising such an algorithm at present.

A second option is that PSTN videophone pictures could be designed to have lower spatial and/or temporal resolution while still using the algorithm of Rec. H.261. Yet a third option is that PSTN videophones with lower picture (and speech) quality and proprietary algorithms will be launched by different manufacturers, leaving market forces to determine an eventual 'de facto' standard. However, if incompatible videophones are available at the same time, this can give rise to user uncertainty and dissatisfaction until the de facto standard emerges.

The marketing of PSTN videophones would ideally extend beyond the business community into the residential market, but in the latter case the terminal costs need to be about 3 to 5 times lower than the ISDN terminal costs. To reduce costs significantly manufacturers need to be convinced of the prospects for large volume sales to enable them to recover the substantial investment in VLSI necessary.

Two different PSTN vidoephone products (one in the USA and the other in the UK) were announced in the first few months of 1992.

3.5.4 Multipoint operation

In general, telecommunications systems have been designed to operate on a point to point basis between two end users. Some form of multipoint operation is necessary when 3 or more users are required to be involved at the same time, and this is usually provided as a network based service via a multipoint control unit (MCU) embedded in the network (Clark, 1990).

The simplest example of an MCU is a telephone conference bridge, located either at a main switching centre or at a private branch exchange. In this instance, the audio signals from all the locations are combined in such a way that each location does not receive its own audio but does receive a mix of all the other signals. Although the speech in a multipoint audio visual connection is treated in exactly the same way, the video signals have obviously to be treated differently.

In a 'switched' audio visual MCU, the video signals are voice switched and forwarded from the MCU to each location according to the following rules:

1.   The picture of the person currently speaking is forwarded to all the other locations.
2.   The person currently speaking is sent the picture of the previous speaker.

Such a system has the advantages of relative simplicity, operates automatically and, apart from some additional control features, uses the same terminals and transmission capacity as point to point connections. The ITU-T is drafting a new Recommendation (current document number AV.231) for a multipoint control unit for use with H.261 codecs at rates from 64kbit/s to 2048kbit/s. The multipoint control data is transmitted in the message channel in the H.221 framing structure.

If all the other participants are required to be seen all of the time, so called 'continuous presence' multipoint operation, a more complex solution is required. One way of achieving this would be by increasing the number of receive channels and decoders at each location, and either increasing the number of displays or accepting the fact that all the incoming pictures will be displayed at smaller sizes on the existing display screen. A second solution is to have a single receive channel and decoder but a more complex MCU which could generate a composite picture of all the other incoming pictures, with the picture of the current speaker being of higher resolution than the others and therefore allocated a greater proportion of the channel capacity. Further research and development in this area is continuing.

3.6 References

Barker, R. and Paradiso, T. (1994) Integrating video at the desktop, *Telecommunications*, December.

Bauer, W. (1995) The next best thing to being there, *Siemens Review*, (1).

Bermingham, A. et al. (1990) *The Video Studio*, 2nd edn, Focal Press.

Calvet, J.D. et al. (1994) Interactive videocommunication evolution, *Electrical Communication*, 3rd Quarter.

Cervenka, D. (1995) Cablephone not ringing yet, *Communications Engineering & Design*, March.

CCIR (1986) Interfaces for digital component video signals in 525-line and 625-line television systems, *Recommendation 656*, Dubrovnik.

CCIR (1990a) Encoding parameters of digital television for studios, *Recommendation 601-2*, Dusseldorf.

CCIR (1990b) Transmission of component-coded digital television signals for contribution-quality applications at bit rates near 140Mbit/s, *Recommendation G.721*, Dusseldorf.

CCIR (1990c) Transmission of component-coded digital television signals for contribution-quality applications at the third hierarchical level of CCITT Recommendation G.702, *Recommendation 723*, Dusseldorf.

CCIR (1990d) Bit-rate reduction for digital television signals, *Report 1089*, Dusseldorf.

CCIR (1990e) Transmission performance of television circuits designed for use in international connections, *Recommendation 567*, Dusseldorf.

CCIR (1990f) Tolerances for transmission time differences between the vision and sound components of a television signal, *Recommendation 717*, Dusseldorf.

CCITT (1984a) Basic rate user-network interface, *Recommendation I.420*, Malaga-Torremolinos.

CCITT (1984b) Primary rate user-network interface, *Recommendation I.421*, Malaga-Torremolinos.

CCITT (1984c) Pulse code modulation (PCM) of voice frequencies, *Recommendation G.711*, Malaga-Torremolinos.

CCITT (1985) Guidelines for placement of microphones and loudspeakers in telephone conference room, Supplement No. 25, p. 335, Fascicle III.1, CCITT Red Book, Geneva.

CCITT (1988a) Characteristics of visual telephone systems, *Recommendation H.100*, Melbourne.

CCITT (1988b) Infrastructure for audiovisual services, *Recommendation H.200*, Melbourne.

CCITT (1988c) 7kHz audio coding within 64kbit/s, *Recommendation G.722*, Melbourne.

CCITT (1988d) System aspects for the use of the 7kHz audio codec within 64kbit/s, *Recommendation G.725*, Melbourne.

CCITT (1988e) Codecs for videoconferencing using primary digital group transmission, *Recommendation H.120*, Melbourne.

CCITT (1990a) Video codec for audio-visual services at p × 64kbit/s, *Recommendation H.261*, Geneva.

CCITT (1990b) Broadband aspects of ISDN, *Recommendation I.121*, Matsuyama.

CCITT (1990c) Narrowband visual telephone systems and terminal equipment, *Recommendation H.320*, Geneva.

CCITT (1990d) Frame structure for a 64 to 1920kbit/s channel in audiovisual teleservices, *Recommendation H.221*, Geneva.

CCITT (1990e) System for establishing communication between audiovisual terminals using digital channels up to 2Mbit/s, *Recommendation H.242*, Geneva.

CCITT (1990f) Frame-synchronous control and indication signals for audiovisual systems, *Recommendation H.230*, Geneva.

Clarke, R.J. (1985) *Transform Coding of Images*, Academic Press, London.

Clark, W.J. et al. (1990) Multipoint audiovisual telecommunications, *Br. Telecom Tech. Jn.*, **8** (3).

ETSI (1991) ISDN and other telecom. networks — Audiovisual services — Narrowband visual telephone system, *European Telecomms. Standards Inst. provisional standard ETS 300 145*.

Gharavi, H. and Tabatabai, A. (1988) Sub-band coding of monochrome and colour images, *IEEE Trans. Circuits and Systems*, **35** (2) pp. 207-204.

Griffiths, J.M. (1990) *ISDN Explained*, Wiley, Chichester, UK.

Horton, M. (1995) Cosy local carriers with big bandwidths, *Communications News*, May.

Huffman, D. (1952) A method for the construction of minimum redundancy codes, *Proc. IRE*, September, pp. 1098-1101.

IEEE (1990a) *IEEE LCS (Lightwave communication systems) — Special Issue on Optical Fibre Video Delivery Systems of the Future*, **1** (1), February.

IEEE (1990b) Specification for the implementation of 8×8 Inverse Discrete Cosine Transform, *Draft Standard P1180/D2*.

ISO/IEC (1991) Digital compression and coding of continuous-tone still images: Part 1: Requirements and guide-lines, *Draft International Standard 10918-1*.

ISO/IEC (1992) Coding of moving pictures and associated audio for digital storage media at up to about 1.5Mbit/s, *Draft International Standard 11172-1*.

International Broadcasting Convention (1980–1990) *IEE Conference Publications*, Nos. 327 (1990), 293 (1988), 268 (1986), 240 (1984), 220 (1982), 191 (1980) etc.

International Journal (1989) *Int. Journal of Digital & Analog Cabled Systems — Special Issue on Cable TV*, **2** (2), April–June.

Jacquin, A. (1990) Fractal image coding based on a theory of iterated contractive image transformations, *SPIE Proc. Visual Communications and Image Processing 90*, **1360** (1), pp. 227-239.

Jayant, N.S. and Noll, P. (1984) *Digital Coding of Waveforms — Principles and Applications to Speech and Video*, Prentice-Hall, New Jersey.

Kafka, G. (1993) Video communications offer viable alternatives, *Networking Management Europe*, March/April.

Kim, G. (1995) Carriers solve service needs with hybrid networks, *Lightwave*, January.

Lawton, G. (1995) Cable-TV industry advances its expertise in hybrid networks, products and services, *Lightwave*, February.

Luther, A.C. (1988) *Digital Video in the PC Environment*, McGraw-Hill, New York.

Morrison, D.G. and Beaumont, D.O. (1991) Two-layer video coding for ATM networks, *Signal Processing: Image Communication*, (3) pp. 179-195.

Mothersole, P. and White, W. (1990) *Broadcast Data Systems: Teletext and RDS*, Butterworths.

NCTA (1990) *1990 NCTA Technical Papers*, Atlanta (May) (see also 1989 papers, Dallas, May) and previous annual conferences.

Paff, A. (1995a) Hybrid fibre/coax in the public telecommunications infrastructure, *IEEE Communications Magazine*, April.

Paff, A. (1995b) Hybrid fibre/coaxial cable networks to expand into interactive global platforms, *Lightwave*, May.

Pearson, D.E. (1989) Model-based image coding, *Proc. Globecom 1989*, pp. 554-558.

Pearson, D. (1991) (ed.) *Image Processing*, McGraw-Hill, Maidenhead, UK.

Ratliff, P.A. and Stott, M.A. (1983) Digital television transmission: 34Mbit/s PAL investigation, *BBC Research Department Report No. RD 1983/9*.

Rioul, O. and Vetterli, M. (1991) Wavelets and signal processing, *IEEE Signal Processing Magazine*, October, pp. 14-38.

Roberts, R.S. (ed.) (1985) *Television Engineering — Broadcast, Cable & Satellite*, Part 1 — Fundamentals, Part 2 — Applications, Pentech Press for Royal TV Society.

Sandbank, C.P. (ed.) (1990) *Digital Television*, John Wiley & Sons.

Shandle, J. (1991) Wringing out the bits: analogue or digital HDTV? *Electronics*, April.

Shetty, V. (1995) Squabbles at the crossroads, *Communications International*, January.

Slater, J.N. (1988) *Cable Television Technology*, Ellis-Horwood, Chichester, UK.

Slater, J. (1994) Coded channels: digital television by satellite, *IEE Review*, July.

Snell, M. (1994) Motion picture commotion, *Communications International*, October.

Stewart, A. (1993) Digital puts the squeeze on television, *TE&M*, 1 June.

Swager, A.W. (1994) Digital HDTV system links computers with telecommunications, *EDN*, 3 February.

Thompson, V. (1994) Videoconferencing: the next step? *Telecommunications*, January.

Townsend, B. and Jankson, K.G. (eds.) (1991) *TV & Video Engineer's Reference Book*, Butterworth-Heinemann.

TV (1988) *15th International TV Symposium*, Montreux (June) (see also previous symposia held at 2 yearly intervals at Montreux).

Watkinson, J. (1990a) *The D2 Digital Video Recorder*, Focal Press.

Watkinson, J. (1990b) *The Art of Digital Video*, Focal Press.

Weaver, L.E. (1979) *Television Video Transmission Measurements*, Marconi Instruments, St. Albans, UK.

White, J.C. (1988) Colour LCD TV, *Phys. Tech*, **19**.

Wilson, D. (1995) British cable-TV operators resist the installation of fibre to the home, *Lightwave*, May.

Wilson, R. (1995) Network in demand, *Electronics Weekly*, 5 April.

4. Telex communications

4.1 Introduction

Telex has its roots in telegraphy and the first practical telegraph was installed by Wheatstone and Cooke in 1857. The development of telegraphy has been marked by continuous mechanical improvements. Hand sending of Morse code was laborious and so an electric typewriter was developed to a point where it could be connected to a telephone line and operated by a typist (the teleprinter).

The ability to send/receive typed messages from one part of the world to the other became of enormous importance to business and as the machine was able to acknowledge receipt of the transmission of the information in some areas the telex message was accepted as legally binding. The first telex machines were connected to the telephone network alongside a telephone, by setting up a telephone call and then transferring the line to a teleprinter. As the need for the service grew in business the need for a separate telex network became apparent. Initially the telex networks were switched via manual switchboards, but as they were exclusive to business use the networks were quickly converted to automatic working in the late 1950s.

4.2 Characteristics of telex

Telex differs from telephony in that it carries the written rather than spoken communication and is almost exclusively used in the business world. A key element of telex communication is the production of a local record, exactly duplicating the message sent to and received at the distant end. Further, telex can be operated with the distant end completely unattended, which makes it ideal for international working where businesses operate in differing time zones. As telex transmits the written word, then it also makes it ideal for communication between people of different languages, as time can be spent on translating the message and then formulating the reply. Since most countries that adopted telex also had a telephony network, they naturally used the telephony network as the basis for the design of the telex network, which in turn led to a wide variety of signalling systems to communicate between telex machines and the network.

4.3 Telex signalling

To send the written word, a character set had to be produced and standardised by all users of the telex system. As the teleprinter grew out of telegraphy and Morse code, then so did the telex character set. The Murray code, unlike the Morse code, is composed in such a manner that all characters contain the same number of units and each unit takes exactly the same time to transmit. The unequal dot and dash of Morse code is replaced by equal duration 'mark' and 'space'. Each character requires 5 units giving 32 characters in total. The character set is extended by defining two shift characters, figures shift and letters shift.

This code makes up the basis of ITU-T (formerly CCITT) International Alphabet Number 2 which is fundamental to the operation of all telex machines (see Figure 4.1). As the telex service grew, the need for a more comprehensive character set was required, particularly when operating over high frequency radio circuits. The ITU-T International Alphabet Number 5, with its 7 unit error detecting code and automatic retransmission to correct errors, was adopted for telex working and a translation defined between both character sets. In essence this meant that a TELEX machine sending in ITU-T ITA 2 would be translated via a code conversion to ITU-T ITA 5.

When a character is sent to line it is preceded with one start element followed by 5 information elements and then one stop element (see Figure 4.2). With the pulse durations shown in Figure 4.1, the telex operates at 50 bits per second.

A variety of line signalling systems exist for telex operation, using voltage and current signalling and mainly designed around the needs of electromagnetic systems, where the transmit and receive elements were contacts and electromagnets respectively. Later single channel

Start — Stop Signal Code

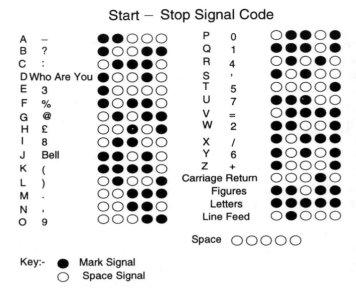

Figure 4.1 ITU-T International Alphabet Number 2

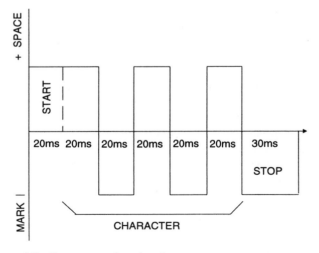

Figure 4.2 Start-stop telex signal

voice frequency signalling was added to the telex system. There are therefore three major signalling systems in use throughout the world all with minor country differences depending on the type of telex exchange operating in the local country. These are double current signalling, single current signalling, single channel voice frequency signalling, as described in the following sections. In addition some telex machines are connected to private networks or point to point private wires using similar signalling systems. The mode of working is also important i.e. full duplex discrete send and receive paths and half duplex common send and receive path. Public telex networks are invariably half duplex in operation.

4.3.1 Single current signalling

This describes a system using the presence or absence of current to indicate a start or stop polarity on the line. Usually the transmitter and receiver are connected in series to obtain the local record. The current source is fed from the telex exchange to the machine, down the telex line. The polarity of the current can change during signalling as well as being at an intermediate level. Single current operation normally works from a 120 volt exchange feed (Figure 4.3).

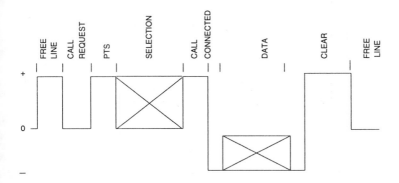

Figure 4.3 Single current call progression

4.3.2 Double current signalling

This describes a system using voltage/currents of equal magnitude but opposite polarity, to indicate start or stop information on the line. The system generally has discrete send and receive paths with a common return and is inherently full duplex in operation. However for normal telex use the local record is generated by linking the transmitter to the receive path in the machine and hence making this system effectively half duplex. Telex machines operate at the following voltages and currents at 20mA, 40mA, and 60mA Line currents for negative mark or positive space (Figure 4.4):

1.   80-0-80 volts.
2.   60-0-60 volts.
3.   48-0-48 volts.

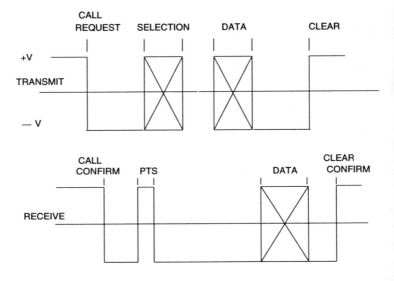

Figure 4.4   Double current call progression

4.3.3 Single channel voice frequency signalling

Single channel voice frequency signalling (SCVF) was adopted by ITU-T R.20 to improve the telex network for the following reasons:

1.	To reduce the incidence of single or double current high level signals, inducing noise in adjacent cable pairs.
2.	To reduce the power consumption of the telex exchange.
3.	To enable connections to be made between telex machines over non-metallic circuits.
4.	To achieve full duplex transmission using relatively inexpensive ITU-T V21 modems over 2 wire circuits.

The method of signalling is based on ITU-T V21 with the following frequency allocations:

1.	Telex exchange to telex machine, Space 0 = 1180Hz; Mark 1 = 980Hz.
2.	Telex machine to telex exchange, Space 0 = 1850Hz; Mark 1 = 1650Hz.

Introduction of this signalling system also gave the opportunity for telex machines to operate at speeds up to 300 baud.

4.3.4 Type A and Type B signalling

Two further subdivisions of the signalling systems have evolved, corresponding to the different types of national network employed. It has been agreed that, where two countries with different types of signalling system are trying to make connection, the country setting up the call will convert its outgoing signals to that of the country receiving the call. Both types of signals convey the same information, the difference is in the detail of implementation.

In general Type A signalling has been used where the telex keyboard has been used to send the address signals to the network and Type B signalling where the address signals were sent to the network

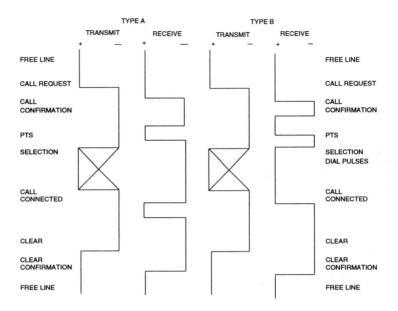

Figure 4.5   Type A and B signalling

with dial pulses, much like a telephone. Figure 4.5 shows the sequence of signals in each system.

4.4 Answerback

ITU-T recommendation F.60 specifies that every telex machine will have a unique answerback code made up of a one or two letter country code, telex line number and abbreviated subscriber's name. Sending a 'who are you' when connected through to the distant end will trigger the distant telex to transmit the answerback code embedded in the distant telex to the sending telex. This technique enables telex users to confirm that they have reached the correct distant party, before message transmission can begin, so protecting the confidentiality of the message.

4.5 Telex protocol

As telex signalling is machine to machine operation and the distant end may be unattended, then a protocol has been established. Several exist but the ones given in Table 4.1 are generally internationally understood.

All telex messages should commence with the sender's answer-back so that the distant end can easily find the caller. The sequence of setting up a call on the telex network is seizing the line, receiving call confirmation and proceed to select indication from the telex network. The telex terminal then transmits the address information and if the call set up is successful the distant machine will automatically transmit to the caller the answerback code indicating it is ready to accept the message. If the call is unsuccessful for any reason the failure will be indicated by a service code of up to 3 letters transmitted from the telex network to the originating machine and printed out on the local record of the telex message.

The telex network has facilities for testing the telex lines and can detect if a machine has its power disconnected or the line is out of order, and then send the corresponding service message from the network to the originating machine.

4.6 Telex terminals

Modern telex terminals are highly sophisticated pieces of equipment built around the principles of the personal computer. They comprise a microprocessor, disk drive, keyboard, VDU, and heavy duty printer with paper roll holder. These machines are still required to interwork with the older electromechanical machines, or paper tape transmitters or receivers, that exist on the telex networks.

The modern telex terminal has in addition the ability to communicate with the telex network word processing software, to enable the telex operator to prepare messages, edit, store and finally transmit the messages.

This makes the telex terminal a very powerful communication tool for business use.

Table 4.1 Telex protocol (* indicates some of the typical service codes)

Code	Meaning
* ABS	Absent subscriber; power switched off the machine
BK	I cut off (break the line)
CFM	Please confirm or I confirm
COL	Collation
CRV	Do you receive/I receive
* DER	Out of order
DF	You are in communication with the called party
GA	You may transmit
* INF	Subscriber temporarily unavailable; call information service
JFE	Office closed because of holiday
MNS	Minutes
* MOM	Wait for reply
MUT	Mutilated
* NA	Number not accessible
* NC	No circuits; trunks busy
* NCH	Number changed
* NP	Called party ceased or spare line
NR	Indicate your called number
* OCC	Subscriber busy
OK	Agree
Tor5	Stop the transmission
PPR	Paper
R	Received

Table 4.1 (Continued from previous page) Telex protocols

Code	Meaning
RAP	I will call again
SSSS	Here ready for data transmission
SVP	Please
TAX	What is the charge?
TEST	Please send test message
THRU	You are in communication with a telex position
IPR	Teleprinter
W	Words
WRU	Who are you?
+	Finished
+?	I have finished, do you wish to transmit?

4.7 References

Barton, R.W. (1968) *Telex*, Pitman.

Corbishley, P. and Hunt, P.G. (1980) Telexcommunication, *Electronics & Power*, September.

Costello, J. (1990) Telex answers back, *Communications*, April.

Gleisberg, H. and Gutman, M. (1989) New terminals for international telex communication, *Electrical Communication*, **63** (1).

Renaud, J.L. and Meredith, P. (1989) The prospects for telex, *Communications International*, June.

Renton, R. (1974) *The International Telex Service*, Pitman.

5. Facsimile transmission

5.1 Introduction

Facsimile, or fax, as it is known for short, is the technique for transmitting a copy of an original page or document to a remote location. It is not taken in the original full sense of an exact copy or reproduction but is a scanned and reproduced copy. The received copy is usually desired as a crisp, clean, good contrast document regardless of the original state, a requirement usually met by modern equipment.

The initial invention was by Alexander Bain in 1843 using a pendulum scanner which made contact with characters of raised metal type. The current flowing was passed by the pendulum in synchronisation at the receiver, through damp chemically impregnated paper which then discoloured. This invention operated on telegraph wires complementary to Morse and predating the telephone.

One of the early uses of facsimile commercially was for the transmission of photographs for newspapers. In this case it was not just to mark the paper or not, but to mark with a density similar to the original photograph. These were dedicated users with skilled operators, at a time when almost any effort was justified to obtain pictures, not to be compared with today's operation.

Technical problems such as synchronisation, detection of the image at the transmitter and exposure at the recorder, amplification and the transmission by radio and telephone line, were solved step by step.

In parallel with these solutions the search continued for an ideal recording medium with the advantages/disadvantages of photographic, electrolytic, carbon, wax coated, electrostatic, thermal and now plain paper recording, being tested in products and voted on by the users.

Throughout these equipment designs a continuous compromise was necessary concerning resolution and transmission time. The results had to be good but not too good because speed was always of the essence.

Facsimile development, like all communication evolutions, wanted higher bandwidth on existing circuits or faster circuits at the same cost. It may not be too high a claim to make that facsimile developments have pressed network use to its highest efficiency, often exceeding the expectations of the network providers.

The development of weather map transmission equipment from the mid 1940s allowed meteorologists access to international charts, compiled in National Centres, so they could make their own local forecasts. A clear case for the immediate distribution of information in the format preferred by the user. Yesterday's weather forecast is not of much value.

In the mid 1950s page facsimile units for the transmission of whole newspaper pages started to become available. These large format machines, with high resolution to preserve the half tone dot structure, are used to transmit the page layouts for remote printing prior to local distribution. With printing deadlines paramount, high scanning rates and wideband networks encouraged facsimile development and manufacturing teams to keep pressing at the then known limits.

In the years before 1980 (when the ITU-T G3 Recommendations were published) there were really only specialist applications for facsimile. Apart from those mentioned there were uses by government, military, police, for telegrams, colour transmissions received as separations and as colour prints, cloud photograph receptions from weather satellites etc. Many of these applications had different standards and formats, as demanded by the application, and were acceptable since interworking was not necessary.

For document facsimile a different approach was necessary. Interoperation had been the desired aim since 1968 when Group 1 was standardised. No one manufacturer expected to supply the whole requirement and it was expected that business facsimile use, like the telephone, could be to new destinations as yet unknown.

The growth in G3 machines after 1980 was due to the right combination of features:

1.   Ease of operation.
2.   Adequate quality, convenient size and compatibility with the working environment.
3.   Ability to transmit the documents already available in the office.
4.   Reasonable operating costs, both line and consumables.
5.   Reliable operation.
6.   Growing business base.

G3 equipment is stand alone and easy to connect to telephone line and to the power source. Its growth in use has been due to the application of practical ITU-T recommendations which reflect the technological and manufacturing possibilities. Coupled with this was the development and availability of high sensitivity thermal paper, which ensured the realistic equipment purchase price and operating costs.

Group 3 fax has developed into a digital version, known broadly as G3/Digital and a new digital standard Group 4 (Costello, 1993).

5.2 Facsimile types

Excluding the document facsimile equipment, all other types perform specialist functions and are exclusively separate transmit and receive units, for transmission in one direction. Document facsimile types are almost exclusively transceivers.

Table 5.1 summarises the characteristics of the different types of facsimile equipment.

5.2.1 Photofax equipment

Photofax equipment is used for the transmission of full tone photographs of size normally less than A4. Often the received picture is printed on photographic paper. The important requirements are not image size but correct aspect ratio, which is preserved by using the same index of co-operation.

Some scanners are designed to transmit colour separations from 35mm colour negatives using sequential transmission. Photofax

Table 5.1 Comparison of facsimile terminal types: [1]Continuous grey scale response. [2]Analogue in scanning direction. [3]Continuous but limited grey scale. [4]Includes various grey scale and compression options

Type and standard	Page size (mm)	Nominal resolution (lines/mm)	Index of co-operation	Trans-mission time
Photofax[1] CCITT T.1	210 × 210 to 254 × 270	4 and 8 or 5 and 10 [2]	352 and 704	8 to 30 min
Weather-fax [3] WMO	450 × 560	4 and 2	576 and 288	4 to 36 min
Pagefax proprietary	Up to 450 × 625	15 to 100 [2]	Not specified (1600 upwards)	1 to 3 min
Mobilefax[3] proprietary	108 × 150	4 [2]	132	1 min
Military[4] NATO Stanag 5000	215 × 297	4 and 8	Not specified (264/528)	20 sec to 20 min

equipment may be used, one transmitter to one receiver for example for sending news photographs from field locations, or one transmitter broadcasting on a wirephoto distribution network to many receivers. The transmission is simplex; there is no equipment confirmation of reception.

Analogue transmission is used and may be by PSTN, speech band private circuit, high frequency (h.f.) or long wave radio. There are several higher speed proprietary standards for equipment on broadcast distribution networks. Received image may be taken into an editorial workstation for cropping, manipulation and onward processing before printing.

Moves towards a digital standard for compressed images progresses slowly, relying on the ITU-T/ISO JPEG work. Interworking may be possible at the application layer, but there seems no agreement on the communication layers at present.

Indications are that compression around 1 bit/picture element (8:1) could be achieved for monochrome images.

5.2.2 Weatherfax equipment

These equipments are usually operated on private circuits or radio networks on a simplex broadcast basis. The analogue transmission involved limits transmission speed and this method of operation is being superseded by point to multipoint computer data transfer. Providing the raw data to the local processor allows action replays of changing conditions, which are not easily appreciated from the printed meteorological charts. The existing network base continues in operation supplementing the data network.

5.2.3 Pagefax equipment

In this area there are no standards, the equipment being tailored to suit individual newspaper requirements. Compression and transmission characteristics, reproduction ratio, and image processing are all selected to suit production requirements in the remote printing of the full newspaper pages.

The savings in transportation costs and time, by using this equipment, funds sophisticated high speed transmission developments, including the transmission of colour separation with sequential receptions on the same receive mechanism.

5.2.4 Mobile equipment

There have been several attempts at mobile facsimile, some using narrow format (100cm) machines. The most popular method was to split the radio speech channel to keep the mobile units in speech contact during facsimile operation, normally transmitting in the direction towards the mobile terminal. These units were costly for their mobile environment and suffered as a result of needing specialised radio equipment.

With the use of the TACS cellular radio system normal G3 equipment can operate when a telephone type interface is available. The Cellular Line Interface connection can be sophisticated and allows automatic answering and call origination by the G3 machine. Calls made between the mobile and normal PSTN connections provide access to the large G3 installed base.

Opinions differ about operations above 4.8kbit/s. Some believe in operating as fast as possible, while the connection is good, whilst others prefer to rely on the improved signal/noise performance at lower modem rates. Most opinions however recommend the use of ITU-T ECM.

The question of facsimile use on GSM is another matter because the system codes the voice and there is no synchronous transparent channel available for facsimile. The topic is well studied but no clear proposal has emerged.

5.2.5 Government and military equipment

Similar requirements exist for the transmission of documents, maps, drawings, photographs etc. as in other market segments. One major difference is that for the transmission of documents classified for national security, additional high performance data encryption equipment is required. Further, to avoid plain language signals from the fax equipment itself being intercepted, and to avoid compromising the encryption key generator codes, significant precautions must be taken in equipment design to reduce the relevant radiated and conductive electromagnetic emissions. These security requirements are not normally published.

5.2.5.1 *Strategic requirements*

These machines normally operate in regular office environments and apart from interoperational requirements for secure fax or tactical machines, communication can usually be met by standard ITU-T G3 models.

5.2.5.2 *Tactical requirements*

Machines for this use include military battlefield equipment to operate under inhospitable environmental conditions, fast, reliably and securely. Standards are desirable to ensure interoperation between allies of different national forces.

Typical features of the NATO standard are:

1.   Up to 16 grey shades for photographs.
2.   G3 standard and fine resolution equivalents.
3.   Broadcast and duplex network operations.
4.   G3 MH compression, also uncompressed and BCH forward error correction.

To be acceptable this equipment should be lightweight, easy to operate in arduous conditions and capable of various communication modes, including high speed burst mode to avoid radio location when necessary.

5.3 ITU-T document facsimile equipment

This is principally for the transmission of business and commercial papers, letters, drawings and general office documentation around A4 size (210mm × 297mm). The pages are often black or dark coloured text or handwritten characters on white or pastel backgrounds, although machines handle a wide range of original documents.

ITU-T has produced and continues to develop recommendations for operation on the public telephone and public data networks, which are summarised in Table 5.2.

5.4 G3 facsimile equipment

Worldwide there are many millions of compatible facsimile transceivers capable of interoperation using the Public Switched Telephone Network. Designs and implementations vary but the most popular

Table 5.2 Document facsimile types

	Network			
	Public telephone (analogue)		*Public data (digital)*	
CCITT Group/ recommendation	G1/T.2	G2/T.3	G3/T.4/T.30	G4 Class 1/T.563
Transmission time	6 min (4 min option)	3 min	Around 30 sec (at 9.6kbit/s)	Around 5 sec (at 64kbit/s)
Data rate	Analogue		14.4–2.4kbit/s	64–2.4kbit/s
Modulation	FM	AM/VSB (vestige of upper sideband)	V.17/V.29/V.27 ter	None (line driver and coder to suit network)
White	1300Hz (US 1500Hz)	Maximum carrier reversing phase		
Black	2100Hz (US 2400Hz)	26dB below white		
Synchronisation	±10 parts in 10^6	±5 parts in 10^6	Derived from data rate and sequence	
Index of co-operation	264 (176 option)	264	Not specified (264/528 option)	Not specified (549)
Scan line frequency	3Hz	6Hz	Not specified (around 100Hz)	Not specified (around 600Hz)
Horizontal resolution	Not applicable		1728 pels/215mm (8.04 pels/mm)	200 pels/25.4mm (option 240/300/400)
Scan line length	215mm		215/255/303mm	219/260/308mm
Vertical resolution	3.85 lines/mm (2.57 opt)	3.85 lines/mm	3.85 lines/mm (7.7 lines/mm option)	Square with horizontal
Data compression encoding	None		One dimensional MH 2 dim MR & MMR Uncompressed	2 dimensional MMR Uncompressed

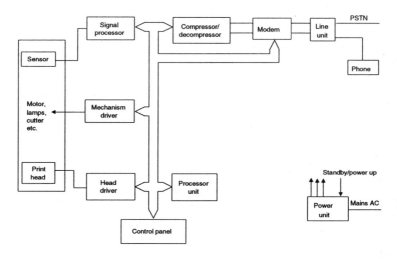

Figure 5.1   Simplified G3 block digaram

scanning method is by CCD (charge coupled device) and printing by thermal head on heat sensitive paper.

Figure 5.1 shows a block diagram of a G3 machine. Discrete LSI is often used for online signal processing, to ensure a manageable load for the main CPU which takes care of the user interface, dialling functions, mechanism control housekeeping and reporting.

The ITU-T G3 recommendations include a number of options, for example fine resolution, MR coding, V29 modem, ECM. For these to be used they must be available in both send and receive machines and are usually negotiated automatically.

5.4.1 Scanner

In a typical CCD scanner a section of the original is illuminated by a fluorescent or cold cathode tube. The facsimile line to be scanned is focused onto a 1728 (A4 width) or 2048 (B4) element CCD single line image sensor. The independent elements are discharged by radiated light from the original which is focused on to them. After a suitable time (1ms) the elements are recharged sequentially. By monitoring the current for this recharge the video signal amplitude is obtained. The signal is then processed to allow for background and level variations, and to preserve character size, then converted to binary levels for normal transmission, as a black/white image. It may be converted to amplitude bits for processing for pseudo half tone/grey scale transmission. The original is then advanced 1/3.85mm or 1/7.7mm for the next line to be scanned. If the line transmission buffers are full the scanning may then wait until further data is required.

A second popular method of scanning uses CIS (Contact Image Sensor). This is a single line sensor assembly fitted close to the paper at the document scanning point. It requires an array the full width of the paper, but it saves the space taken up by the CCD optical path. The copy is illuminated by LEDs (Light Emitting Diodes) within the unit and the radiated light from the area being scanned is collected by a multiple lens assembly and focused on to the image sensor array. If the sensors are brought almost into contact with the paper, the multiple lens is not required and in this case there are holes in the sensor array to allow the LED illumination from behind.

The detection of black or white at a particular picture element depends on the density and the position of the edge of the image with reference to the sensor element. The resolution in G3 is adequate to preserve character shape but there is almost always a difference between the raster images of identical characters even when adjacent.

To provide facsimile copy with a similar appearance to computer generated printer output, the resolution needs to be greater by about 30%. This has led to resolution incompatibility problems for facsimile and computer interoperation.

5.4.2 Data compression

An A4 scanned page of 297mm at 3.85 lines/mm is 1144 facsimile lines. This together with 1728 elements per line gives 1976832 elements per page, which if sent uncompressed to line at 9.6kbit/s would take 206 seconds, a time which can be significantly reduced by using run length coding.

5.4.2.1 *Modified Huffman*

With data compression a code is transmitted to represent the number of black or white bits to be sent, rather than transmitting the 1 or 0 for the appropriate scanning time. The basic G3 compression is Modified Huffman (MH) where, in a limited code table, the most frequent run lengths are represented by the shortest length codes. Because of the different distributions of black run lengths and white run lengths in typical documents, different code tables and make up codes for the runs longer than 63 elements are used. This is illustrated in Figure 5.2 and Table 5.3, where the compression is 1728:132 or 13:1 for this particular line.

Tables 5.4 and 5.5 provide extracts from Modified Huffman code tables.

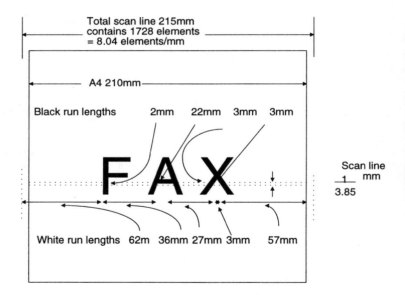

Figure 5.2   G3 resolution and Modified Huffman coding (see Table 5.2)

Table 5.3   G3 resolution and modified Huffman Coding (see Figure 5.2)

Run length mm	No. of pels	Make up code	Terminating code	No. of bits
W62	498	01100100	01010011	16
B2	16	—	0000010111	10
W36	289	0110111	00010010	15
B22	177	000011001000	000001100101	24
W27	217	010111	0101011	13
B3	24	—	00000010111	11
W3	24	—	0101000	7
B3	24	—	00000010111	11
W57	459	01100100	01000	13
215	1728			120
End of line		000000000001		12
			Total bits	132

An end of line code is added to provide synchronisation and allow the receiver to check that the decoded line is 1728 elements. Typically a compression of about 7:1 can be obtained.

5.4.2.2 *Modified READ*

ITU-T allows two optional two dimensional coding schemes. These are both RElative ADdress or READ techniques where the new line to be coded is based on the previous line. The first ITU-T option of the modified version of READ (MR) was standardised before ECM (error correction mode) was available. It had to operate in the presence of network errors and ensure that the remainder of the data on the page could be decoded. To provide for this only one two

Table 5.4   Extract from Modified Huffman code table (terminating codes)

White run length	Code word	Black run length	Code word
0	00110101	0	0000110111
1	000111	1	010
2	0111	2	11
3	1000	3	10
4	1011	4	011
5	1100	5	0011
6	1110	6	0010
7	1111	7	00011
8	10011	8	000101
9	10100	9	000100
10	00111	10	0000100
11	01000	11	0000101
12	001000	12	0000111
13	000011	13	00000100
14	110100	14	00000111
15	110101	15	000011000
16	101010	16	0000010111
17	101011	17	0000011000
18	0100111	18	0000001000
19	0001100	19	00001100111
20	0001000	20	00001101000
.	.	.	.
.	.	.	.
60	01001011	60	000000101100
61	00110010	61	000001011010
62	00110011	62	000001100110
63	00110100	63	000001100111

Table 5.5   Extract from Modified Huffman code table
(make up code)

White run lengths	Code word	Black run lengths	Code word
64	11011	64	0000001111
128	10010	128	000011001000
192	010111	192	000011001001,
256	0110111	256	000001011011
.	.	.	.
.	.	.	.
.	.	.	.
1600	010011010	1600	0000001011011
1664	011000	1664	0000001100100
1728	010011011	1728	0000001100101
EOL	000000000001	EOL	000000000001

dimensional line was permitted to follow the one dimensional MH line in standard resolution, and 3 lines were permitted in fine resolution.

Inclusion of this redundant data in an MH line allows decoder recovery.

Figure 5.3 and Table 5.6 illustrate the Modified READ coding technique.

A pair of points either between reference and coding lines or on one or other of the lines are recognised and the appropriate code transmitted with the addition of an MH code for longer runs.

MR coding is successful because of the high degree of correlation between facsimile lines in documents and typically a compression of about 10:1 can be obtained.

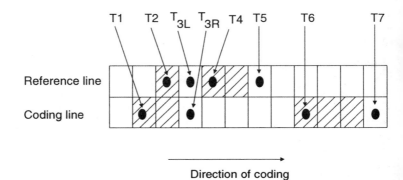

Direction of coding

Figure 5.3   Modified READ coding (see Table 5.6)

Table 5.6   Modified READ coding (see Figure 5.3)

Mode	*Points*	*Use*	*Code*
Vertical (VO) (V$_L$) (V$_R$)	T$_1$ & T$_2$ T$_{3L}$ & T$_{3R}$	Up to ±3 changing elements offset coded otherwise use horizontal	7 code words allocated (1 to 7 bits)
Pass (P)	T$_4$ & T$_5$	When no accompanying changes on coding line	Single code allocated (0001)
Horizontal (H)	T$_6$ & T$_7$	When no reference for the change on coding line	Single identifying code (001) followed by normal MH black and white run pair

5.4.2.3 *Modified Modified READ*

When the G3 ECM option is used the reference lines in MR are redundant and ITU-T permit the Modified Modified READ (MMR) option. In this case the line before the first line of the page is assumed white and all subsequent lines are referenced to their previous line. This coding is the same as T.6 used in G4 and can give compressions of the order of 14:1.

MMR is particularly suited to higher resolutions where the correlation between lines increases. For twice the vertical resolution with MH the number of bits to be transmitted doubles but with MMR the increase reduces to around 1.4:1.

5.4.3 Modulation and demodulation

Digital signals from the data compression encoder are unsuitable for direct transmission to the telephone network. For 9.6kbit/s the necessary transmission frequencies extend from d.c. to 4800Hz, too wide for the telephone network's nominal bandwidth of 300Hz to 3000Hz. For transmission the digital signals are transformed by the modem to analogue voice band signals which can tolerate the frequency shift, noise, amplitude and group delay variation with frequency, and also the echo and phase jitter of the international telephone network. G3 line signals are analogue. They vary in amplitude as a speech signal, but they are generated from digital signals and may be completely and accurately recovered providing line conditions permit.

5.4.3.1 *G3 signal transmission*

G3 is a half duplex transmission which uses 2 types of modulation/demodulation; the first of 300bit/s for the T.30 protocol and handshaking between terminals. This 300bit/s V.21 modem is a robust FSK transmission. It is easily implemented and does not require training. It is used for the relatively low volume of data establishing machine parameters and providing feedback from receiver to transmitter.

The second is the high speed modem used for the compressed image data transfer. In G3 there is a basic V.27 mode of 4.8kbit/s with

Table 5.7   Comparison of G3 modulation methods

	Bit rate (kbit/s)	Carrier (Hz)	Modu- lation	Baud rate (sym- bols/s)	Bits/ symbol	States in con- stella- tion
V.21 chan- nel 2	0.3	1750	FM ±100Hz	300	1	
V.27 ter	2.4 4.8	1800	QAM	1200 1600	2 3	4 8
V.29	7.2 9.6	1700	QAM	2400	3 4	8 16
V.17	7.2 9.6 12 14.4	1800	QAM (Trellis coded)	2400	4 5 6 7	16 32 64 128

2.4kbit/s fallback where the lines are poor, and optional modes up to 9.6kbit/s and up to 14.4kbit/s for use where terminals and networks permit. It is generally acknowledged that over 80% of transmissions used these higher rates.

Table 5.7 compares the G3 modulation methods, where QAM refers to quadrature amplitude modulation.

5.4.3.2 *Modem operation*

The data rate modem takes a number of bits of the incoming data (e.g. 4 bits for V.29 9.6kbit/s), and for the symbol time (1/2400 second for V.29 9.6kbit/s) generates the relevant modulation condition for these bits (16 conditions for V.29 9.6kbit/s).

The modulation condition may be generated by a controlled combination of sine and cosine modulated carriers which are then filtered before application to the network to limit damaging out of band signals. The receiving modem tracks the carrier to correct for network frequency shift and recovers the symbol timing. It then studies the signal during this symbol period to decide which of the possible states the received signal most closely matches and decodes that state to provide the digital bit stream.

To establish the symbol timing, and allow the receive modem to set equaliser conditions to compensate for the network impairments, an initial training signal is sent from the transmit modem. In G3 this is followed by a 1.5s period all '0' TCF, so that the machine can decide if it can correctly receive at this rate. If not the 300bit/s handshake reply initiates a new training sequence, which the transmitter may choose to send at a lower rate. With ECM it is often found desirable to operate at the higher data rates, accepting that a limited number of errors which can be rapidly corrected may provide an overall increase in transmission efficiency.

5.4.3.3 *14.4kbit/s option*

The ITU-T option at 14.4kbit/s uses V.17 TCM (Trellis Coded Modulation). The symbol rate is the same as V.29 9.6kbit/s which appears optimum for the telephone network, but the bits per symbol increase not to 6 as expected but to 7 to allow FEC (Forward Error Correction) data to be included. The 7th bit, bringing the number of states to be decoded at the receiver to 128, is generated from 2 of the data bits in each symbol interval. This introduced redundancy means that only certain decoded sequences are valid. The receiver knows from the recent signal history when an unlikely condition occurs and can make an educated guess at the correct data. It is this difference in operation which gives a 3dB signal/noise improvement in Gaussian noise tests, and noticeable end to end improvement over QAM in actual use.

5.4.4 Error correction mode

In ITU-T ECM the transmitted signal is separated into HDLC frames so that on receive the FCS bytes allow the data accuracy to be checked. G3 transmission is half duplex and when the transmission stops the receiver replies giving the condition for each of the frames.

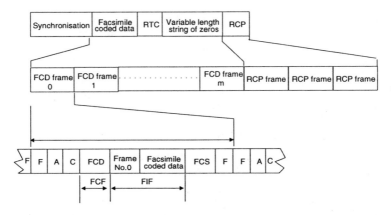

Figure 5.4   ECM transmitted frame structure

The transmitter then selectively repeats the frames which the receiver advised were in error.

Figure 5.4 shows the ECM transmitted frame structure. Each frame contains 256 octets of image plus its frame number. A block can have up to 256 frames, equivalent to around 0.5Mbits of data, sufficient for most facsimile pages. In this case, if there are no errors, there are no additional turn rounds above a standard G3 transmission.

If the pages are of greater data content than 0.5Mbit (about 50s at 9.6kbit/s) a partial page is generated at 256 frames. This partial page is corrected before proceeding with the next block. Following the image transmission a PPS is sent at 300bit/s to tell the receiver the page and block number and the actual number of frames in that block, for checking and recovery purposes.

5.4.4.1 *ECM receiver operation*

The receiver knows by the FCS which frames are correctly received. Often, in a thermal paper receiver, the machine will print the copy as received until such time as an error is recognised. It then stops with the data going to memory until corrected data is available. In most practical cases this procedure, and the availability in the receiver of

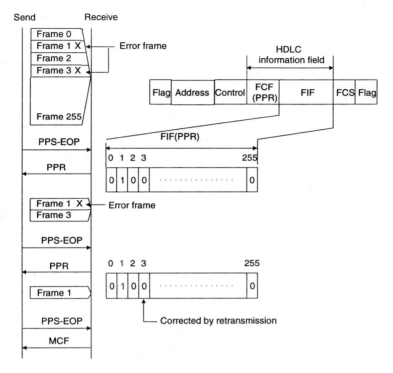

Figure 5.5 ECM operation with errors

sufficient memory for the next page/partial page, avoids waiting between pages due to printer unavailability.

With the page/partial page correctly received the receiver replies with MCF and the transmitter continues with the next data.

Figure 5.5 shows ECM operation with errors. If errors are detected the receiver sends PPR which has an information field of 256 bits, one for each frame of the transmitted block. The receiver sets each bit of PPR to 'O' for a correctly received frame and waits for the transmitter to selectively repeat the unacceptable frames. Pages/partial pages are often corrected with a single retransmission but the cycle is repeated for the then outstanding error frames. When the receiver has all frames correct it finishes printing the page and returns MCF for the next block to follow.

5.4.4.2 *ECM performance*

The overhead for G3 ECM is in the transmit direction and is approximately 5% when there are no errors. Normally in non-ECM facsimile transmission a limited number of errors are tolerated due to the image redundancy remaining in the MH and MR coding. The reception at the transmitter of MCF confirms that the document has been satisfactorily received but not necessarily that it is free of errors.

There are 2 main user advantages with ECM:

1.   The sender is 100% confident that acknowledged pages are complete and received free of error.
2.   As errors are efficiently corrected transmission time (and cost) can be reduced by using higher transmission rates together with MMR coding.

The transmitter has the opportunity from studying the pattern of errors in PPR to reduce the frame size to 64 octets or to change the data rate to maximise throughput. The selective retransmission and large window with minimum turnarounds providing efficient long haul communication even including 3 satellite links.

5.4.5 Printer

There are several methods of printing the facsimile image including electrophotographic (laser or LED), ink jet, thermal transfer and, the most popular, recording on thermal paper.

5.4.5.1 *Thermal printers*

Heat sensitive paper is passed over a single line thermal head having a heater element for each of the 1728 (A4) picture elements.

A typical method of operation in a thermal printer is at the start of reception to step the paper back from its normal guillotine or tear off position, so that the start of the page is under the thermal head. To avoid having a driver for each element the head may be electrically divided into sections for printing in a matrix. The data is latched into a section and printer in 1 to 2.5ms. When all sections of the line are printed the paper is either advanced 1/3.85mm for a standard line or 1/7.7mm for a fineline.

A standard line may be achieved by printing 2 identical fine resolution lines. The print energy required is about 1/4mJ per black dot, at a temperature on the paper of around 90°C. Print times of between 5ms and 20ms per line are typical, with automatic compensation for ambient and head temperature by varying the supply voltage or the print pulse time.

5.4.5.2 *Plain paper printers*

A number of technologies are available to produce the printed image on plain, office type paper. The advantages of this is that copies feel like other office documents and are generally archival.

Thermal transfer

The paper is usually in roll form to simplify machine handling. It moves through the machine with, and generally at the same rate as, a thermal transfer film. The thermal head prints in a similar way to normal thermal paper printing and the film is a donor, transferring its image to the plain paper. The thermal transfer film, collected on a take up roll, is used at the same rate as the paper and retains a negative image which may need careful handling for security reasons.

The facsimile printer is otherwise identical to a thermal paper printer.

Electrophotographic

A well established technology in office printers uses either a laser or an LED array to discharge a photoconductive drum for offset printing. The latent image on the drum is developed by the attraction of charged normally black toner powder. This image is transferred to a cut sheet and fixed by the combination of heat and pressure at the output rollers.

The additional hardware required for a facsimile machine is bulky, expensive and significantly increases the size and cost. The paper, normal copier type paper, is much cheaper than thermal paper but when allowing for toner, drum replacement and other consumables this saving is much reduced.

Ink jet

Ink is a simple way to print on plain paper. The problem has been to keep the ink fluid and flowing until printed and then for it to dry rapidly. This technique is being used in facsimile equipment with a replaceable bubble jet ink cartridge. The cartridge is moved across the paper to print several facsimile lines (typically 16 fine mode lines) at once and the ink bubbled appropriately through a series of apertures, one for each facsimile line. The hardware is not complicated or bulky and a range of low cost plain paper machines may emerge for use at about 30 seconds for an A4 page.

5.4.6 G3 handshake protocol

ITU-T G3 uses signals generated in an HDLC frame structure exchanged in half duplex mode. A preamble of a series of flags starting each transmission ensures that valuable data is preserved when truncation occurs at echo suppressor turnaround. The flag octet 01111110 is a unique signal that is preserved by a '10' insertion after a fifth '1' occurring in the data. A 2-byte FCS is used to allow the receiver to check data validity.

Figure 5.6 gives the T.30 G3 handshake signal format showing DIS.

5.4.6.1 *G3 handshake basic operation*

This is usually started by a call originated from the transmit machine. However, the significant signal flow is initiated when the receiver answers the ringing current by sending a DIS to indicate its capa-

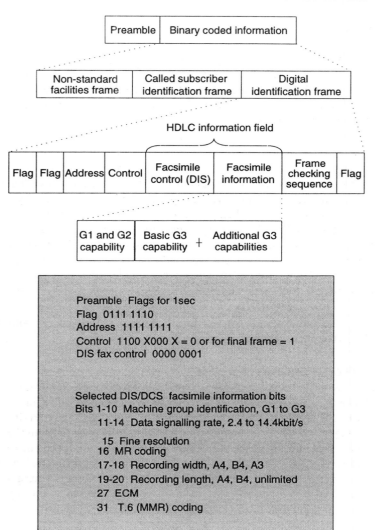

Figure 5.6 T.30 G3 handshake signal format showing DIS

bilities. These include the paper size, coding schemes and modem rates it has available. The transmit machine selects appropriate conditions in conjunction with document size and operator selections, commands the receiver using DCS and sends the modem training signal and TCF at the high speed data rate.

The receiver attempts to train, checks the performance on TCF and replies either CFR or FTT. The transmitter then either starts the image transmission or sends DCS and training again.

Figure 5.7 shows a typical G3 signal flow chart, and Table 5.8 gives popular G3 handshake signals.

When the transmitter indicates the end of page the receiver replies with MCF for a correctly received page, or one of the retrain signals indicating that it requires retraining for any further pages.

If the transmitter signalled MPS, advising more pages to be sent, it continues with the following pages, finishing with EOP and DCN in response to MCF before releasing the connection.

5.4.6.2 *G3 machine identification*

Identification of terminals is a useful feature in G3 equipment with several popular methods implemented.

ITU-T CSI/CIG/TSI signals

These are optional T.30 signals completely defined to allow interoperation between different manufacturers' machines. They are intended by ITU-T to contain a '+' sign followed by up to 20 numeric digits giving the subscriber's international telephone number. In most implementations the user can insert/update the number freely. The way the machine receiving the number uses it varies with manufacturer; it may be reported on the machine display, listed in an activity report or printed by the receive machine on the received copy.

Messages on the transmitted facsimile page

Numeric, alphanumeric or graphical messages held in a transmit memory and sent as part of the facsimile transmission. They are not

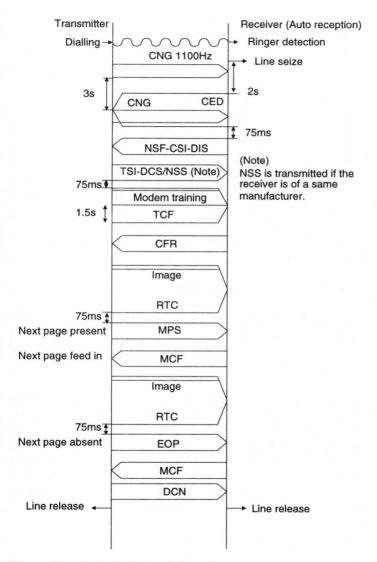

Figure 5.7   Typical G3 signal flow chart

Table 5.8 Popular G3 handshake signals

Abbreviation	Function
CED	Called station identification
CFR	Confirmation to receive
CIG	Calling subscriber identification
CNG	Calling tone
CSI	Called subscriber identification
DCN	Disconnect
DCS	Digital command signal
DIS	Digital identification signal
DTC	Digital transmit command
EOM	End of message
EOP	End of procedure
ERR	Response for end of retransmission
FCD	Facsimile coded date
FCF	Facsimile control field
FCS	Frame checking sequence
FIF	Facsimile information field
FTT	Failure to train
HDLC	High level data link control
MCF	Message confirmation
MPS	Multi-page signal
NSF	Non-standard facilities
NSS	Non-standard set-up
PPS	Partial page signal
PPR	Partial page request

Table 5.8   (Continued from previous page)

RCP	Return to control for partial page
RNR	Receive not ready
RR	Receive ready
RTC	Return to control
RTN	Retrain negative
RTP	Retrain positive
TCF	Training check
TSI	Transmitting subscriber identification

sent in T.30 format. Because they are facsimile encoded the receive machine remains ignorant of the content and cannot record them in the reports.

The information may contain:

1.   Document number, time and date of sending.
2.   Sender's name or TSI.
3.   Urgent or priority comment.

Although the implementation may be proprietary to the manufacture it is printed on all receivers because it is included in the facsimile message. It is often transmitted outside the regular A4 page increasing the received page length.

ITU-T NSF signals

Under the non-standard facilities procedure a manufacturer may implement any proprietary identification form desired. When transmitting to another machine of the same manufacturer it may include alpha as well as numeric characters. This can enable the name of the communicating machine to be shown on the display or recorded in the activity report. It is not recognised between machines of different manufacturers.

NSF covers a wide range of proprietary features but in the identification area it also allows the transmission of passwords for confidential operation.

Received copy with typical identification

In addition to the text at the top (date, time and sender identification) transmitted as part of the facsimile image, other information, compiled at the receiver from the transmitted TSI/NSS and from locally available information in the receiver, may be added.

The word 'END' is sometimes inserted at the bottom of the facsimile image to confirm that this is the last page of the document.

5.5 64kbit/s facsimile equipment

The availability of switched digital networks with 64kbit/s channels continues to increase with basic rate and primary rate ISDN. The I Series recommendations developed by ITU-T have established international standards for 64kbit/s intercommunication.

The G3 transmissions use the voice speech band which, when converted to PCM digital signals for transmission within the public network, use the complete 64kbit/s channel. This means 9.6kbit/s or 14.4kbit/s maximum rate on a 64kbit/s channel.

Clearly where 64kbit/s digital access is available, as through the ISDN connection, a direct digital input at 64kbit/s machine data rate is desirable giving an improvement of four to six times in speed and reduction in transmission cost. To take advantage of this a 64kbit/s data rate facsimile machine is required.

5.5.1 G4 equipment

ITU-T has produced recommendations for G4 digital equipment in 3 classes based on the ISO 7 layer model for interoperation with open systems communication standards.

Class 1 is for the transmission of facsimile documents only and is a higher performance equivalent to G3. Class 2 has the transmission capabilities of class 1 and the receive capabilities of class 3. It is similar in operation to class 1 but can take advantage of the increased efficiency of character transmission where available.

Class 3 provides for the transmission of characters and facsimile data, either separately or combined in a mixed mode format. This is a more complex terminal giving the possibility of keyboard and scanner input with the document architecture to support interoperation with ISO hierarchical models.

The requirements of classes 2 and 3 will continue to develop as necessary to track the evolution of document architecture standards. Class 1 machines are already being implemented to provide higher performance facsimile with direct digital access to the ISDN network, 3 seconds/page transmission and higher resolutions operation to 400 × 400 pels/inch.

5.5.2 64kbit/s G3 type equipment

With the tremendous growth in G3 an enhancement is being discussed in ITU-T to provide a similar operation at the faster digital interface rate of 64kbit/s to that recommended on the analogue network interface at between 14.4kbit/s and 2.4kbit/s.

This will simplify implementation and provide the user with current G3 facilities at the faster and more efficient digital interface rate. G3-64kbit/s is proposed as an option to the basic G3 mode which is essential for interworking with the existing G3 machine population. In this machine the basic G3 operation is likely to be provided on the I series port by the implementation of the equivalent of a codec converting the G3 modem signals to the ISDN speech equivalent.

5.6 G3 networks, switches, gateways and PC fax

The success of G3 facsimile has encouraged the provision of additional equipment/facilities to enhance operation and provide cost savings. The communication interfaces are based on T.4 and T.30 recommendations and follow standard facsimile protocols. Where these units are provided by suppliers different from the machine suppliers, the NSF proprietary operation is often precluded. This can result in a loss of facilities and an increase in transmission time. It may also mean that because of simple interfaces used, MR, ECM, 14.4kbit/s ITU-T options are not implemented and transmission efficiency is limited.

5.6.1 Managed network use

By the provision of store and forward units with multiline PSTN access, a network operator or value added supplier can relieve the user of major distribution tasks and free the user's machine for other work. With multiline access it is realistic to consider a regular broadcast transmission to 10000 recipients from a single originator transmission to the store. To some extent the network operator can schedule the traffic to suit network loading and therefore offer practical tariffs which could compensate for the delay in delivery and the subsequent confirmation report necessary.

5.6.2 Facsimile switches

The requirements of some major users include facsimile traffic control and costing, archival recording of all transferred facsimile messages and controlled distribution of centrally received incoming messages. By routeing the facsimile traffic through an intelligent central switch, possibly associated with the company PBX, the required monitoring and control functions can be provided with cost and traffic reporting developed to suit the individual needs of the user. (Figure 5.8.)

One main area of concern for facsimile users is that the onward distribution of documents received at central machines may be located in the mail room. Onward distribution is often delayed waiting for the next mail round, and onward transmission by facsimile to the department in question is sometimes not felt desirable.

One solution being considered is that the facsimile switch can have a soft copy display of the facsimile message on a VDU. An operator would then display and readdress the document for onward transmission from memory. Clearly, for efficient operations, a suitable

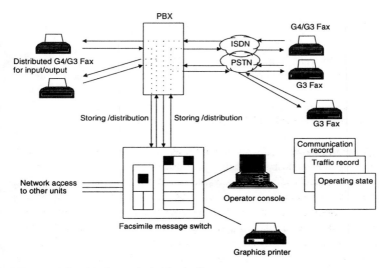

Figure 5.8   G3 fax switch block diagram

compromise must be made between the switch capital cost and the time required by the operator, to re-route the document.

5.6.3 Facsimile gateways

The transmission of facsimile documents and of electronic mail or computer generated text are usually kept separate. However the wide population of G3 machines has encouraged users on electronic mail or local area networks to request interoperation. This is usually achieved by fitting a gateway on the computer network to convert the information to the T.4 and T.30 facsimile format for onward transmission.

The problem is for incoming documents in the facsimile domain. These are virtually impossible to convert to the text environment and require onward transmission in a graphics mode with the high bandwidth and large storage capacity associated with raw image data. These facsimile documents are most conveniently printed out on a local facsimile unit and kept separate from the data system.

5.6.4 PC fax cards

The widespread availability of G3 machines and the expansion card provision in desktop personal computers, has encouraged the development of specialised fax cards. With the addition of a dedicated PSTN interface card and support software, it is possible to make facsimile transmissions directly from PC memory without the image being printed. The performance depends on the balance between PC software capability, for example speed of compression, and the processing and memory capability of the card itself.

User expectations that the simple operation of fax machines be available in PC fax are beginning to be met together with background operation of the PC in fax mode. However there are similar incoming document problem, as for gateways:

1.   Difficult to provide adequate soft copy memory.
2.   Slow to print received pages.
3.   Limitations of screen resolution or of whole page display.
4.   Time to decode/display compressed image limits search mode.

One of the benefits of PC fax cards or fax gateways is their ability to send the equivalent of personalised mailshots by facsimile, a feature not normally available in the broadcast mode of facsimile transceivers which send identical documents to all destinations.

The fax modem fitted to these cards can also be used for PC to PC communication for file transfer over the PSTN. If the growth in this requirement continues, then discussions in ITU-T are likely to provide an additional option within the G3 fax recommendations.

The convenience of communicating by facsimile can be extended to operation with the computer in the briefcase. Transmission directly from the keyboard (actually from memory) and soft copy reception without printing are easily possible with existing fax standards over the PSTN.

Customer requirements dominate facsimile developments and the increase in use of the G3 interface in non-fax products is expected to continue although the replacement of documents in the briefcase by facsimile files in the laptop/notebook PC seems remote.

5.7 Facsimile futures

The PSTN remains the major communication network for the fore-seeable future with increasing opportunities on the ISDN. Facsimile terminals G3, G3-64kbit/s and G4 will continue to operate on these networks.

Facsimile transmission is particularly appropriate for the future because of the large compatible equipment base and because of the vast and continuing information base on paper and film.

Documents are required on paper for convenience, for availability (even in power failure) and for use when out of communication away from the office.

Development continues in ITU-T with higher speed, higher resolution transmission and with high speed character and mixed mode functions.

The potential for communication with this ubiquitous terminal is hardly touched. Interfaces into the facsimile domain to use the proven reliable transmission method are increasing. The terminals provide reliable input/output devices into other applications and systems using the current ITU-T recommendations. Continued growth in the number of terminals, including the domestic environment, is expected.

5.8 References

Buerms, F. (1995) Computer-based fax: the hard facts, *Voice International*, June/July.

Costello, J. (1993) Will politics rule fax revolution? *Communications International*, March.

Costigan, D.M. (1971) *The Principles and Practice of Facsimile Communication*, Philadelphia, Chilton.

Halton, Jones and Treece (1991) Facsimile — the essential image, *Br. Telecom Technol J.*, **9** (1), January.

ITU-T (1989) *Blue Book Volume VII Fascicle VII.3*, International Telecommunication Union, Geneva, ISBN 92-61-03611-2

McConnell, Bodson, and Schaphorst (1992) *Fax*, 2nd ed., Artech House, ISBN 0-89006-310-9.

McDermott, R. (1994) Fax software evolves? *Telecommunications*, December.

Payton and Qureshi (1985) Trellis encoding, *Data Communications*, May.

Pugh, A. (1991) Facsimile Today, *Electronics & Communication Engineering Journal*, October.

Reardon, R. (Ed.) (1990) *Facsimile Networks for the 1990s*, Online Publications, ISBN 0-86353-131-8.

Wittering, S. (1993) As a matter of fax, *Communications International*, December.

6. Modems

6.1 Introduction

With a long and illustrious history behind them, one might be forgiven for thinking that the humble modem should be firmly consigned to the electronic scrap heap. Indeed, it was not so long ago that the majority of industry pundits believed that ISDN would eventually finish off the modem for good.

But the modem is a survivor and in the 1990s, some twenty years after its first appearance, those same pundits agree that far from being finished, the modem is still firmly fighting back and looking forward to another decade of life. This renewed enthusiasm is based on two fundamental reasons:

1. The introduction of ISDN, the Integrated Services Digital Network. The hype of the eighties delivered little in the way of actual service, so that towards the end of that decade it was viewed with an increasing amount of cynicism and scepticism. Now, ISDN has turned the corner and is a key element in the strategies of networking companies, but although BT are rolling out 90,000 Basic Rate or ISDN2 circuits (2×64kbit/s bearer channels plus 1×16kbit/s signalling channel), it is still a drop in the ocean compared to some 24 million analogue lines installed in the UK. While reasonably priced switched digital circuits are hard to come by, there remain many applications for which the modem will be eminently suited, and areas where ISDN will never be available.

2. The modem's resilience and stability as a product. The modem has benefited from the same advances in microelectronics as the rest of the computing industry. This has allowed it to change radically but remain reliable enough to more than keep pace with alternative transmission systems.

When the ITU-T (formerly CCITT) introduced the V.32 standard in 1986 for operation at 9000 bit/s, it was hailed as the last, great modem standard. By February 1991 the ITU-T had approved the V.32bis standard and was working on an even faster standard called, appropriately, V.fast or V.34 (Vadgama, 1993; Bright, 1993; Wright, 1994; Taylor, 1995).

Whilst this quest for sheer performance continues apace, shipments of V.22bis modems operating at a stately 2.4kbit/s expect to top 2.5 million in 1994, roughly two and a half times that of the V.32 product.

With faster operation, greater functionality and reducing prices, the outlook, for the consumer at least, is rosy indeed (Reed, 1994; King, 1995).

6.2 Principles of operation

The principles of modem operation were fashioned by the limitations of the telephone network for which they were originally designed (Figure 6.1). The telephone circuits of the Public Switched Telephone Network (PSTN) are designed to reproduce speech of a quality that is reliably understandable to the human ear.

Most of the intelligible sound generated by vocal chords can be contained in a frequency range of 300Hz to 3400Hz, although generating sounds both higher and lower in frequency. The restriction of frequencies to this range also eliminates a lot of interference and extraneous noise.

In order to provide a constant response to sounds within this range, telephone circuits are 'loaded' with extra inductance to offset the cables' natural capacitance. Add to this the effect of switching and the variation in route from call to call and it can be readily appreciated that it is not an environment conducive to digital transmission, where acceptable bit error rates are typically less than one in a million.

The humble dial up modem must deal with all of this, but is limited as a result to a maximum speed of around 30kbit/s for today's dial up line according to Shannon's Law. Contrast this with a digital KiloStream circuit delivering 64kbit/s and digital MegaStream circuits delivering 2.048Mbit/s.

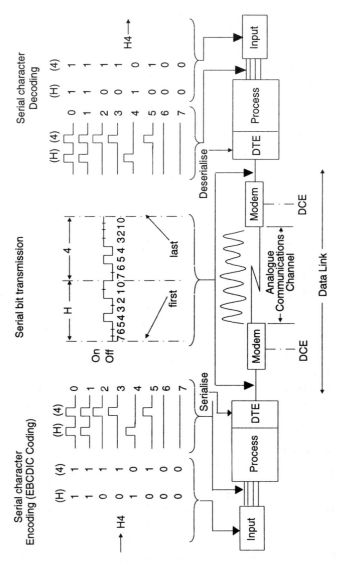

Figure 6.1 A complete end to end data communication system using a modem link

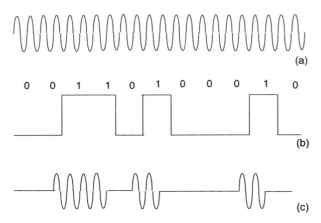

Figure 6.2   Amplitude modulation: (a) carrier; (b) modulating waveform; (c) modulated waveform

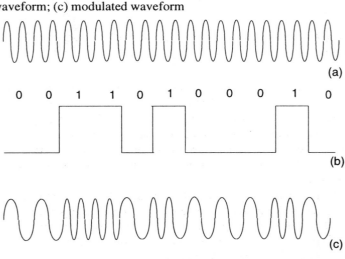

Figure 6.3   Frequency modulation: (a) carrier; (b) modulating waveform; (c) modulated waveform

An analogue signal has an amplitude, a frequency and a phase. Each can be varied to modulate the waveform (Figures 6.2 to 6.4). In practice, simple amplitude modulation is not used on its own because

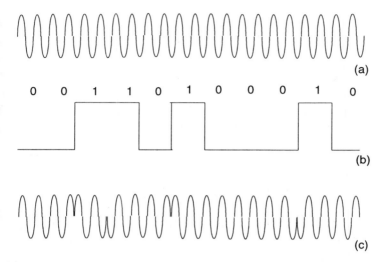

Figure 6.4 Phase modulation: (a) carrier; (b) modulating waveform; (c) modulated waveform

of its sensitivity to noise. Crackles on the line may not impair the ability of a human ear to understand speech, but they certainly impair a computer's ability to understand a digital signal if it is corrupted by them during transmission. Frequency modulation changes the frequency of the basic carrier wave (unmodulated signal) according to the state of the digital signal generated by the computing or terminal equipment.

All the signals or tones generated remain in-band. In phase modulation, the carrier frequency remains constant, but the phase can be shifted in increments over a complete cycle of the waveform. Dibit Phase Shift Keying for example allows two bits of information to be represented by a single cycle. The rate of the waveform is called the baud rate. The information rate in bits per second is twice the baud rate, since each signal level represents two bits.

Other modulation techniques provide for far greater throughput. Quadrature Amplitude Modulation, for example, combines amplitude modulation with phase modulation to generate 16 different signal combinations, so that each signal element transmitted on the line represents a 4 bit digital sequence. The ITU-T V.29 standard uses this modulation technique over 4 wire lines at a baud rate of 2400. Since each baud represents 4bit/s, the resulting speed of operation is rated at 4×2400 or 9600bits/s.

Having outlined how a digital signal can be encoded into a signal suitable for transmission over the telephone line, what happens when the modem has used its dial up telephony capabilities to establish a transmission path? (Figure 6.5; Scott, 1980.) The digital equipment originating the call uses the interface signals presented to it by the modem to raise the Request To Send (RTS) signal. If the modem is ready, it responds with Clear To Send (CTS) and turns on its Data Carrier Detect (DCD).

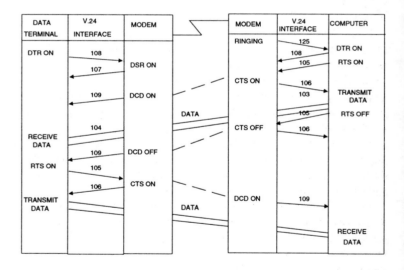

Figure 6.5   Simplified timings for data transmission between a data terminal and a remote computer over the telephone network. The terminal initiates a PSTN call to the computer which responds to set up a two way dialogue

Having raised CTS, transmit data is applied to the encoder where the modulation of the carrier wave we have previously described takes place. The modulated wave is filtered to eliminate unnecessary frequencies and the level of transmission is adjusted to suit the line before it is actually transmitted. When transmission has been completed, the RTS signal is turned off by the digital equipment. At the destination end, the signal is filtered again to remove unwanted frequencies generated as the signal propagates along the line, before being applied to an amplitude and delay equaliser.

Although speech circuits are 'loaded' to give an even response to in-band frequencies, distortion does take place. Private leased lines can be conditioned or fine tuned to reduce this distortion, but dial up circuits can deliver a different path, quality and response on each connection. The faster the modem operates, the more complex this becomes.

From the equaliser an automatic gain control amplifier compensates for different levels of received signal before the analogue signal is demodulated to reconstruct the original digital signal. In the example of Dibit Phase Shift Keying used earlier, the demodulator measures the phase of the incoming signal and the corresponding 2 bit digital signal is output at the Receive Data (RD) line at the modem interface to the receiving digital equipment.

So far data has been serially transmitted from source to destination. But data only went one way, and while the source transmitted the destination listened. This is half duplex operation and is inefficient since the line has to clear before transmission in the opposite direction can take place, limiting the speed of operation. The use of four wire lines, instead of two, reduces the turnaround time. Modems that operate full duplex permit simultaneous operation in both directions and is accomplished by using four wire lines or much more commonly by dividing the bandwidth of two wire lines using different transmit signals frequencies. ITU-T V.32 echo cancellation techniques broke new ground by providing full duplex operation over two wires with the full bandwidth available in each direction.

The patterns of 1s and 0s of course have to be arranged in a way that makes sense to the digital equipment. Modems operating asynchronously do this by sending a start bit. The modem can then count off the required number of bits that make up a byte or character, including a parity and stop bit before sending the next start bit. Synchronous modems on the other hand solve this timing problem by synchronising their clocks. Instead of having to re-synchronise after each character, synchronous modems send timing information along with the data in a continuous sequence. A protocol is used to define these synchronising sequences, block sizes and formatting characters. The extra circuitry and logic to achieve this provides greater through-put but at a price premium compared to asynchronous modes.

6.3 Modem standards

Standardisation in modem operation is important to guarantee that a user can connect to a modem attached to the same link or network (Tables 6.1 to 6.3).

This is particularly important in the dial up environment where the modem model operating at the distant end may not even be known. At one time, high speed modems would only operate at peak perfor-mance when talking to another modem of the same type, typically operating a proprietary transmission standard. When connected to a different modem, they would have to accept the lowest common level of operation, often significantly less than their individual optimum performance.

The main force for standards in Europe and increasingly more in the United States is the ITU-T. Over the years they have developed standards from the 300bit/s V.21 operation of the early 1970s to the recently agreed 14400bit/s V.32bis standard and beyond. Digital signal processing technology now delivers chip sets covering multiple standards in an attempt to provide universal connectivity. Since optimum performance of links may depend not only on a common transmission standard but a common error correction and data compression standard, connecting modems must undergo a se-quential negotiation before actual transmission can take place.

The V.32 transmission standard introduced 5 years ago pushed full duplex operation over 2 wires up to 9600bit/s. The first to use a technique called echo cancellation, it was made possible only be-cause of the development of Digital Signal Processing (DSP) technol-

Table 6.1 ITU-T V Series transmission standards

Standard	Transmission rate	Duplex capability	Mode	Media
V.21	300bit/s	Full duplex	Asynchronous	2 wire PSTN
V.22	1200bit/s	Full duplex	Asynchronous	2 wire PSTN
V.22bis	2400bit/s	Full duplex	Asynchronous/ synchronous	2 wire PSTN
V.23	1200/ 75bit/s	Full duplex	Asynchronous	4 wire leased
		Half duplex	Asynchronous	2 wire PSTN
V.26bis	2400bit/s	Full duplex	Synchronous	2 wire leased
		Half duplex	Synchronous	2 wire PSTN
V.27ter	4800bit/s	Half duplex	Synchronous	2 wire PSTN
V.29	9600bit/s	Full duplex	Synchronous	4 wire leased
V.32	9600bit/s	Full duplex	Asynchronous/ synchronous	2 wire PSTN
V.32bis	14400bit/s	Full duplex	Asynchronous/ synchronous	2 wire PSTN
V.33	14400bit/s	Full duplex	Synchronous	4 wire leased
V.34	28800bit/s	Full duplex	Asynchronous/ synchronous	4 wire leased

Table 6.2 Error correction standards

Standard		Description
CCITT V.42		Standard for error correcting protocols including LAP/M and MNP4
MNP	Level 1	Error correcting/Throughput reduced to 70%
	Level 2	Error correcting/Throughput reduced to 84%
	Level 3	Error correcting/Throughput up to 108%
	Level 4	Error correcting/Throughput up to 120%

Table 6.3 Data compression standards

Standard		Description
CCITT V.42bis		Standard for data compression using BTLZ for throughput up to 400%
MNP	Level 5	Data compression/Throughput up to 200%
	Level 6	Data compression with V.29 technology/ Throughput up to 200%
	Level 7	Predictive data compression/ Throughput up to 300%
	Level 8	Predictive data compression with V.29/Throughput up to 300%
	Level 9	Predictive data compression with V.32/Throughput up to 300%
	Level 10	Enhanced Level 9/Throughput up to 300%

ogy. Previously, full duplex operation required the available bandwidth to be split into two frequency bands so that simultaneous transmission in both directions was possible. Echo cancellation made the full bandwidth available in both directions by allowing the transmitting modem to detect its own signal mixed in with the received signal of the distant modem and remove it.

V.32 also uses a second technique called Trellis encoding which uses an extra bit to help identify and correct errors. This extra bit, added to those multiple bit per baud sequences for improving throughput described earlier, do not carry information. Although this appears as a simple signal overhead, their presence can actually further increase throughput.

A V.32 signal space diagram, or constellation, shows pictorially all the 32 signalling combinations possible from a 5 bit digital sequence (Figures 6.6 and 6.7). To show how this relates in performance terms, the baud rate for V.22bis is 600bit/s. Each baud contains a 4 bit digital code (or 16 combinations), 600 baud × 4 bits equals 2400bit/s. The baud rate for V.32 is much higher i.e. 2400bit/s. Four of the five bit V.32 code is used for information, the fifth for Trellis encoding. 2400 baud × 4 bits equals 9600bit/s performance.

The V.32bis standard builds on V.32 by using a 7 bit digital sequence per baud. With six bits for information and a similar baud rate, V.32bis performance is pushed up to 14400bit/s over 2 wires.

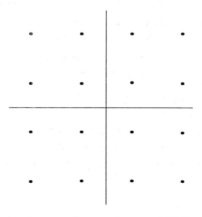

Figure 6.6   A signal space diagram (or constellation) for V.22 bis modems

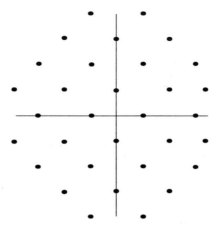

Figure 6.7   A signal space diagram for V.32 modems

Standards must equally be applied to the DTE-DCE boundary (Table 6.4; Enslow, 1988). Although perceived as a mundane subject, specifications and standards are in a continual state of flux and merit some discussion. On the simplest level, an interface consists of three parts, a protocol, an electrical specification and a mechanical connector. The protocol describes the logical attributes which typically include the meaning of the electrical signals on each pin, the interrelationship between the signals and the means to exchange information.

The electrical and mechanical specification in turn specify the physical attributes of the electrical signals on the pins and the dimensions and construction of the connector itself. A successful connection is dependent on the combination of all three. The best known of these is the ubiquitous Electronic Industries Association (EIA) RS232C specification which formed the basis of the ITU-T V.24 recommendation. Whereas RS232C described both physical and logical attributes, V.24 describes only the logical and is supplemented by recommendations V.28 and ISO2110 for electrical and mechanical characteristics.

Table 6.4 Interface standards

	Electrical Signals Interface	Mechanical Interface	Functional Protocols	Procedure Protocols
RS-232-C	*	*	*	*
(V.24)			*	*
(V.28)	*			
(ISO-2110)		*		
(X.21bis)		*	*	*
X.24			*	
X.21		*	*	*
(ISO 4903)		*		
RS-422-A	*			
(V.11/X.27)	*			
(ISO 4902)		*		
(V.24)			*	*
(V.54)				*
RS-423-A	*			
(V.10/X.26)	*			
V.35	*		*	*
(ISO 2593)		*		

The use of the term V.24 popularly implies the use of the other two. Specified for operation up to 20kbit/s via a 25 way D type connector it provides a set of unbalanced (one leg goes to ground potential), double current (current may flow in either the go or return path depending on voltage polarity) interchange circuits. Unbalanced circuits are susceptible to crosstalk and other interference. The operating distance is capacitance limited to 2500pF but, when the specification was written, cable technology imposed a limit of about 50 feet.

Improvements made since can deliver four times that distance without exceeding the capacitance limit, although V.28 sets no such limitation. The second interface in common usage is the V.35 recommendation supplied via a 34 way connector, its electrical characteristics providing for balanced (carrying equal and opposite voltages) interchange circuits. Neither lead is at ground potential.

Balanced circuits provide a cancellation effect which bestows higher immunity to interference and, due to lower capacitance, allows extended transmission distances in comparison to RS232C. Originally specified at 48kbit/s operation, it is common to find US developed equipment rated at up to MegaStream speeds. Later standards developed for higher rates and operating distances originated initially as EIA RS423 and RS422 which were subsequently adopted by the ITU-T as recommendations V.10 and V.11 respectively. Because their electrical characteristics were suitable for public data network interfaces they have also been assigned as X.26 and X.27 respectively.

The potential for confusion increased when EIA released RS449 to cover the non-electrical aspects, as well as updating RS232C. RS449 was designed to overcome limitations in RS232C but because it arrived late and specified pins for ten additional circuits it has not become widely adopted. V.10 delivers an unbalanced interface, with maximum ratings of 100kbit/s and 1000 metres and V.11 a balanced interface with maximum ratings of 10Mbit/s and 1000 metres. Maximum distance and speed are mutually exclusive. V.11 electrical interface signals are commonly combined with a 15 way D type connector in common use as the method of connection to BT's KiloStream service.

The goal for the future is to reduce the number and size of these interfaces, ideally to an universal DTE/DCE standard, so a DTE would not care if it were connected to a DCE or another DTE. Various issues of control signal pass through and timing are the principle problems.

Supremacy in error connection and data compression standards is currently a straight race between ITU-T international standards, and proprietary standards developed by Microcom called the Microcom Networking Protocol MNP (TM). ITU-T recommendations specify a negotiation process that attempts error correction using the V.42 standard or Link Access Protocol for Modems (LAPM).

If LAPM (Clark, 1991) is not available in both devices attempting communication, MNP class 4 is attempted. MNP up to level 4 is included as an addendum to this international standard owing to the large installed base of modems using it, but higher levels will not be included in further developments. If neither is acceptable, simple asynchronous operation is used.

Once error correction is established, modems operating ITU-T standards will attempt to instigate compression using V.42bis. Failing this, the fallback is to MNP level 5 (2:1 compression) and from there to uncompressed operation. V.42bis uses a technique called the Lempel-Ziv algorithm (Section 6.3.1). This, like other techniques, builds dictionaries of code words for recurring characters in the data stream. The code words are abbreviations, so that it takes fewer bits to transmit, thereby increasing throughput and lowering cost over dial up lines.

Unlike other techniques, Lempel-Ziv develops these dictionaries dynamically as it goes along and stores them in Random Access Memory in both modems. Providing up to a fourfold performance increase, its choice as the ITU-T adopted international standard was due to efficient use of both memory and processing power and perhaps more importantly its ability to shut the compression algorithm down when incompressible scrambled, encrypted or random data is presented to it.

Figure 6.8 shows examples of compression ratios possible for various applications. From a commercial viewpoint, V.42bis is an expensive proposition for vendors. Three companies, BT, IBM and the Unisys Corporation, all patented their contributions to it and charge licence fees.

6.3.1 The V42.bis algorithm

In order to compress data, the V.42bis algorithm must first identify recurring strings of characters in the data stream. These code words

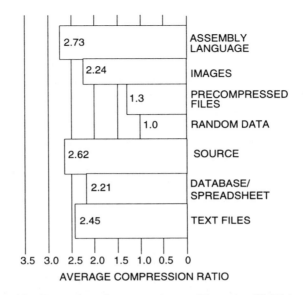

Figure 6.8 Examples of compression on files using V.42bis

are used to compile dictionaries which are duplicated at both ends of the transmission link and are accessed by a common synchronised index system.

This process is dynamic and the dictionaries are constantly being updated and modified. As data is transferred to the modem for transmission, a complex string matching or 'parsing' process must take place requiring an extensive dictionary search. It is easy to see how less efficient compression techniques could consume large amounts of memory and why it is necessary to disable the algorithm when presented with incompressible or encrypted data.

V.42bis dictionaries do not search from start to finish but use a 'tree' type data structure somewhat similar to a telephone directory. In that way the same information will be identically stored whenever it is placed in either the encoding or decoding dictionaries.

V.42bis uses the concepts of nodes to store information. The initial character is stored as a 'root' node which has 'leaf' nodes associated

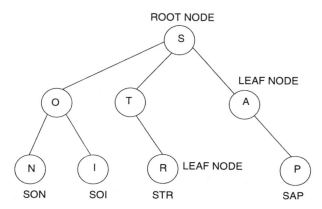

ROOT NODE

LEAF NODE

LEAF NODE

SON   SOI   STR   SAP

Figure 6.9   V.42bis dictionary tree

with it on paths radiating out from the root. Suppose the modem tries to find the code word 'STRING'. The initial character S is read and the entry located. T, the next character, is read and a search started amongst the immediate offshoots or 'leaves' of the root node (see Figure 6.9). If found, the location is recorded and the next character read. This is repeated until the 'I' character when this particular root node has been exhausted. At this time the compressed index value of the location for 'STR' is transmitted, the algorithm adds an 'I' leaf node to the string 'STR' and starts afresh to look for a new root node associated with 'I' which may be elsewhere in the dictionary.

Implementing this concept into a memory structure is shown in Figure 6.10. V.42bis devices commonly use a method called the 'trie', which uses both a character and three pointers to identify information by location. Starting again with our initial character 'S', the right hand pointer designates the alternative characters at the second level, 'T', 'A' and 'O'. These are the dependent characters of the parent character 'S'. Similarly 'N' and 'I' are dependent characters of the 'SO' string.

Since the index value built up by the pointer locations are unique, the far end modem can use the transmitted, compressed, index value to locate the entry in its own dictionary, with the parent (upward

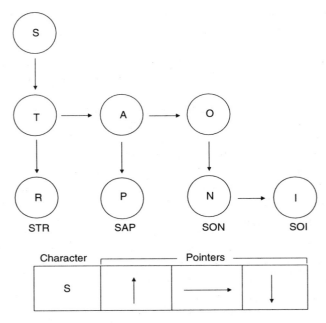

Figure 6.10 V.42bis data structure

facing pointer) used to locate the preceding entry. By following the pointers backwards to the root the whole string is reconstructed in its uncompressed form. To maintain synchronisation of information the encoding dictionary updates are delayed by one string to allow the decoder to store new index values before attempting to decode them. In our example, the first time the index value for 'STRI' is transmitted, it is not recognised. The new index value is stored for subsequent use by the decoder and instead decodes the index value already stored for 'STR'.

6.4 Types of modem

When modems first appeared providing terminal to mainframe computer connection over the PSTN, the definition of a modem was clear.

The modem was required to take the computer's digital binary signals and use them to modulate an analogue signal capable of being transmitted down a telephone line, where another modem could demodulate the analogue signal and reproduce the computer's original digital signal faithfully. The modem took its name from this MODulating and DEModulating process.

Today there are a number of devices called modems that do not modulate or demodulate a carrier signal in the same way as the original dial up modem. In order to classify devices, we have to consider the type of line they use, the mode of transmission and the distances over which they operate.

The most commonly used medium is still the telephone network. Links are made by dialling over the PSTN or by using private point to point circuits leased from the telephone company. Dial up and leased line modems using these voice grade circuits, sometimes collectively referred to as long haul modems, must compensate for the frequency limitations and the variable quality of the transmission media. Distance however is unlimited.

Baseband modems are not 'true' modems, because they do not modulate signals in the normally accepted sense of the word. Baseband signals contain frequencies outside the normal 300–3400Hz voice grade circuits going right down to DC. Voice grade circuits are loaded so that performance for speech is optimised. Baseband modems therefore cannot use them, because they act like low pass filters, eliminating the higher baseband frequencies. Instead they use unloaded cable where they have the entire bandwidth at their disposal, but are subject to the linear relationship between frequency and attenuation which limits the operating distance.

The baseband modem takes the digital signal it is presented with and either transmits it directly or in a slightly modified form to the line. In Figure 6.11 each time cell represents one information bit. The first half represents the complement of the bit value, the second half the bit value. By ensuring a signal change half way through each cell, synchronisation is maintained without separate synchronisation signals.

End users can provide their own unloaded circuits by laying twisted pair cable within the confines of private property or lease

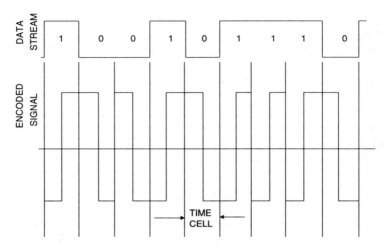

Figure 6.11 Baseband signalling (Manchester encoding)

from carriers like BT. Unloaded circuits are restricted to local exchange areas which means a maximum distance of approximately 7
miles. Short haul modems and local data sets are two popular terms
for devices using baseband techniques over short distance unloaded
lines, providing both synchronous and asychronous operation up to
19.2kbit/s, and up to 64kbit/s in special applications. The maximum
operating speed is usually distance dependent.

Limited distance modems are hybrid devices. Some offer the same
performance as ITU-T standard modems over shorter distances by
using less sophisticated, non-standard modulation and equalisation
techniques. Indeed some US developed modems converted for the
UK market provide nationwide operation over dedicated and wire
leased lines at speeds up to 19.2kbit/s. From the US perspective,
coverage of the UK would constitute a limited distance! Some modems, described as limited distance devices, use the baseband technique and are subsequently limited to the local exchange operating
restrictions.

The types of modem so far have dealt exclusively with digital data
using baseband techniques that carry one channel per line. Broadband

signalling has its origins in the cable television industry and carries many channels per cable (Minoli, 1991). A 300MHz broadband system can handle seventy five thousand 4kHz voice channels, but can also carry data, text and image. Using a two cable implementation to link devices to the network, the interface is provided by a radio frequency transmitter/receiver called an RF modem. Radio modems are now being developed for data transmission over cellular links and packet radio. Packet radio accommodates asynchronous and synchronous data transmission at 9.6kbit/s over mobile land channels and is set to foster a new generation of wireless local area networks.

6.5 Typical modem features

The years have seen a tremendous change in modem features and functionality. Although quite adequate at the time, the 300 baud modem of the early 70s is a far cry from the sophisticated and powerful, multi-transmission standard, error correcting and data compressing products of today. Techniques like multi-layer printed circuit boards, surface mount technology and DSP (digital signal processing) have combined increasing functionality with decreasing physical size.

The range of options, once available only in hardware, can now be programmed by software, and each year brings a new diversity of applications and a relentless downward trend in pricing. Features can be categorised into three groups. Some enhance the basic group's modem performance itself. Some actually restrict performance in order to better accomplish a specialised task, whilst others aid user operation independent of performance. The features emphasise dial up modems since they incorporate such a wide range of functionality.

6.5.1 Transmission

The most common standards are those of the ITU-T. The ITU-T transmission standards are covered by the V series, the code designation for data transmission over the telephone network. Digital signal processors now deliver multiple transmission standard capability in a single chipset.

Two of the most popular combinations today are the low speed 'quad' combination covering V.22bis, V.22, V.23 and V.21 and the high speed 'quin', V.32, V.22bis, V.22, V.23 and V.21. Although demanding ever more powerful processing to be able to provide and negotiate the inter-modem communication for this automatic multi-standard capability, the user benefits of universal connectivity are a powerful selling point.

6.5.2 Operating modes

A modem will typically offer a range of operating modes over a variety of lines, as described in following sections.

6.5.2.1 *Half duplex vs full duplex*

A train travelling on a single track illustrates half duplex operation over two wire circuits, because while it is travelling in one direction, travel in the other direction is not possible. The train would have to be removed from the track at its destination before another could be sent in the opposite direction. Half duplex operation on four wire circuits can also be illustrated using the same analogy if we now have a second track, so there is one for each direction, but one train is not allowed to start before the other is finished.

Continuing with two parallel tracks, full duplex operation is equivalent to the trains being able to operate independently of each other on their own track. In practice, full-duplex operation is provided over four wire lines where the outward and inward 'tracks' are physically separate or over two wires where either the modem splits the physical circuit into two channels of different frequency or uses echo cancellation.

6.5.2.2 *Dial up vs leased lines*

Calls over the PSTN are routed by tone or pulse signals generated by the modem which duplicate those of an ordinary telephone. The advantages are that one modem can connect to any other modem on the same network no matter where it is and charges are based on distance and connection time, not the amount of data transmitted. Disadvantages are that the line quality varies because the circuits are switched through exchanges which introduce transmission loss and noise. Even if the same destination is dialled, the route may be different, so the line cannot be 'tuned' for better quality.

Leased lines or private lines obtained from telephone companies are permanent connections between two points. Because the quality of the line is constant and the route is fixed, it can be fine tuned or conditioned to carry high volumes of data, at higher speeds than dial up lines and with lower error rates. Most of today's sophisticated dial up modems incorporate 2 or 4 leased line operation as standard.

6.5.2.3 *Synchronous or asychronous*

Controlled by the transmission standard invoked on call set up, typically both asynchronous and synchronous operation is provided within a single unit. Synchronous operation is usually protocol transparent, whereas asynchronous operation will be possible over a variety of character lengths, parity and stop bit combinations under software programme control.

6.5.2.4 *Equalisation*

Equalisation circuitry compensates for the distortion caused as different frequencies travel at different rates down a transmission line changing the shape of the signal waveform. Fixed equalisers used in lower speed modems are designed to compensate for average line conditions, which include frequency response and envelope delay. For higher speed operation, automatic adaptive equalisers are used which continually re-adjust for changes in line quality, especially useful in dial up operation.

6.5.2.5 *Error correction*

As speeds of operation increase, modem links become more prone to errors, because a line disturbance that corrupts one bit at 300bit/s corrupts thirty two at 9.6kbit/s. At higher speeds, errors may less obviously be generated by communications software or lower quality cables.

Error correction need not necessarily take place in the modem. In fact, most dial up modems have an operating mode where error correction is disabled. For example, if a workstation or computer uses a built in synchronous error control protocol like that used by an X.25 Packet Assembler/Disassembler (PAD), data is presented to the modem and just transmitted. Further error correction from the modem would simply increase the overhead and degrade throughput.

Where error correction does occur in the modem, the most basic form is the parity bit where an extra bit, either 1 or 0, is added to each character so that the sum of the bits is always odd or even. When bits are corrupted during transmission, the receiving modem can detect it and ask for a retransmission. This is known as Automatic Retransmission Request (ARQ).

Because its ability to detect errors is limited (two compensating errors within a single character would go undetected) the next stage is to incorporate a checksum. Here a number of characters are grouped together into a frame and certain bits of it are combined together according to a mathematical algorithm to generate a checksum, often called a Cyclical Redundancy Check (CRC). This is then transmitted with the frame. The receiver does the same computation on the transmitted frame and compares its own checksum with that transmitted to it. Depending on the result it sends an acknowledgement or a retransmission request back to the originating modem.

Although a typical 16 bit checksum is far more efficient at detecting errors it cannot detect all. As the move towards standards has been consolidated these techniques have been incorporated into standards. The two major players are the international ITU-T V.42 standard and the Microcom Networking Protocol. V.42 uses a 32 bit CRC option.

6.5.2.6 *Data compression*

Data compression schemes are a way of increasing throughput as it gets increasingly difficult to improve the modem's basic operating speed as upper limits of performance over analogue telephone lines are approached.

Data compression relies on encoding recurring sequences more efficiently. If more information can be represented by fewer bits, the faster it can be transmitted. Although vendors' data sheets always quote the maximum compression rates, they vary with the type of data being transmitted and the quality of line being used. The two standards battling it out in the marketplace are again the V.42bis and the MNP standard, currently at level 10.

6.5.2.7 *Call control*

Originally dial up operations could only be performed by a telephone attached directly into the modem, the use of internal relays preventing the phone from disturbing the data call, once it was in progress, as well as allowing normal phone operation at all other times. It is now common to find manual call control possible by using front panel buttons which initiate a call stored in internal registers. Automatic calling can be programmed through the connected terminal, PC or workstation so that a number, or sequence of numbers, is dialled on a typed command.

For even simpler usage, some can initiate dialling to a stored number location on power up, typically by raising the DSR signal on the V.24 modem interface. Varying with available memory, storage is typically between 10 to 20 fourteen digit numbers, although up to 100 are available. For dialling behind a PABX, a pause function in the dialling sequence is often still required, to allow the public line to be accessed.

Both the pulse dialling of the older Strowger telephone exchanges and the dual tone multifrequency signalling of the new generation are standard features. Software programming can limit the modem to originating calls only. Standards for automatic dialling include the proprietary Hayes 'AT' protocol, specifically designed for asynchronous personal computers communications, or the ITU-T's V.25bis command set covering both asynchronous and synchronous environments. Vendors are finding it necessary to include both these to satisfy user demands on connectivity.

6.5.2.8 *Auto answer*

When a modem requires an operator to receive a call and switch from voice to data it is called attended operation. Unattended operation is when the modem turns on its associated equipment and commences operation from a distance, especially useful in overnight data collection by a central computer from geographically dispersed locations.

6.5.2.9 *Auto call back and line restoral*

For the leased line application, transferring large amounts of data between two points, a PSTN link can be used as a back up in the event of the leased line failure. Dial up to one or more destinations can be initiated automatically by the modem keeping the network on line. Leased line restoral is either attempted after the expiry of a simple time out function when the back up line is inactive, or the modem incorporates active circuitry that monitors and tests the leased line continuously and restores at the first available opportunity.

The second method is far superior, because it eliminates switching back to a faulty line and avoids using the back up circuit any longer than necessary. Ideally a visual indication of this back up mode is desirable to avoid excessive call charges generated by a consistently poor leased line service.

6.5.2.10 *Speed conversion flow control*

Increasingly included in the feature list is the ability to automatically cater for communicating devices operating at different speeds, essential for modem pool applications where a host computer running at a fixed speed is accessed by a multi-speed environment.

6.5.2.11 *Visual audio indications*

To allow a simple and instantaneous check on status, front panel indications are typically provided for transmit, receive, carrier detect, terminal ready, off hook and power on signals. This is increasingly complemented by an internal speaker which monitors the call set up tones.

The introduction of sophisticated liquid crystal displays has spawned a new generation of intelligent front panels which can be used to programme both local and remotely connected units without the need to attach a separate programming terminal via a console port. This is a boon in the synchronous environment allowing in situ reprogramming and diagnostics.

6.5.2.12 *Diagnostics*

Once proprietary but now conforming increasingly to the ITU-T V.54 standard, diagnostic tests typically include the local analogue and digital loop, and remote digital loop often with a test pattern generator and decoder to simplify both the initial installation and subsequent fault isolation.

6.5.2.13 *Timing*

To allow for both synchronous and asynchronous operation, modems must be capable of being driven by a range of clock sources.

Asynchronous operation uses the clock internal to the modem. Synchronous operation, which requires timing information to be passed with the data, uses a combination of internal, system and external clock sources. A synchronous link requires a master clock source, either generated internally by the modem or externally by data terminal equipment at one end. At the remote end the modem uses the system clock option to synchronise its received and transmitted data to the master.

6.5.2.14 *Management*

Essential for the corporate network running business critical applications, modem management is sold as either a software package or a complete hardware and software solution. Typically locally attached to a centrally sited racking system and driven by a personal computer, management packages offer port traffic monitoring and statics coupled with local and remote diagnostics and configuration. A management system monitor displays information either textually or as dynamic graphical information, whilst hard copy output tends to be limited and textual only. Largely proprietary, these systems lag behind in terms of open systems standards compliance as vendors development budgets focus on local area network management.

6.5.2.15 *Security*

A rapidly developing market as companies provide increasing access to their networks from either the high street outlet or direct to the customer, modem security is typically delivered as a basic password system which can be optionally combined with a dial back facility. On connection the called modem requests a password. If the password is validated by the modem's directory, it will disconnect the line and redial outwards to the telephone number associated with it in memory. Once reconnected, the password is again requested. If successful the user is connected to the service. Modem security is often integrated within a management system and may be supplemented by modem identification codes.

6.6 Applications

The future of modem applications depends on a variety of tariffing, technological, business and political factors operating at both national and international level and the extent to which any one of them can dominate.

The short haul modem suffers the least from pressures like public network digitisation and tariffing. Technologically it is characterised by a level of miniaturisation and cost reduction that further development would be hard pressed to improve, where medium speed, limited distance interoffice and on premise intersite connectivity is required. Commercially it is firmly established as a commodity product and is becoming an integrated part of structured cabling systems. The only real threat to its existence is the demand on bandwidth to the desktop of new computing and workstation applications.

By contrast, the long haul dial up and leased line modem suffers more, reflected by the effort put into its technological advancement. The last few years have seen an upsurge in dial up applications, triggered by the introduction of 2 wire V.32 technology coupled with echo cancellation, Trellis encoding, error correction and data compression techniques.

Satisfying a user need for faster, less error prone communications and underpinned by cost savings achieved in switching from 4 wire leased circuits to 2 wire dial up circuits, the upper modem limit of 30kbit/s imposed by the copper loop is however rapidly being reached. Compensating for this are a number of new emerging markets.

At the low speed V.22bis commodity end where ISDN, for the time being at least, is less of a threat, a new market place has developed for the portable, laptop and now palm top computer. Miniaturised battery powered and increasingly integrated modems are being used to connect the business traveller from the home, hotel or even the car to the office for data transfer. These will inevitably be looking to upgrade to V.32 technology and beyond.

In the high speed modem sector, the 15 million Group III analogue fax terminals installed worldwide represent a major opportunity (Braue, 1991). Currently using V.29 and V.27 technology they are expected to upgrade to V.32 and V.32bis within one year. Some vendors have already grasped the facsimile opportunity by building these facilities onto battery powered, pocket size V.22bis modems with a view to keeping the mobile business man in constant touch.

New standards are being developed by the ITU-T for transferring digital data over Group III analogue connections and improvements in both speed and error correcting capability have been recommended. ITU-T study groups are currently looking at connectivity between digital Group IV fax and Group III fax, a sure sign of a healthy market.

Apart from the fax boom, other applications, which improvements in dial up technology have made possible, include local area network interconnection. Formerly the sole province of analogue or digital leased lines, dial up technology now provides for Internet Protocol (IP) addressing over switched circuits. The continuing viability of this trend from leased circuit to dial up circuit, typically for back up applications, is the speed with which ISDN can erode this technological advance.

Increasingly there will be a choice to be made between high speed modems over switched analogue lines and ISDN over switched digital lines, as PTTs fulfil their promises on basic rate ISDN availability. For the moment, costing up analogue switched, digital leased and ISDN alternatives is easy but potentially misleading. Connecting and installing ISDN is expensive, whereas the call charges are identical to analogue dial up lines, being based on distance and time but independent of the volume.

By comparison with analogue voice lines, they offer considerably more bandwidth, the quality of end to end digital connections and practically instantaneous call set up. So in reality it is not a like for like comparison.

Based purely on today's tariffs, and compared with a V.32 alternative, ISDN can only be justified by substantial use, where its greater bandwidth can reduce call charges to recoup the much higher initial outlay. By comparison, used on a single location for more than three hours a day, it could well be cheaper to use digital leased lines like KiloStream.

For a genuine comparison, the nature of the application, the expected traffic, connection and equipment charges must all be carefully considered. If the 30kbit/s limit on modems is achieved and can successfully be combined with compression techniques operating a 4:1 reduction in line transmission requirements, potential throughputs of 120kbit/s will provide modems with ISDN basic rate performance. The question is, will they need to?

Already products are having to be developed to help computer serial communications ports keep up with current modem performance as users fall into the speed trap of assuming their desktop equipment can run fast enough to make full use of it. Significantly those vendors who have a foot in both the modem and ISDN camps still believe there is a lot of mileage left in the modem. Their future is not in trying to match ISDN in terms of performance, but providing innovative, added functionality for increasingly cost effective communications.

6.7 References

Braue, J. (1991) The state of the modem, *Data Communications International*.

Bright, J. (1993) V.Fast: probing the limits, *Telecommunications*, June.

Clark, A. (1991) Error control and modem communications, *Communication and Computer News*, May.

Communicate (1994) Out of the office, but not out of pocket, *Communicate*, March.

Dennis, T. (1990) Dial up modems, *Datacom*, June.

Doll, D. (1978) *Data Communications; Facilities, Networks and System Design*, John Wiley & Sons.

Enslow, P. (1988) *The OSI Reference Model and Network Architectures*, Frost & Sullivan, London.

King, J. (1995) Model modems, *Communications Networks*, June.

Minoli, D. (1991) *Telecommunications Technology Handbook*, Artech House, Boston.

Read, R.J. et al. (1994) Modems for the general switched telephone network: development, design and the future, *Electronics & Communication Engineering Journal*, February.

Scott, P.R.D. (1980) *Modems in Data Communication*, NCC Publications, Manchester.

Taylor, K. (1995) V.34 modems: you get what you pay for, *Data Communications*, June.

Vadgama, J. (1993) A slow start for V.Fast, *Communications Networks*, September.

Wright, R. (1994) Putting V.34 to work, *Telecommunications*, July.

7. Multiplexers

7.1 Introduction

The multiplexer is one of the most important components in communications networking. Its central function, from the network manager's viewpoint, is to concentrate many users (or information channels) on to a single transmission channel in order to maximise the efficiency of that channel: it is used in almost every aspect of networking digital data, voice and video. This section will describe the advantages and disadvantages of different data multiplexing techniques, why these different techniques evolved to solve particular network engineering problems and how they fit in to modern networks.

Figure 7.1 shows the basic theoretical model for a multiplexer with the composite line speed exactly equal to the aggregate speed of the inputs.

Given a transmission channel, there are two ways the available bandwidth can be used: firstly by dividing the available bandwidth frequency spectrum into a subset of frequencies, each of which can then simultaneously use the transmission channel and allocate each

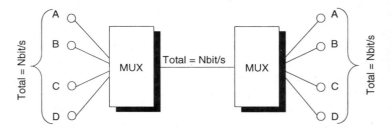

Figure 7.1   Basic model for a multiplexer

frequency band to an input channel that needs to be multiplexed; or secondly, allocate all the available bandwidth to each channel for a fixed discrete time period. The first of these methods would be Frequency Division Multiplexing (FDM) and the latter Time Division Multiplexing (TDM). FDM is used primarily as an analogue solution to multiplexing and, for example, has been used extensively in telephony; indeed many of the FDM standards and techniques such as the multiplexing ratios dictated by the early designs of telephone exchange multiplexers (such as 24:1) are still in evidence in some of the latter digital exchanges.

This chapter is concerned however with the use and applications of the latter type of multiplexing technique, Time Division Multiplexing, which can be used in one of two modes, deterministic or non-deterministic. Deterministic TDM (which is more commonly known just as TDM) allocates the available transmission channel bandwidth of a fixed regular basis to the input channels, whether they have data to send or not. Non- deterministic TDM or statistical TDM (which is more commonly just statistical multiplexing) allocates the available bandwidth to input channels only on demand when data is present.

7.2 Time division multiplexers

7.2.1 Principles

Time division multiplexing is the earliest and simplest form of digital multiplexing. It was developed to solve the communications problem created by the growth in remote computer processing during the 1960s. Computer terminals (or consoles) were locally attached in early computers but as computers became multi-user, so the need grew for more users gaining remote access over a single transmission line. Single users could gain access by simply attaching their terminal to a modem that converted the digital information by modulation into a voice frequency that could then be transmitted down a telephone to a modem at the receiving end that demodulated the signals back into digital form and hence onto the computer. However the need for groups of co-located users to gain access to computing resources meant that multiplexing techniques had to be applied to maximise the utilisation of rented PTT lease line circuits or costly dial up calls.

The early forms of multiplexers, which evolved to meet this growth in computing power, were designed for use with asynchronous data as this was the most commonly available type of terminal and printer. Typically running at speeds of up to 1200bit/s and with code formats of 5 and 7 bits (Baudot and ASCII respectively). As computer manufacturers moved to synchronous data, as a more efficient form of communications, so the design of multiplexers was adapted for handling this type of traffic. It was in this period that many of the design techniques to overcome specific engineering and networking problems evolved.

In common with all multiplexing techniques the primary requirement was for the two multiplexers to have some form of synchronisation procedure whereby they could calculate the location of each channel. This was done by defining a fixed length composite frame format, as in Figure 7.2, that had a unique synchronisation code at the start. When the link was first started the multiplexers would enter into a 'training' period, with only empty frames plus the synchronisation 'header' code being sent to each other to determine the frame boundaries. The composite overhead or bandwidth needed could be taken by reducing the available aggregate from the input channels.

Starting with the first commercially available asynchronous multiplexers the initial multiplexing technique was bit interleaved. In this method, the incoming data on each channel is sampled bit by bit and stored in a transitory central buffer before being assembled on to a composite.

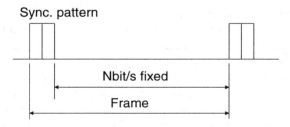

Figure 7.2   The basic operation of framing

This is the simplest technique that can be employed as it only requires that the multiplexer recognises the bit boundaries of the incoming data. Providing that the sequence of data bits is then forwarded to the remote end and demultiplexed without losing integrity, then any type of data format can be handled. However, as this meant sending all data bits for an asynchronous character including the stop, start and parity bits, the multiplexing technique adopted quickly moved to byte interleaved. In this method the ancillary bits could be stripped off and only the data sent.

At the receiving end they could be reconstituted. The byte was 8 bits with data requiring 7 bits and the 8th bit in each byte indicating whether data or controls were being sent. Although it meant that 5 bit data such as Baudot had 2 bits per byte wasted and that 8 bit codes could not be sent, as the majority of traffic was based on 7 bit code (ASCII), the overall gains made it worthwhile.

As stated above, the original design was for handling asynchronous traffic and the only rules for configuration would involve working out the total aggregate input and formulating the best 'scanning' method to cater for all the different speeds, so that they could mapped on to the available composite bandwidth. According to the design of the multiplexer a small percentage of the bandwidth had to be allocated for the synchronisation pattern, or sequence, so the general design rule was to limit the overhead to around 1% or 2 bits in a 200 bit frame. In addition, if the status of the V.24 (RS232) control lines such as Data Terminal Ready (circuit 108/1 or 2) or Request to Send (circuit 105), then this had to be allocated bandwidth as if it were data.

As an example, if a half duplex circuit is being employed, which means that the data and control signals have to be kept contiguous, then the control information could require as much bandwidth as the data. The result is that the bandwidth actually available for data could be less than the theoretical maximum by up to 50%. The technique developed to overcome this problem is to use multi-frames with two types of controls, high and low priority. High priority is dealt with as described above. Low priority control information is sent every N frames, where N could be from 4 to 64 depending on the frame size and speed of the composite.

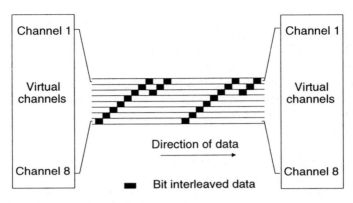

Figure 7.3   Ideal model of a TDM

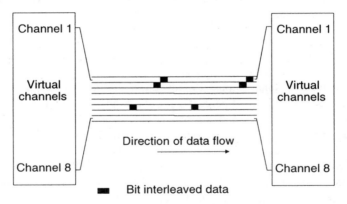

Figure 7.4   Line utilisation in a typical TDM

Figure 7.3 shows the ideal model of time division multiplexing operation, where all eight channels are being efficiently multiplexed onto a composite line. At any one instant in time there is always one of the channels using the available bandwidth. Figure 7.4 shows the realistic utilisation of the line. Note that only channels 1, 2 and 6 have any data to send. However, time slots in the form of bandwidth still have to be allocated since the TDM cannot recognise the absence of real data; this is the trade-off against data transparency and speed.

To summarise, the technique of sending asynchronous data by TDM is to use a frame synchronised, byte interleaved method with facilities for control information using redundant bits.

The advantage is transparency to data format; any format of asynchronous data can be sent, at any speed.

The disadvantages are:

1. Fixed speeds; it was usually difficult to change any speeds without completely re-programming the multiplexers.
2. Poor efficiency; input channels always have a fixed allocation of composite bandwidth, whether they have data to send or not. As asynchronous data is by definition 'bursty' interactive type traffic, there will almost certainly be long periods of inactivity which still have bandwidth being allocated to them.
3. Prone to errors; in the process of being transmitted, any errors generated on the composite circuit are passed to the receiving end without any indication to the end device (in fact the parity recovery method makes this worse as it hides dual bit errors). Unless the link synchronisation actually fails the remote end has no indication that there is a problem on the line.

7.2.2 Synchronous TDM

As synchronous protocols evolved the need to multiplex them grew; networks with remote sites that had a mix of asynchronous and synchronous terminals needed to connect them to the central site computing resource.

For synchronous TDMs, the bit-interleaved method was adopted as the most superior technique. The main difference from asynchronous multiplexing being that as well as keeping data integrity, the multiplexers had to keep the associated clock timing synchronisation so that the demultiplexed recovered data could have a regenerated clock associated with it. This point will be referred to later as it imposes major restrictions on the design and operation of networks and techniques have been developed to solve the problem. Apart from timing considerations, the synchronisation header in the composite frame has to be included in the overall bandwidth calculation.

In asynchronous data the actual speed of transmission can vary, according to the manufacturer's specification, by up to ±15%, therefore devices running overspeed were a particular problem. Synchronous data has a much tighter specification and may only vary by 0.1%, as recommended by ITU-T (formerly CCITT) V.28. This is particularly important for synchronous modems which cannot tolerate any deviation from the specified speed.

The technique of 'robbing' the low speed input channels and allocating it to the composite was normally only applied within these constraints. Two alternatives were:

1.   To designate one of the input channels as a 'vari-speed' input which may be attached to non-critical devices. This approach, for obvious reasons, has to be handled with caution.
2.   By the preferred technique used by latter designs to permanently allocate a synchronisation overhead.

A mixture of bit and byte interleaving with a fixed synchronisation header was also adopted by some high order multiplexers, where multiple voice channels needed to be multiplexed after being digitally encoded; the US Bell D1 system for example. The basic technique employed is for an analogue sample of the voice signal to be converted into an 8 bit code word, after being manipulated through a compander circuit operating on a logarithmic law to reduce the signal to noise level. The Bell D2 system used bit robbing for signalling purposes. The standards which have been adopted for this type of high order multiplexing are discussed later in this chapter e.g. the ITU-T standard G.711 for pulse code modulation.

From the viewpoint of line efficiency between two point to point multiplexers, the advantages and disadvantages of synchronous TDM compared to asynchronous TDM are almost identical. The main exception is that error detection and correction is not an issue with a synchronous data, as it will be enveloped in its own protocol independent from the multiplexer and therefore will have its own error recovery mechanisms via retransmission. However, from a network-

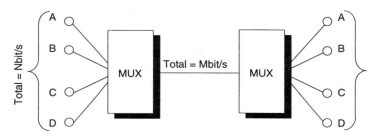

Figure 7.5 Model of a multiplexer with overheads considered

ing viewpoint, the network timing recovery mechanisms and the methods by which the nodes in a network can be synchronised together are major issues.

Figure 7.5 shows a more realistic model of a multiplexer, with the overheads taken into account, that results in a composite that must be faster than the input aggregate. The value of M is given by Equation 7.1, therefore M > N.

$$M = A + B + C + C$$
$$+ \text{ synchronisation header} + \text{control information} \qquad (7.1)$$

In summary it can be stated that time division multiplexing has established itself as the most efficient technique for handling synchronous protocols and data at different speeds, even though it suffered from the fact that bandwidth is always wasted. It is not however very effective at handing asynchronous data due to the inflexibility and lack of error detection and correction. It is from this major disadvantage that the use of statistical multiplexers evolved.

7.3 Statistical time division multiplexing

7.3.1 Principle of operation

Caught between the exponential growth of computing power and the use of asynchronous terminals as a cheap and convenient way of accessing computers, the statistical TDM was developed. It was first formulated in the early 1970s and in particular on the Arpanet network in the USA from which the X.25 packet switch standard evolved (Davis, 1973).

As stated above, the main problems with using TDM techniques on asynchronous data were lack of error detection and correction, and poor efficiency on the composite line, especially since the average asynchronous device is only active for 5 to 10% of the time.

The solution for asynchronous multiplexers was to use a formal protocol between the multiplexer nodes which could concentrate the data and provide the means of detecting and recovering from errors on the line. The protocol invariably chosen was based on a High Level Data Link Control (HDLC) which in turn had been derived from IBM's SDLC protocol. This protocol had several design advantages over previous synchronous protocols such as IBM's 3270, as follows:

1.   It was solely concerned with the maintenance of the data link and did not have to get involved with device control.
2.   It had one common frame format for data, control and supervision with a unique flag indentifier for synchronisation.
3.   It was bit oriented and therefore inherently transparent to data structures. However, it used byte aligned boundaries to permit byte interleaving, if required.
4.   It had a Frame Check Sequence (FCS), in the form of a Cyclic Redundancy Check (CRC), that allowed error checking of the complete contents of all frames and thereby providing a mechanism for error recovery.
5.   It was being considered as an international standard.

There were still drawbacks, however, in that early versions of HDLC only allowed one virtual circuit (or user) per frame, and therefore modifications were made by many manufacturers to allow several users to share the same frame. In addition the multiplexers needed to pass not just data but also various other types of information such as:

1.   The status conditions of the V.24 (RS232) interface controls.

Flag	Address	Control	128 bytes of user data	CRC	CRC	Flag

Figure 7.6 Basic HDLC information frame

2.   Test information, such as setting a specific remote channel into loopback for testing purposes.
3.   Information for validation of a channel connection, to check that it is working end to end.
4.   A SPACE condition for so many milliseconds.
5.   Information to set remote buffers into an XOFF state so that no more data should be sent until further notification.

It also had to allow the input channels to locally emulate some asynchronous polled protocols e.g. HP3000, so that polling could be locally acknowledged rather than end-to-end. The link need only carry a poll count and report polling exceptions.

The standard HDLC format has no inherent mechanism for allowing these facilities as it was designed purely to control the link level functions. It is up to the designer to implement this in the information (data) fields in order to make the product as flexible as possible.

Figure 7.6 shows a basic HDLC information frame with the unique flag identifier 7E (hexadecimal), the address field and the control field, which in this case is indicating that the frame contains data.

Figure 7.7 shows a modified HDLC information frame format, used by a proprietary STDM manufactured by Dowty Case, other manufacturers using different encoding techniques. Here the information frame does not require an address field. It does, however, require a mapping field for each block of 4 bytes for a given channel, which indicates whether the following bytes are data or control and timing codes e.g. DTR dropped, set channel loopbacks, set SPACE condition for 100mS.

Given the mechanisms of a link protocol it was a small step to design a multiplexer that only transmitted data when there was data to sent. By scanning the input channels for activity and placing any

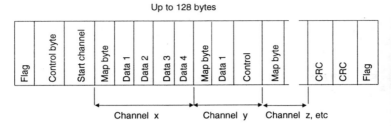

Figure 7.7   Proprietary HDLC information frame format. (Dowty Case Communications Ltd)

data present into a common buffer pool, a frame could be assembled with data from different channels, plus any control information, and transmitted to the multiplexer at the other end of the link for demultiplexing.

Since HDLC uses a go-back-N frame sequencing count, any errors on the line due to a bad CRC or out of sequence frame would be detected and a request for the frame to be retransmitted issued from the remote end (also known as Automatic Repeat Request or ARQ). At that time, no standards existed for describing how the frames should be constructed for multiple users and interface control information, so every manufacturer developed their own proprietary standard, compared to the present development of LAPD which overcomes these restrictions. The outcome of this was to see a generation of proprietary statistical multiplexers before the establishment of X.25.

Figure 7.8 shows the simplified operation of a statistical multiplexer which operates by scanning the input buffers for data presence (indicated by the flag). Data is transferred into a buffer queue waiting to be assembled and transmitted as a frame.

7.3.2 Features

By definition, statistical multiplexers have to concentrate many input channels onto a composite link, where the aggregate input speeds may temporarily exceed the available composite bandwidth. In this situation it is essential that the multiplexer has the facility to flow

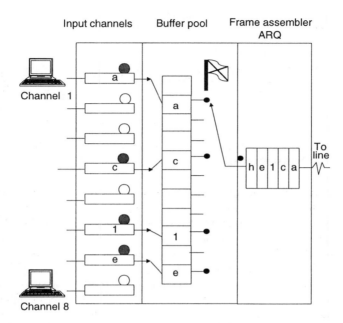

Input channels   Buffer pool   Frame assembler ARQ

Figure 7.8 Simplified operation of a statistical multiplexer

control the data input, either by use of XON/XOFF or V.24 control signals such as DTR or CTS. The decisions by which the network designer decided how to size a network with the mix of input speeds and output speeds were assisted by queuing theory.

In summary, statistical time division multiplexers offer asynchronous users the advantages of:

1.   Better use of the composite line by only allocating bandwidth when sending data.
2.   Techniques for encoding additional control and timing information to make the system more flexible.
3.   Speed translation end to end.
4.   Intelligent interaction to allow some asynchronous protocols to be emulated locally rather than over the whole link.

However one of the disadvantages is:

1.　　Only asynchronous data was practical. Synchronous protocols could be handled in the same manner as some asynchronous protocols in that local emulation of the host end and terminal end would result in only the actual data being transmitted over the link and the majority of the control information could be handled locally.

7.3.3 Networking

Only point to point multiplexers have been considered so far, as they illustrate the basic principles of multiplexing. However, a major development in the mid 1970s was to give a user on a terminal the facility to select more than one destination. The requirement grew out of the development in computing power, which meant that many companies were expanding on the number of computers they used and were perhaps dropping the mainframes in favour of distributed minis. To allow these to be accessible the users required the multiplexers to become networked. In effect rather than let the computer switch the user to an application it was left to the network.

7.4　High order multiplexing

7.4.1　Standards

The term high order multiplexing is used to describe the technique for multiplexing multiplexers. By successively taking input channels of fixed speed and creating a hierarchy of 'groups' of multiplexers, a final high speed output composite is produced that is logically structured to contain all the input channels in a defined sequence.

High order multiplexers were originally developed as described above to allow voice circuits to be multiplexed. This simple statement is the underlying design principle for all the decisions that have been made on PTT digital speeds and frame structures throughout the world in the past 20 years. Although today they can be used for any type of digitally encoded data, including fax and video, these are the result of data communications manufacturers, and lately PTTs, 'high-jacking' the circuits developed for digitised voice and using them for pure data.

The lowest input speed for high order multiplexing contained within ITU-T is 64kbit/s. This is the speed arrived at from encoding voice, with a maximum frequency of 3.4kHz, at 8000 samples a second (which is above the Nyquist sampling rate) and then converting each sample into an 8 bit word or byte. The original technique used by the PTTs was to use frequency division multiplexing with 12 or 24 voice channels being frequency multiplied. For example, in the ITU-T 960 channel system, channel 1 would be frequency translated to 62kHz in the first group and then to 420kHz in the second or supergroup.

At present the three principal hierarchical systems in existence are from Europe, the US and Japan.

From Table 7.1 (based on ITU-T G.702) it can be seen that each system, from a base speed of 64kbit/s, multiplexes in fixed, discrete bands, up to the gigahertz bands, suitable for transmission over microwave and satellite carriers.

Table 7.1 High order systems

Multiplex level	Europe (kbit/s)	USA (kbit/s)	Japan (kbit/s)
0	64	64	64
1	2048	1544	1544
2	8448	6312	7876
3	34368	44736	32064
4	139264	274176	97728
5	565148		397200

The underlying system employed is bit interleaved, although the framing structure is byte oriented. Analysis of the framing structures gives more detail on how they were used as general purpose data multiplexers. In general the input channels were constructed in frames, each consisting of 12, 24 or 30 voice channels or 'timeslots' depending on the system. This gave the first hierarchical grouping. Within this group the frames could be assembled together in super-frames to contain signalling and control information.

The early US systems need to be examined separately as they used a technique that was completely alien to pure data use. The original Bell D1 system had an input rate of 56kbit/s (7 times 8000 samples per second) because the timeslots used a 'bit robbing' technique whereby the 8th bit in every slot was used for maintaining timing information on the line. By always setting the 8th bit to zero and inverting the PCM data sample so that it was normally set to all 1s i.e. no speech signal, the line signal could be guaranteed to have data transitions which kept the timing content. When the D2 system was introduced using HDB3 (high density bipolar 3) line encoding, this allowed 8 bits per slot. However, the system used part of the old standard in that it again allowed the same 'bit robbing' to take place in the same way but only every 6th frame and in this case it was used for passing control and signalling information. For speech purposes this did not impose a reduction in the quality of service as the human ear will not detect this impairment, but for pure data it introduced an unacceptable error rate.

The speeds which became standard offerings were derived in the following ways. US Bell system D2 (usually known as T1) used a frame made of 24 timeslots (or input channels) at 8 bits each i.e. 192 bits: an additional bit was added on to each of the frames for syn-chronisation purposes giving 193 bits per frame. The 'sweep' rate or number of frames per second was 8000 (the voice encoding, or codec, sampling rate) giving an overall speed of 1.544Mbit/s.

In the version adopted by the ITU-T the frame consisted of 32 timeslots, of which 30 were for voice and two for synchronisation and signalling information, giving a total of 256 bits. At a sweep rate of 8000 frames per second this gives a speed of 2.048Mbit/s.

All digital exchanges and the space/time switches used these speeds at the core of their design.

As with all synchronous TDM networks timing is a major consideration in all network design. Simply put, in order to maintain data integrity, the whole network must run off a single clock or timing source, with every node 'slaved' to that clock designated the 'master'. Failure to do so results in 'bit slippage' in the frames, with data loss. On a small network, geographically spread over a small area, this may not present a serious implementation problem. On a national network it requires careful planning with contingency back up clocks available automatically if the master fails. International networks resolve the problem by clocking parts of the network independently or plesiochronously, that is off a clock that is so stable (1 part in 10^{-12}) that the slippages are low enough to be acceptable.

7.4.2 Synchronous Digital Hierarchy (SDH)

In an attempt to reconcile the different high order multiplexers a new set of G. standards have been defined which can support the US and European variants. ITU-T have initially defined G.708, G.708, and G.709 to offer a ultra high speed Synchronous TDM system based on the US SONET. (See Chapter 1.)

7.5 Multiplexing and packet switching

The evolution of multiplexing over the past 20 years has seen the generalisation of the original design techniques into two distinct types: circuit switching and packet switching.

Circuit switching has developed out of the synchronous digital techniques and, as its name implies, supports network source to destination connections as a single, end-to-end circuit. Bandwidth over the network links is permanently allocated for the duration of the call. It is then set aside whether information is being sent or not. In this it is analogous to a telephone connection.

Circuit switching is implemented using space/time switches that move the timeslots from one frame to another. Timeslot access is through multiplexers which operate in 'drop and insert' mode. This

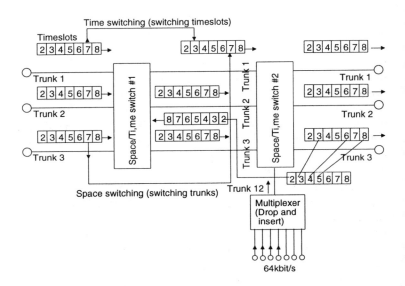

Figure 7.9 Circuit switching used to route frames

works by taking a timeslot that terminates on one channel, and therefore becomes free, and allowing another channel to use that timeslot for sending data back out. It can be seen that no method to dynamically allocate bandwidth is available.

Figure 7.9 shows how circuit switching is implemented using space/time switches that route the timeslots in high-speed T1/E1 frames around a network.

Packet switching, on the other hand, does not require permanent bandwidth to be allocated. Data is sent through the network in discrete packets, each packet only demanding bandwidth on any specific link for the time it is being transmitted. In this it is similar to statistical multiplexing. There are, however, two ways in which packet switch connections can be tracked through a network for the duration of a call or session. These are Connection (CON) and Connectionless (CLNS) oriented. The differences between these two methods are so important to networking that they will be explained in detail here.

The first method (CON) requires that the destination address only be sent in the first packet, when the call is first set up. The network merely has to assign virtual links to that call so that subsequent packets have a route assigned to them through the network. CLNS packets, on the other hand, have the destination address in every packet, and as such do not require a virtual network path to be set up in advance. In fact each packet can take a different route through the network, even arriving out of sequence at the far end and relying on the protocol to reassemble them in the correct sequence.

Connection oriented networks such as X.25 packet switching derive their design methodology from telephony techniques, while connectionless techniques, which are now widely used on LANs, were derived from Ethernet radio broadcast systems, such as the Aloha system developed by the University of Hawaii.

Today the single most important multiplexing technique is packet switching as defined in the ITU-T X.25 worldwide accepted standard. From 1976 when it was first ratified it has become a fundamental part of the Open Systems Interconnection model as one of the primary standards in layer three, the network layer.

In its basic form, as an independent networking standard, it is designed to allow asynchronous devices to make and clear network connections by a defined calling procedure. It uses the ITU-T stand-ards for defining how the asynchronous device should interface (X.3); how to interpret network messages (X.28); the numbering system for setting up international calls (X.121); and negotiation parameters for end to end session compliance (X.29).

The strength of X.25 lies in the fact that it relies on other standards for interfacing into the lower layers. It resolves the logical and physical link connection problems by utilising an HDLC format LAPB and an X.21bis physical interface.

In order to use X.25 in a packet switch network two components are required: a Packet Switch Exchange (PSE) and a Packet Assem-bler/Disassembler (PAD). The former takes in X.25 formatted pac-kets and, after reading the addressing information in the header, routes it to its destination down the appropriate link. Terminals gain

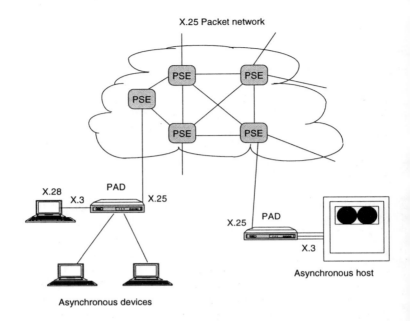

Figure 7.10 A packet switch network

access onto the network through the PAD which may typically handle up to 32 terminals or other devices (the upper limit is restricted only by physical constraints). Figure 7.10 shows the basic components of a packet switch network.

X.3 is the terminal profile standard that helps to define exactly how the asynchronous device (printer or terminal) should communicate with the PAD. There are a range of parameters that must be set, such as speed, flow control, how to edit and when to wrap around the screen. The parameters were originally designed to include the totally 'dumb' terminal (such as an electromechanical Teletype) so that to a modern device they appear unnecessary. However, in an international context, such a device may still be in use and connected to the network in some remote region of the world. The X.28 set of com-

mands and messages are essential for controlling and monitoring the
PAD functions.

7.6 X.25 and OSI

X.25 goes a long way towards being OSI compatible and is a recognised standard. Figure 7.11 shows how X.25 and its associated layers
fits into the OSI model. The physical layers of both X.25 and the OSI
reference model are similar though X.21 and X.21bis only cater for
point to point full duplex links. These physical layer standards, which
are common to other forms of multiplexing, are described in a later
section.

The data link layers are very close with minor differences. The
most significant difference is that the X.25 link layer only deals with
full duplex single links. This has been mostly remedied by the 1984
version of X.25 which caters for multiple links, though X.25 still does
not cater for multi-point connections.

The X.25 packet layer provides the majority of the functions
specified in the OSI network layer and some of the functions specified in the OSI transport layer. The network layer functions which are
not provided are routeing and switching. This is because X.25 is a
network interface specification and not an internal network specifica-

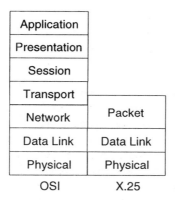

Figure 7.11 X.25 and the OSI model

tion as mentioned previously. The transport layer function provided for in the X.25 packet layer is end to end data acknowledgement.

7.6.1 The benefits of X.25

The advantages of using X.25 are as follows:

1. Flexibility. A user can make and break communication sessions with many destinations.
2. Economical. A user only pays for the resources used. It is possible for a user to establish many concurrent communication sessions with the same or different destinations over one physical connection to the network. A network administration can produce a cost reduced system because not every user wishes to communicate at the same time, or continually.
3. Reliability. The probability of a fault occurring on a relatively short leased line is far less than for a long distance line. If an inter-node link fails within the network the communication sessions can be re-routed and data recovered with little or no inconvenience to the end users.
4. Maintainability. The node or network is intelligent and can provide statistical and diagnostic information to aid fault tracing.
5. OSI compatible. X.25 is part of the OSI model and as such can be used as part of an OSI networking strategy.

The disadvantages of X.25 are:

1. Network delay. Although networks can provide the same (or very close) throughput figures to private wires, there is always a finite delay caused as packets are routed (stored and forwarded) through the network. This is a product of the number of nodes in the route across the network, the traffic load on different parts of the network and various other factors.
2. Poor efficiency with interactive traffic. Because of the way in which packets are built up with the data from a single user per packet, X.25 tends to become inefficient with network band-

width if a predominance of single character enquiry traffic is being sent. (Compare this with the statistical multiplexer frame with multiple users per frame). However X.25 becomes very efficient for file transfer type applications where the packets can be filled to a maximum. It should be pointed out that in OSI, the layer 4 functionality does include the facility for enveloping multiple channels into a single packet.

3.   Network congestion. It is not economically viable for a network administration to run a network sized to provide enough bandwidth for the worse case traffic load. Therefore at peak times network congestion conditions occur causing existing sessions to slow down and preventing new sessions from starting. This is analogous to the public telephone networks i.e. 'All lines to Cityville are engaged please try later'.

4.   Wrong numbers. Expensive as generally all outgoing calls are billed.

5.   Network variance. Not all networks obey the protocol in the same way. This is due to grey areas in the ITU-T X.25 Recommendations and to individual manufacturer's interpretations on how to handle exception conditions.

6.   Bureaucracy. Most PTTs insist that X.25 products must pass a set of certification or conformance tests in order to gain permission to connect to their network. This can take a considerable period of time and money. This problem will be resolved to a certain degree in EC countries as the NETs attachment testing regime becomes law.

7.6.2 Using X.25

X.25 can be used in many different ways for communication. Figure 7.12 shows how an X.25 based network can operate with different components such as:

1.   Asynchronous terminals and hosts communicating via PADs.
2.   X.25 based devices connected directly to the network.
3.   Synchronous devices communicating via protocol converts.
4.   Gateways to non-X.25 based networks.

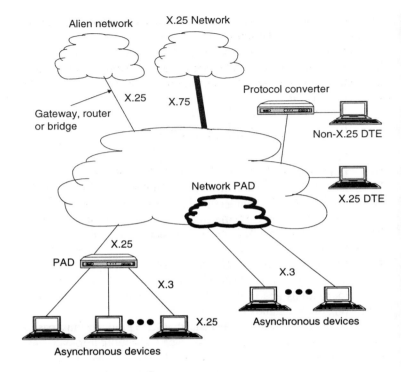

Figure 7.12 An X.25 based network

5.   Connection to international networks using the X.75 protocol.

Note that all devices can communicate through using X.25 as the common carrier.

X.25 networks can be bolted on to other X.25 networks simply by making one look like an X.25 terminal or by using the X.75 protocol (a protocol similar to X.25). X.25 networks can be connected to non-X.25 networks via a gateway or router which is just a type of protocol converter. Some of the larger public networks offer an integrated PAD service. A large PAD is resident at the node and subscribers rent stop/start lines to the PAD (dial up or modem link).

In this configuration the X.25 interface is actually within the network and not available to the subscribers.

Another method of accessing an X.25 network is via a high speed leased line link, such as KiloStream in the UK. KiloStream operates at speeds of up to 64kbit/s (but only 48kbit/s when connecting to the PSS X.25 network).

7.6.3 Services provided by X.25

Recommendation X.25 defines three types of data transmission services for use with PDNs: leased circuit, circuit switched, packet switched. The packet switched service is primarily considered here.

The packet switched service is subdivided into three services: Permanent Virtual Circuits (PVCs), Switched Virtual Circuits (SVCs) and Datagrams. PVCs and SVCs are essential services i.e. all networks should provide them (although not all provide PVC services). Datagrams are now being made obsolete within connection oriented (CON) X.25 and will be replaced by a connectionless (CLNS) version of X.25.

Recommendations X.25 defines the user facilities for each of the three types of data transmission services. These facilities provide capabilities beyond the basic service, a few examples are: reverse charging, preventing incoming calls and call re-direction.

7.6.3.1 *Virtual circuits*

The packet level interface comprises a set of logical channels, each with a unique identifier. Each logical channel can be associated with a single virtual circuit. A virtual circuit provides a connection based service similar to that of circuit switched services but with the added advantage of statistical multiplexing.

For every physical link, the number of possible logical channels is given by sixteen groups of two hundred and fifty six channels. The relevant group and channel number are contained in each packet header. There is a one to one correspondence between DTE and DCE channel numbers.

Each virtual circuit can support at least one communication session, so in the most extreme (but unrealistic) case a single DTE/DCE link can support 4095 concurrent virtual circuits. The available virtual circuits are utilised to offer two facilities, namely the Permanent Virtual Circuit (PVC) and the Virtual Call (VC) or Switched Virtual Circuit (SVC).

7.6.3.2 *Switched virtual circuits*

Switched virtual circuits, or virtual calls, must be dynamically established between DTEs at extreme ends of a network by the exchange of command packets between the two DTEs and the network.

A virtual call is a temporary association between two DTEs. It is initiated by a DTE sending a Call Request packet to the network on a free logical channel. The logical channel should be the highest free channel available. A Call Request packet must contain either the destination address or a reference to it.

When a Call Request packet is received by a network it will send the called DTE an incoming call packet on the lowest free logical channel number available at that interface. The called DTE then has the option of accepting or refusing the call.

The calling DTE will subsequently receive a response indicating whether or not the called DTE has accepted the call. If the call is accepted the virtual circuit is established and enters the data transfer mode. At this point either DTE can send packets containing data, via the network, to the other DTE. If however a virtual call cannot be established the network will return a call clearing packet to the calling DTE to indicate that the virtual circuit has not been established. Either DTE can clear an established call.

7.6.3.3 *Permanent virtual circuit*

A permanent virtual circuit is a logical connection between two DTEs at extreme ends of a network which is constant for an agreed period of time. When the lower levels of X.25 are operational, either DTE can send packets containing data via the network to the other DTE without the need for the Virtual Call establishment procedures mentioned above.

7.6.3.4 *Virtual circuit services*

A virtual circuit service (connection oriented) is considered superior to a connectionless service for handling long messages. Virtual circuits are analogous to the telephone service in that messages are delivered in the order in which they are sent. The full destination and source network addresses as well as the information required in order to deliver a packet are only required to establish a circuit.

Once a virtual circuit has been established the logical channel numbers allow either of the DTEs on the virtual circuit to send data to the other. Network congestion is controlled by limiting the inputs to a virtual circuit (or controlling the flow of data) rather than by discarding packets.

Individual packets on a virtual circuit are rarely autonomous; generally they are only part of a message.

7.7 Physical layer standards

There are two standards applicable to the physical layer X.21 and X.21bis. X.21 allows the user to access the network via a high speed serial interface. X.21bis allows the user to access the network using a lower speed (<20000bit/s) serial interface. X.21bis is the most common method of connection to an X.25 network.

The full X.21 protocol provides all the services of the first three layers: physical, data link, and network services. X.25 only uses the X.21 physical interface specifications.

7.7.1 X.21bis

X.21bis is based upon ITU-T Recommendations V.24/V.28 where V.24 specifies the control signals such as Request to Send (RTS circuit 104) and Clear to Send (CTS circuit 105). V.28 specifies the electrical interface in terms of voltage levels, impedances and the rise and fall times of the signals. It is suitable for speeds up to 19200bits/s.

Higher speeds can be achieved using the V.35 and V.36 interfaces which were specifically designed for that purpose. The EIA RS232-C and D standards are almost identical to the V.24/V.28 standard but also include the connector specification which is a 25 way D type.

7.7.2 V.35

The V.35 interface provides for speeds up to 48000bits/s at a distance of up to 1 kilometre incorporating a partially balanced interface to give a higher noise immunity. The V.35 connector is significantly different from the D type V.28 connector. It has a square profile with a staggered pin layout to prevent it being coupled incorrectly and is known as the MRAC connector. V.35 uses a balanced interface for T×D, R×D and the clocks but not the control signals. V.35 is however no longer recommended by ITU-T who suggest using V.36 in its place for all new developments.

7.7.3 V.36

The V.36 (similar to RS-449) interface provides for speeds up to 72kbit/s at a distance of 1 kilometre. All control, data and clock signals have balanced interfaces which gives greater noise immunity. V.36 uses the 37 pin D type connector.

7.7.4 X.21

X.21 operates over eight interchange circuits, and this is shown in Table 7.2.

The circuit's function is defined in ITU-T Recommendations X.24 and their electrical characteristics are defined in ITU-T Recommendations X.27 for DCE and X.26 for DTE.

Signal Element Timing provides bit timing. Byte Timing is optional and therefore not always supplied. All timing is provided by the DCE.

The DTE uses the Transmit and Receive circuits to exchange data and control messages with the DCE. Unlike the V.24 and RS232-C/D standards X.21 specifies that control information be exchanged using

Table 7.2   X.21 interchange circuits

Circuit		Direction to DCE	Direction to DTE
G	Signal Ground		
Ga	DTE Common Return		
T	Transmit	***	
R	Receive		***
C	Control	***	
I	Indication		***
S	Signal Element Timing		***
B	Byte Timing		***

characters transferred on the interchange circuits, rather than using circuit states.

The Control and Indication circuits are used in conjunction with the Transmit and Receive circuits to indicate the state of the DTE or DCE respectively. No characters are transmitted or received on these circuits; they are simply turned ON or OFF to indicate their current state.

The Byte Timing circuit provides information pertaining to the grouping of bits into characters. When the byte timing circuit is not available a synchronising character is inserted before each string of characters. Byte timing and SYNC characters are only required when exchanging physical layer control characters. When the physical layer is being used to transmit link layer information on the Transmit and Receive circuits byte timing and synchronising characters are not used.

7.7.5 Physical interface

The X.21 physical interface is specified by V.11 and is basically a cut-down version of the V.36 interface. There are only two control signals (one in each direction), other than that the interface is the same. The physical interface for X.21 is the 15 pin D type connector.

7.8 Multiplexers in communications networks

This section will focus on the more practical aspects of network design giving attention to performance, configuration, routeing, traffic requirements, expansion and topology. Some of these areas are interrelated and there is a degree of overlap in functionality.

7.8.1 Specification

The first consideration when specifying any data communications network is to establish the nature and rates of traffic which the network will be expected to support both in the short and the long term. This is crucial to all network design and is the starting point of all network decisions. If errors are made here, the network cannot be expanded to meet new (and possibly unexpected) requirements.

7.8.2 Traffic types

There are numerous different types of traffic, some of which are:

1.   Stop-start traffic in the form of lots of short packets travelling in one direction often with slightly longer packets in the reverse direction. A characteristic of this type of traffic is that it is often associated with a requirement for very short turn-around and transit delays (e.g. word-processing). This is a classic form of asynchronous traffic.
2.   'Forms' traffic where a small amount of data travels in one direction on an ad hoc basis, but it is answered with a stream of traffic in the other direction (database enquiry).
3.   Block mode traffic, where there is a stream of large full packets travelling in one direction with short packets travelling in the other (file transfer).

4.   Transaction traffic where there are high numbers of calls with limited data transfer, often done with the Fast Select facility (e.g. credit card checks, holiday booking lounges).

5.   Optimised traffic, where many users are sharing a single connection (often using a Transport connection). Optimisation is achieved by filling the packets as full as possible without degrading the class of service below the user requirements (OSI).

6.   Priority traffic. This may be any of the traffic types described above but takes precedence over the normal data flowing in the network.

7.   Management traffic, which is an overhead in any network.

A corporate or public data network would handle all these types of traffic (and more). Most small private networks will only have one or two types of traffic and are often designed and tuned to those specific requirements.

The list above is not intended to be conclusive, but to give an idea of the differing traffic types that exist.

7.8.3 Topology

The construction of a network is very dependent on the distribution of the users and the resources. In the past large organisations centralised computing centres to which the users were linked to using private communications circuits.

Today, distributed processing has created the WAN/LAN topology network structure where the LANs provide high speed local connectivity between the users and the local computing resources such as file servers, local electronic mail servers, local computers, printers etc. The wide area network provides connectivity and interoperability between the LANs and to centralised computing resources i.e. a centralised stock distribution system or an aircraft booking system.

Often the geographic distribution of the users and the information technology resources dictates the basic topology of the network which serves to interconnect them.

A typical network topology comprises a set of very high speed low intelligence backbone switches, such as synchronous TDMs, which serve to interconnect lower speed high functionality packet switching nodes, or statistical multiplexers, to which LAN users are connected (via modems or KiloStream links) through bridges.

7.8.4 Performance requirements

A common misconception is that performance is all about line rates. This is only a part of the equation. Hop counts, accumulative transit delays, turn around times, congestion level, congestion handling and the actual end systems all contribute to the performance of the network as a whole.

The performance requirements of a network depend on the types of traffic running over it, the time of day traffic requirements, the distribution of the traffic, the cost of the resources, the reliability requirements.

7.8.5 Traffic requirements

Obviously the different traffic types mentioned above place differing requirements on the network equipment.

A transaction system (such as a booking system) will require fast call establishment and termination, high call capacity, but not necessarily fast data throughput as it will only be the occasional screen.

A network with a large community of stop-start terminal applications (typically the ITU-T triple X PAD) requires fairly low transit delays and low hop counts, but again not necessarily high data performance.

Block mode traffic, such as file transfer or database enquiry systems, probably do not require low transit delays but do require high data performance.

Certainly, as technology progresses, users are becoming more and more aware of the different jobs that IT can do for them and consequently the dumb terminal is being replaced by the intelligent terminal which in turn is being replaced by the personal workstation.

Ultimately users will be transferring files, sending electronic mail, booking holidays, home banking, home shopping, paying bills and making directory enquiries all from the same (pocket) workstations!

7.8.6 Traffic variance

Traffic type and load can vary with the time of day. This must be considered when estimating the performance requirements of a system.

An example is that of a large company with many retail outlets. During the day the traffic is almost completely local to the individual retail outlets, as they process data onto the local processor with just a few interactive enquiries to head office.

At the end of the day's business the local processors up load the stock requirements for the next day's trading to regional main frames, which arrange for the goods to be on the shelves for the following day's trading. This change in traffic conditions needs to be calculated in the overall network design.

7.8.7 Load balancing

The most basic (and most used) form of traffic balancing comes in the form of local load balancing across links connecting adjacent nodes within a network.

In the most basic form the traffic is evenly balanced across all the links connecting two devices. Some systems apply a weighting factor to the links based on the link speed. The next step is to dynamically adjust the weighting factor based on the real time performance of the link.

This ensures that a link which is performing badly (perhaps due to noise on the line) is only allocated the amount of traffic that it can reasonably transfer.

The X.25 multi-link procedures can achieve a reasonable load balancing and can, depending on the implementation, provide dynamic load balancing.

The most basic requirement is that load balancing takes account of the link speed.

7.8.8 Hop counts and lifetimes

Hop counts and lifetimes are used to ensure that a particular traffic element does not spend too much time traversing the network. The hop count is set in a message when it enters a communications network, to a pre-defined value. Every time the message is switched (i.e. passes through a node) the hop counter is decreased. If the hop counter reaches zero the message is either cleared or discarded.

Life times are very similar. The message lifetime is set up when it enters the network and if it is not acknowledged within its lifetime the originator sends another via a different route. Hop counts and lifetimes can be dynamically adjusted to suit the traffic Quality of Service requirements and the real time network characteristics.

7.8.9 Configuration

Configuration of a network is normally proportional to its size, although there are some aspects which seem to increase exponentially in complexity as a network grows. For large networks manual configuration becomes a major issue and in some cases out of the question. A widely distributed network can be a real headache in terms of manpower to manage and support without the complication of configuring links.

Configuration tends to fall into five categories:

1.   Manual configuration using a locally attached terminal or push buttons.
2.   Remote configuration via a virtual call.
3.   Automatic configuration with remote configuration for fine tuning.
4.   Off-line configuration (minimum downtime).
5.   On-line configuration (minimum disturbance).

7.8.10 Fault tracing

There are various tools which a networking product can supply to aid fault tracing. At the simplest level this would be statistical counts of all the frames and packets received and transmitted on each link and trunk. With the appropriate timing information this can be compiled into link utilisation and packet throughput statistics. This information can be used to check the general well being of the network.

7.8.11 Error rate monitors

Errors can be assigned to alarms with various levels of significance from calls being incorrectly sent (users not entering data properly) to link failures.

7.8.12 Call tracing

One of the most common problems is often referred to as call tracing. This is rather like the PSTN namesake. If a user gets connected to a faulty port on a host computer which is connected to a PAD using a hunt group, it is very difficult to ascertain which is the offending port of the computer.

This is because the logical channel identifiers (LCIs) change throughout the network from one link to the next. A network has to provide constantly updated routeing tables, which display this type of information to solve this problem.

7.8.13 Network management

Network management is one of the most important issues in networking today. A badly run network, or one which has been poorly designed so that management is difficult, can cost a company an enormous amount in money and labour to maintain it. The actual definition of network management varies according to the user perspective.

A network operator will have a different list of priorities to the network manager and to the managing director. In OSI network management is being codified to give a common platform so that everyone plays by the same rules and uses the same terminology.

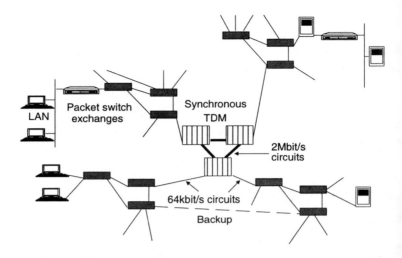

Figure 7.13   A network of TDMs and PSEs

7.8.14 Different multiplexer types in a network

Figure 7.13 shows how time division multiplexers and packet switch exchanges may be intermixed in a network. The multiplexers form a hierarchy from the LANs which are multiplexed on to medium speed 64kbit/s circuits and then on to the high speed 2Mbit/s trunks. Not shown on the diagram is the distance factor, normally the higher speed trunks are geographically much further apart, up to hundreds of miles, than the lower speed circuits.

7.8.15 Network expansion issues

There are various reasons to expand a network:

1.   Geographic changes.
2.   More users.
3.   New facilities.
4.   Higher traffic performance requirements.

Geographic changes, more users and new facilities tend to mean more connections and more or larger user access nodes. This normally means that the traffic requirements change i.e. the aggregate traffic levels per trunk increase. Higher performance can be the result of more users; higher performance end user equipment; lower transit delay requirements; or that existing users are making more use of the network. Performance increases can be addressed by adding links between the nodes or by raising the speed of the existing links between nodes. It is important to note that raising the link speed often means that the network node equipment will require upgrading.

7.8.16 Adding new links

When analysing the statistical information provided by a network it is important to take the historical information into account. A link running at a high utilisation may not necessarily be saturated. X.25 is designed to be more efficient when a link is heavily used.

The first sign that a link is becoming overloaded is when network response times become erratic. X.25 will not lose data; as the network becomes busy it merely delays the transit of that data. The next sign of overloading is when users cannot make new calls and are left with 'busy' messages.

Normal network practice is to design a network for 30% to 40% theoretical usage, which leaves enough capacity to cope with fluctuations in traffic density. Note that this not only includes trunk bandwidth capacity but also the ability to set up and clear calls. Another factor which should be taken into account for sizing the network is that the majority of traffic tends to be local; practical usage suggests that up to 90% of all data on a LAN is between local devices.

7.9 The future of multiplexing

7.9.1 Frame relay

The speeds required by networks increase every year to cope with the increase in computer processing power. Network transmission is

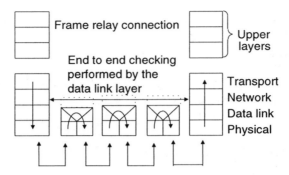

Figure 7.14 Layer model of frame relay

being revolutionised by the availability of high speed fibre systems. Because of the inherent low loss and error free transmission capabilities of fibre a complete rethink on the multiplexing requirements has come about. Instead of relying on the multiplexer to provide an error free path it only need provide a basic routeing path. This is the basis of frame relay. As can be seen from Figure 7.14, the routeing path is part of the link layer and as such network addressing only works on a link by link basis. Each node will have a routeing table indicating where the frame should go but, having transmitted, it does not have any mechanism for checking whether it arrived.

Figure 7.14 shows the layer model of frame relay. Note that it only operates in the lower half of the data link layer. Figure 7.15 shows the standards associated with frame relay and where they fit in the model and Figure 7.16 shows the utilisation on a frame relay circuit with different traffic types. Note that this is almost identical to the format of the statistical multiplexer shown in Figure 7.8.

7.9.2 Synchronous Digital Hierarchy (SDH)

In an attempt to reconcile the three main variants of high order multiplexers a new set of G. standards have been defined, which can transport all types of synchronous traffic. These are G.707, G.708 and G.709 on frame structure; G.781, G.782 and G.783 on SDH multi-

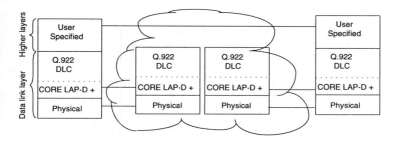

Figure 7.15   Frame relay standards

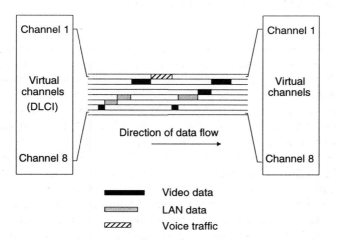

Video data
LAN data
Voice traffic

Figure 7.16   Frame relay utilisation when carrying a mix of traffic types

plexing equipment; G.784 on SDH management; G.957 on SDH optical interfaces; and G.958 on SDH line systems. Other standards are being proposed for network management and digital cross-connect equipment. The underlying rationale for SDH is to provide a transparent 'bit pipe' for synchronous data.

SDH works on the principle of Virtual Containers (VCs) which contain the various services. (See Chapter 1.) These are assembled into Administrative Units (AUs) which can then be assembled as frames into Synchronous Transport Modules (STMs). There is a hierarchy of STMs from STM-1 which runs at 155Mbit/s to STM-16 at 2.488Gbit/s. Again it is the PTTs that are taking the initiative, and services based on this system are on offer in the US as SONET (Synchronous Optical Network).

One of the main benefits of SDH is that it allows plesiochronous networks to operate with relatively inaccurate (1 part in 10^{-4}) and therefore inexpensive clocks. Another is that this service can then be used by other emerging technologies, such as Asynchronous Transfer Mode (ATM) which is the result of the ITU-T work on the I.121 standard.

In ATM data can be transferred without reference to an underlying clock system. Frame relay is an example of an early form of this but ATM is more generally aligned with the switching and multiplexing techniques known as 'cell relay'. Unlike frame relay, which uses variable length frames, cell relay operates with fixed frames (called cells) of 48 octets for the information field and 5 for the header. Because these cells are so simple in structure, they can be implemented in hardware rather than software (as for X.25 packets). This means gigabit speeds will be achievable.

Different data services such as computer data, video and voice, break up their data streams into the cells for transmission over the network where they are recovered at the remote end. As with frame relay, errors are not detected and recovered by the network but by the transport layers in the end systems (OSI layer 4) which initiate the data recovery mechanisms on a peer to peer basis across the network. Obviously such a technique relies on a very efficient high speed, low error transmission path for efficient throughput. This can be provided by fibre optic cables running at the speeds quoted above.

Figure 7.17 shows how fixed length cells, each carrying different types of data, are multiplexed down a link. The VPI/VCI is only assigned on a cell by cell basis. It is the address in the cell header that determines the route taken. This makes for a highly efficient use of bandwidth using the best of TDM and statistical multiplexing.

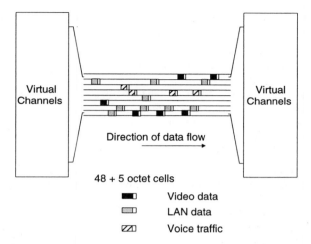

Figure 7.17   Use of fixed length cells for the transport of data. (Compare with Figure 7.16)

7.10 References

Brewster, R.L. (1987) *Telecommunications Technology*, Ellis Horwood Ltd.

CCITT (1988) *Data Communications over the Telephone Network*, Series V Recommendations, Vol. VIII, Fascicle VIII.I.

CCITT (1988) *General Aspects of Digital Transmission Systems*, Recommendations G.700–G.795, Vol. III, Fascicle VIII.4.

CCITT (1990) *Draft Proposals on B-ISDN*, Recommendations I.113, I.150, I.311, May.

Communicate (1993) The veteran technology with a bright future, *Communicate*, September.

Davis, D. and Barbar, D. (1973) *Communication Networks for Computers*, John Wiley and Sons.

Halsall, F. (1988) *Data Communications, Computer Networks and OSI*, Addison Wesley Publishing Co.

Hanning, S. (1993) Getting more out of ISDN, *Communications News*, November.

Hunter, P. (1993) X.25 packs more in, *Datacom*, April.

Jubainville, R. (1994) Congestion control for frame relay, *Telecommunications*, March.

Long, M. (1995) Meeting the challenge presented by ATM, *PC User*, 28 June–11 July.

Lundfall, K. (1993) Packet-switched networks: what protocol do users want? *Telecommunications*, April.

Reeves, J. (1995) Low-speed access: extending the reach of ATM, *Telecommunications*, February.

Ronayne, J. (1991) *Introduction to Digital Communications Switching*, Pitman Publishing.

Tanebaum, A.S. (1989) *Computer Networks*, Prentice Hall.

8. Telecommunication system measurements

8.1 Digital circuit testing

The simplified block diagram (Figure 8.1) shows the connection from one end user to another via various network sections. Measurements will be used to characterise the overall end-to-end transmission performance of the system, known as the digital path. Measurements may also be made on individual network sections, and on the electrical parameters at network interfaces, including PCM codec measurements.

The types of measurement and the associated standards are shown in Table 8.1. Measurements, in common with other telecommunications standards, follow either the ITU-T (formerly CCITT) recommendations or the North American ANSI T1 standards. Note that many of these standards undergo continuous revision to include new technology and operating conditions. It is important to obtain the latest version of documentation from the appropriate standards organisation.

The following sections cover firstly interface measurements, and secondly transmission measurements, particularly error performance criteria.

8.2 Interface measurements

8.2.1 PCM measurements

PCM measurements characterise the analog to digital and digital to analogue conversions that take place at the interface between an analogue telephone line and the digital network. In order to provide the best signal to noise ratio and dynamic range within the digitised

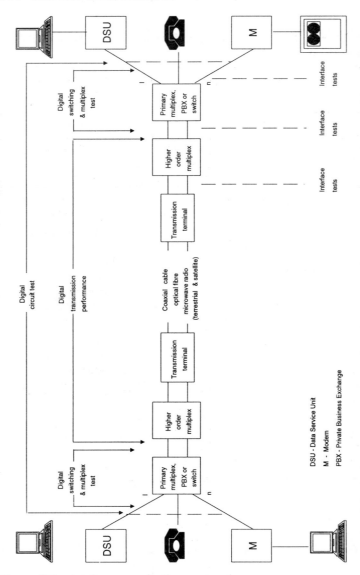

Figure 8.1 A telecommunications network

Table 8.1   Meassurement and performance standards for digital transmission tests

	Measurement type	International standards (ITU-T, ITU-R)	North American standards (ANSI/Bellcore)
Interface measurements	PCM Codec	G.712/713 (A-A) G.714 (A-D D-A) O.131-133 (measurement)	BSTR 43801 (Bellcore TR-NWT-000499)
	Pulse shape	G.703, G.975 (SDH)	T1.403
	Clock frequency		T1.102 (T1X1.4 committee) Bellcore TR-NWT-000499
	Voltage/Imped-ance		T1.105 (SONET)
	Coding		T1X1.6 committee
	Framing	G.704, G.706, G.708	Bellcore GR-253 (Sonet)
	Jitter/Wander/ Timing	G.822/G.823 (European hierarchy) G.824 (N.A. hierarchy) G.825 (SDH) G.958, G.782, G.783 (SDH) O.171 (measurement)	T1.102 T1.403 Bellcore TR-NWT-000499 Bellcore GR253 (Sonet) T1X1.4 committee
Transmission measurements	Error Performance	G.821 (64kbit/s ISDN circuits)	T1M1.3 committee
	Quality of Service	G.826 (primary rate and above) G.921 (digital sections) I.356 (ATM transmission ITU-R Recommenda-tion 594-1 M.2100, M.2110 (limits for bringing into service)	T1.231-1993

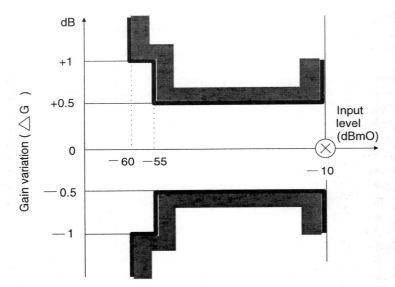

Figure 8.2 ITU-T Recommendation G.712: variation of gain with input level

64kbit/s channel, companding (compression and expansion) of signals is used.

This involves non-linear conversion between analogue amplitude and digital code, which must be exactly matched by the conversion back to analogue at the receive end. Measurements of this characteristic can be made analogue to analogue (A-A), specified in ITU-T Recommendations G.712 and G.713, or as a half channel measurement (A-D and D-A) as specified in G.714. Compliance with half channel specifications ensures interworking between PCM codecs.

Either noise or tone stimulus can be used, with levels at the digital interface being interpreted from the digital 8 bit codes present in the selected 64kbit/s timeslot. The companding algorithm is usually checked by a gain versus level plot (Figure 8.2), or quantising distortion versus level (Figure 8.3). A typical set of PCM codec measurements is shown in Table 8.2.

Table 8.2   PCM measurements in a typical test set

Standard measurements	A-A	A-D	D-A	D-D
Gain	*	*	*	*
Digital mW gain			*	*
Level (including harmonic distortion)	*	*	*	*
Gain vs level (using tone)	*	*	*	*
Gain vs level (using noise)	*	*	*	*
Gain vs level (using synch 2kHz)			*	*
Gain vs frequency	*	*	*	*
Idle state (choice of filters)	*	*	*	*
Coder offset and peak codes		*		*
Noise with tone .	*	*	*	*
Quantising distortion (using tone)	*	*	*	*
Quantising distortion (using noise)	*	*	*	*
Intermodulation (two tone)	*	*	*	*
Intermodulation (four tone)	*	*	*	*

8.2.2 Electrical interface specifications

Electrical interface specifications are usually measured during equipment design and manufacture to ensure compatible interconnection between network elements at a Network Node Interface (NNI) and User Network Interface (UNI). Equipment normally conforms to the electrical characteristics specified in G.703, T1.403, T1.102 or T1.105 (SONET), for the following parameters:

1.   Pulse shape, height, equality of negative/positive pulses.
2.   Voltage and impedance.

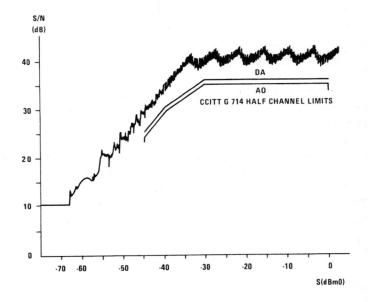

Figure 8.3 S/N characteristic of the A-law for tones

3.   Coding (HDB3, CMI, B3ZS, B6ZS, B8ZS).
4.   Clock frequency.
5.   Framing (G.704, G.706).
6.   Timing jitter and wander (G.823, G.824).

8.2.2.1 *Pulse shape*

The pulse shape of the equipment transmit output is normalised and compared to the mask specified in the standard. This is usually an isolated pulse, typically preceded by 3 zeros to minimise inter-symbol interference (ISI). Either an isolated pulse test pattern is used, or the test receiver (e.g. an oscilloscope) must trigger on the right isolated one bit sequence in a random data stream. The measured signal should be terminated in a well matched resistive load. The pulse is also sometimes specified at a cross connect point after traversing a standard length of coaxial cable.

8.2.2.2 *Voltage and impedance*

Signal voltage is usually measured as part of the pulse shape test, though some specifications quote the average signal power for a particular pattern density.

Impedance is normally 75 ohm unbalanced coaxial, except at the primary rates of 1.544Mbit/s and 2.048Mbit/s where balanced 110 ohm and 120 ohm connections may be used. The return loss should be typically 15 to 20dB and ideally be maintained at 6 to 10dB up to 2 to 3 times the clock frequency, otherwise undesirable overshoot will appear on the pulse transitions.

8.2.2.3 *Coding*

Interface codes are intended to ensure satisfactory clock recovery under varying pattern density. Conformance to the code rules is usually checked automatically with a digital transmission tester. It is also useful to inject code errors on a test pattern to check that the equipment under test recognises this condition.

8.2.2.4 *Clock frequency*

The clock frequency at a hierarchical interface must lie within the specified tolerances shown in Table 8.3, otherwise justification and clock recovery will not operate correctly in terminal equipment.

8.2.2.5 *Framing*

As with interface codes, conformance to the specified frame format is usually checked automatically by a framed digital transmission tester. Likewise, injecting frame errors in a test pattern checks that equipment under test recognises the condition.

Table 8.3 Clock tolerance at hierarchical interfaces

Clock rate	Tolerance
PDH	
64kbit/s	±100ppm
1.544Mbit/s (DS-1)	±50ppm
2.048Mbit/s (E1)	±50ppm
8.448Mbit/s	±30ppm
34.368Mbit/s	±20ppm
44.736Mbit/s (DS-3)	±20ppm
139.264Mbit/s	±15ppm
SONET/SDH	
51.84Mbit/s (STS-1)	< 4.6ppm
155.52Mbit/s (STS-3, STM-1)	< 4.6ppm
622.08Mbit/s (STS-12, STM-3)	< 4.6ppm

Both code errors and frame errors can be used as a simple means of in service error monitoring. Testing may also include a check on the accuracy of these indications.

The standards specify the conditions for loss of frame synchronisation and for regain of synchronisation. These criteria can be tested by injecting a known sequence of frame errors in a test pattern (refer to G.704 and G.706).

8.2.2.6 *Jitter and wander*

Timing jitter is defined as the short term variations of the significant instants of a digital signal from their ideal positions in time. The significant instant might be the rising or falling edge of a pulse. The effect of jitter is shown in Figures 8.4 and 8.5. At certain points in time

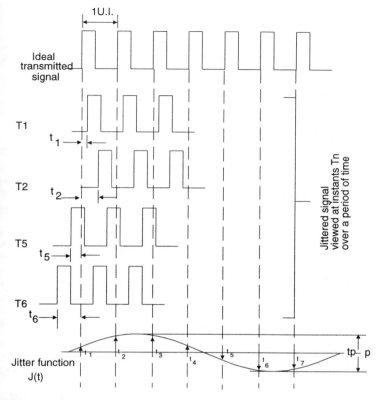

Figure 8.4 Displacement of timing instance of a digital signal due to jitter modulation

the pulse is significantly offset from its correct position. If this offset becomes large, then there will be an error when sampling and decoding the digital signal.

The disturbance or offset of the timing instant is measured in Unit Intervals peak-to-peak (UI), equivalent to one bit period.

One of the advantages of recovering a timing clock from the data stream is that it will tend to track any timing jitter present in the data. Provided this tracking occurs, then no errors will result when the recovered clock is used to sample the data. In view of the limited

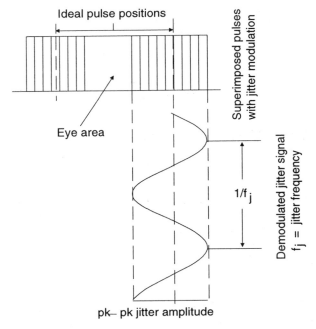

Figure 8.5 Effect of jitter modulation on the eye diagram

bandwidth of clock recovery circuits, this advantage only exists at low jitter modulation frequencies. At higher jitter frequencies, the tracking diminishes and the equipment's tolerance to input jitter is greatly reduced. For this reason, jitter standards are always specified in terms of UI versus jitter frequency for various bit rates.

Timing variations at frequencies below 10Hz are referred to as wander, and are typically caused by changes in phase and propagation delay (e.g. through satellites or long cables subject to temperature changes). Wander is sometimes classified as long term (24 hours, i.e. daily temperature changes) or short term (15 minutes), these definitions being taken from ANSI T1.403.

To fully specify the jitter performance of a piece of equipment, we need to measure the input jitter tolerance, the jitter level at the output

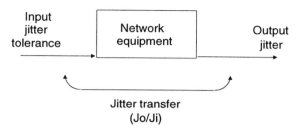

Figure 8.6 Three jitter specifications

and also the jitter transfer function or the degree to which jitter present at the input is amplified or attenuated by the equipment (Figure 8.6). The input jitter tolerance is checked by increasing the level of jitter on a test pattern at a given modulation frequency and determining the level at which the equipment under test starts to generate errors.

The permitted levels for these parameters are specified in ITU-T Recommendation G.823 for European hierarchy and G.824 for North American hierarchy. A similar set of North American specifications will be found in ANSI T1.102 and in Bellcore TR-NWT-000499. The measuring methods and receiver bandwidths are defined in ITU-T Recommendation O.171. An example of the jitter tolerance mask from G.823 is shown in Figure 8.7.

Jitter measurements have become important in the new generation of multiplex equipment for SONET and Synchronous Digital Hierarchy (SDH). Synchronisation of payload signals in the SONET/SDH frame is handled by pointer movements. The pointer movements can lead to significant amounts of jitter at the tributary output of an add/drop multiplexer. Tributary output jitter (e.g. at DS-1 or DS-3) is measured while a SONET/SDH tester forces a specified sequence of pointer movements. These are described in the latest version of Bellcore GR-253 and ITU-T G.783.

When equipment meets the jitter specifications at a hierarchical interface, it should be possible to interconnect network sections without causing bit errors.

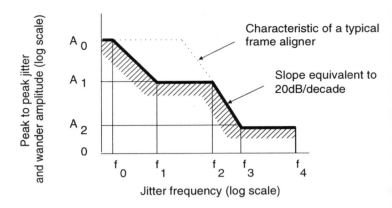

Figure 8.7 Lower limit of maximum tolerable input jitter and wander

8.3 Error performance measurements

8.3.1 Lines, paths and sections

Digital network error performance can be measured over a complete end-to-end connection called a path, or over parts of the network termed lines and sections. These network layers are shown in Figure 8.8. Path measurements indicate the overall quality of service to the customer. Line and section measurements are used for trouble-shooting, installation and maintenance, and for assuring transmission performance objectives are met.

8.3.2 In service and out of service measurements

In service error performance measurements rely on checking known bit patterns in an otherwise random data stream of live traffic. As discussed in Section 8.3.6, some in service measurements are more representative than others of the actual error performance of the traffic signal. Furthermore, some are applicable to the path measure-

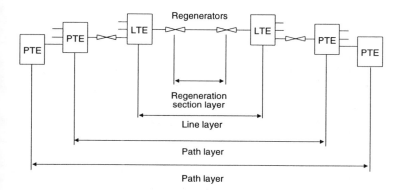

LTE: Line Terminating Equipment
PTE: Path Terminating Equipment

Figure 8.8   Illustration of lines, paths and sections

ment provided the parameters are not reset at an intermediate network interface. Others are only useful at the line or section level.

Out of service measurements involve removing live traffic from the link and replacing it with a known test signal, usually a pseudo-random binary sequence (p.r.b.s.). These tests are disruptive if applied to working networks, but do give very exact performance measurements as every bit is checked for error.

8.3.3 The error performance tester (out of service)

The bit error rate tester (BERT), shown in Figures 8.9 and 8.10, consists of a pattern generator and error detector, often combined in a single instrument though sometimes separate. The p.r.b.s. is generated using a feedback shift register which is driven by a very stable clock source, either internally or derived externally from a frequency synthesiser.

The feedback connections on the shift register determine the p.r.b.s. characteristics, and are defined in ITU-T Recommendation O.151, O.152, and O.153.

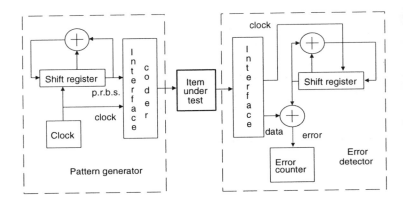

Figure 8.9 Principles of BER tester

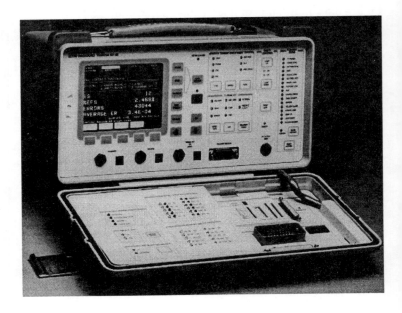

Figure 8.10 A modern error performance analyser

The raw data from the shift register is usually passed through an interface circuit to generate the correct code format and output level (G.703). At the receive side the same type of interface circuit strips off the code and recovers a clock. This clock drives a reference p.r.b.s. generator whose output is compared with the received data.

When the system has synchronised correctly, every bit error in the received data stream will be detected and recorded by the error counter. The error detector can then compute the bit error ratio for a given measurement period as in Equation 8.1 and can also analyse the results statistically to determine how BER varies as a function of time.

$$\text{BER} = \frac{\text{Total number of bit errors}}{\text{Total number of bits received}} \qquad (8.1)$$

The test patterns used at various bit rates are standardised by ITU-T and are summarised in Table 8.4. In addition to p.r.b.s. test patterns, repetitive word patterns with particular 'ones' density can be used to explore pattern dependency when troubleshooting.

Table 8.4 Test pattern versus bit rate (0.151, 0.152, 0.153)

Bit rate	Test pattern
50bit/s – 168kbit/s (0.153)	$2^9 - 1, 2^{11} - 1, 2^{20} - 1$
64kbit/s (0.152)	$2^{11} - 1$
1.544Mbit/s	$2^{15} - 1, 2^{20} - 1$
2.048Mbit/s	$2^{15} - 1$
8.448Mbit/s	$2^{15} - 1$
34.368Mbit/s	$2^{23} - 1$
44.736Mbit/s	$2^{15} - 1, 2^{20} - 1$
139.264Mbit/s	$2^{23} - 1$

8.3.4 ITU-T Recommendation G.821

Error performance, or statistical analysis of error occurrence, is usually evaluated in accordance with ITU-T Recommendation G.821 (Table 8.5) which specifies the percentage of time that certain thresholds can be exceeded. It gives the error performance of an international digital connection forming part of an ISDN, measured over a period T_L (e.g. one month) on a unidirectional 64kbit/s channel of the hypothetical reference connection (HRX) of 27500km.

G.821 refers to the overall performance for the end-to-end 64kbit/s connection on a very long (27500km) international connection. It's the starting point for error performance measurements, but needs interpretation before being applied to a practical transmission system.

G.821 defines how error performance parameters are calculated (Figure 8.11). The total measurement time is divided into 1 second periods, and unavailable time is subtracted to obtain the available time on which the G.821 parameters are calculated.

A period of unavailable time begins when the BER in each second is worse than 10^{-3} for a period of ten consecutive seconds. These ten seconds are then considered to be unavailable time. A new period of

Table 8.5 ITU-T Recommendation G.821

Performance classification	Objectives
Degraded Minutes (DM)	Fewer than 10% of one minute intervals to have a Bit Error Ratio (BER) worse than 10^{-6}
Severely Errored Seconds (SES)	Fewer than 0.2% of one second intervals to have a Bit Error Ratio (BER) worse than 10^{-3}
Errored Seconds (ES)	Fewer than 8% of one second intervals to have any errors — equivalent to 92% error free seconds

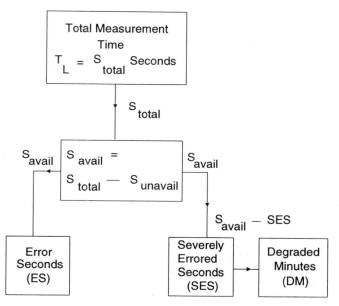

Figure 8.11   G.821 classification

available time begins with the first second of a period of ten consecutive seconds each of which has a BER better than 10^{-3}.

During available time, any second containing one or more errors is logged as an errored second (ES). Any period of 1 second with a BER exceeding 10^{-3} is classified as a severely errored second (SES) and is subtracted from available time. The remainder is grouped into 60 second periods. Any of these 1 minute periods with a BER exceeding 10^{-6} is classified as a degraded minute (DM).

8.3.4.1 *Apportionment*

The hypothetical reference connection (HRX) defined in G.821 is shown in Figure 8.12. The connection consists of a local and medium grade section at each end of the link, and a long distance high grade section in the middle. A high capacity transmission system such as

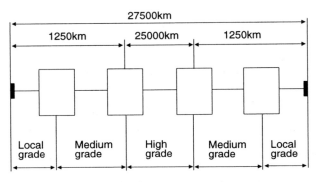

Figure 8.12   Hypothetical reference connection

Table 8.6   Allocation of degraded minutes and errored second objectives

Circuit classification	Allocation of degraded minutes and errored seconds objectives
Local grade (two ends)	15% block allowance to each end
Medium grade (two ends)	15% block allowance to each end
High grade	40% (equivalent to conceptual quality of 0.0016%/km)

microwave or lightwave would be characterised as a high grade section.

Typically a low grade section would be the metallic subscriber loop. Medium grade would be the connection from, say, a local exchange to a trunk switching centre. The three types of section in the network are allocated different portions of the total G.821 specification.

As shown in Tables 8.6 and 8.7, the allocation of degraded minutes and errored seconds is handled slightly differently from severely errored seconds. Low and medium grade sections are allocated a

Table 8.7 Allocation of severely errored seconds

Circuit classification	Allocation of severely errored seconds objectives
Local grade (two ends)	0.015% block allowance to each end
Medium grade (two ends)	0.015% block allowance to each end
High grade	0.04%

block allowance of 15% of the total G.821 specification at each end (i.e. 1.5% DM and 1.2% ES) irrespective of length. The longer high grade section is apportioned on a distance basis so that 40% allowance is reduced in the ratio L/25000.

Thus for a high grade section of length L km, Equations 8.2 and 8.3 give the values for allowable DM and ES.

$$\text{Allowable DM} = 10\% \times 0.4 \times \frac{L}{25000} \quad \text{or} \quad 0.00016\%/\text{km} \qquad (8.2)$$

$$\text{Allowable ES} = 8\% \times 0.4 \times \frac{L}{25000} \quad \text{or} \quad 0.000128\%/\text{km} \qquad (8.3)$$

Severely errored seconds are allocated on a block basis only. 0.1% (of the total 0.2% G.821 specification) is allocated on a block basis as shown in Table 8.7.

The remaining 0.1% SES is allocated to medium and high grade sections to account for adverse operating conditions such as propagation in microwave radio systems. For example, G.821 recommends that an additional 0.05% SES may be allocated to a medium or high grade microwave radio section of 2500km.

8.3.4.2 *Conversion of measurements*

Error performance standards usually refer to measurements at 64kbit/s, whereas practical measurements on transmission systems are invariably made at a higher multiplex rate. The 1988 (Blue Book) version of G.821 (Annex D) gives provisional guidelines for conversion:

1.   Percent DM converted directly.
2.   Percent SES converted directly with the addition of percent time with loss of frame alignment.

Error second estimation is given by Equation 8.4, where n is the number of errors in the i*th* second, N is the higher bit rate divided by 64kbit/s, and j is the total number of seconds.

$$ES_{64kbit/s} = \frac{1}{j} \sum_{i=1}^{i=j} \left(\frac{n}{N} \right)_i \times 100\% \tag{8.4}$$

Y% DM measured at the line rate can be compared directly to Y% DM at 64kbit/s. Y% SES measured at the line rate can be converted directly to Y% SES at 64kbit/s, but if during the test a loss of frame alignment is detected (or a slip), this time as a percentage should be added.

The conversion for errored seconds is more complicated. Since the higher multiplexed bit rate contains many 64kbit/s channels, we need to know how many errors are contained in each errored second at the higher rate in order to estimate how many 64kbit/s channels have been errored.

Assuming errors are distributed evenly within the frame (the worst case condition), then Equation 8.4 is representative.

However, the validity of all these conversion algorithms is being debated in standards committees. Bursts of errors in a high rate transmission stream may cause loss of synchronisation in a subsequent demultiplexer, creating an extended error burst on a tributary output.

Some practical measurements seem to support these conclusions. Refer to the latest version of Recommendation G.821 for guidance on conversion algorithms. The more recent G.826 recommendation should also be consulted.

8.3.5 Related error performance standards

Several other standards exist, however generally these are related to G.821 specifications.

8.3.5.1 *CCIR Recommendation 594-1*

Error performance of digital microwave radio systems is characterised using CCIR (now part of ITU-R) recommendations, notably Recommendation 594-1, for 2500km link (64kbit/s unidirectional channel) as follows:

1.   BER worse than 1×10^{-6} for less than 0.4% of any month.
2.   BER worse than 1×10^{-3} for less than 0.054% of any month.
3.   Errored seconds should not exceed 0.32% of any month.
4.   Residual BER should not exceed 5×10^{-9} (15 minute integration).

Recommendation 594-1 is compatible with the high grade portion of G.821. An additional block allowance of 0.05% SES has been added for adverse propagation conditions and a specification for residual BER has been added.

Both the Residual BER (RBER) threshold and the percentage for G.821 parameters should be reduced in proportion for systems less than 2500km long.

As these recommendations are compatible with G.821, the same measuring instruments and calculation are used to assess performance. The main consideration is that radio propagation is affected by weather and so results could be misleading unless measured over a reasonable period (e.g. 1 month)

8.3.5.2 *Recommendation G.826*

This recommendation (issued at the end of 1993) focuses on the error performance parameters and objectives for international constant bit rate (CBR) digital paths at or above the primary rate (i.e. 1544/2048kbits/s and above).

It is complementary to G.821 and a higher speed transmission system meeting G.826 should in most cases meet the G.821 requirements for the 64kbits/s path carried therein. G.826 applies to PDH and SDH transmission systems and also to ATM transmission paths supported by PDH/SDH framing.

The overall end-to-end ATM performance objectives are defined in ITU-T Recommendation I.356.

The measurement definitions in G.826 are applicable to both in-service and out-of-service testing, and are based on the concept of an errored block. The block check for errors could be generated by a test set or could be the in-service monitoring of CRC or parity errors (see Section 8.3.6).

The error events are defined as follows:

Errored Block (EB): A block in which one or more bits are in error.
Errored Seconds (ES): A one second period with one or more block errors.
Severely Errored Seconds (SES): A one second period which contains 30% errored blocks or at least one Severely Disturbed Period (SDP).

An SDP occurs when over a period of time, equivalent to four contiguous blocks or 1ms, whichever is longer, either all contiguous blocks are affected by a high error density 10^{-2}, or a Defect Event (see Section 8.3.6). The performance parameters are defined as follows:

Errored Second Ratio (ESR): The ratio of ES to total seconds of available time during a fixed measurement interval.
Severely Errored Second Ratio (SESR): The ratio of SES to total available time.
Background Block Error Ratio (BBER): The ratio of errored blocks to total blocks during a fixed measurement interval, excluding all blocks during SES and unavailable time.

Based on these parameters, the G.826 performance criteria as a function of bit rate are shown in Table 8.8.

Table 8.8 End-to-end error performance objectives for a 27500km digital hypothetical reference path

Par-ameter	Rate				
	1.5 to 5	*5 to 15*	*15 to 55*	*55 to 160*	*160 to 3500*
Bits/block	2000–8000	2000–8000	4000–20000	6000–20000	15000–30000
ESR	0.04	0.05	0.075	0.16	Under review
SESR	0.002	0.002	0.222	0.002	0.002
BBER	3×10^{-4}	2×10^{-4}	2×10^{-4}	2×10^{-4}	10^{-4}

8.3.5.3 *Recommendation G.921*

ITU-T Recommendation G.921 defines the performance of a Hypothetical Reference Digital Section (HRDS) and is based on the requirements of G.821.

G.921 considers digital sections of 280km (or multiples of 280km) and assigns percentage allocation of overall G.821 specifications. Shorter medium grade connections are also defined as shown in Table 8.9.

8.3.5.4 *Recommendation M.2100*

ITU-T recommendation M.2100 is titled 'Performance limits for bringing-into-service and maintenance of digital paths, sections and transmission sections'. Error, timing and availability performance are considered. A method for deriving ES and SES from in-service measurements is given for all hierarchical levels.

M.2100 defines practical performance criteria for digital circuits, measured over shorter periods than the 1 month defined in G.821. Periods of 15 minutes, 24 hours and 7 days are recommended. It also

Table 8.9　Digital section quality classifications for error performance

Section quality classification	HRDS length (km)	Allocation	To be used in circuit classification
1	280	0.45%	High grade
2	280	2%	Medium grade
3	50	2%	Medium grade
4	50	5%	Medium grade

recommends margins for ageing so that maintenance intervals can be extended.

Furthermore, M.2100 defines Anomaly Events (AE) and Defect Events (DE) for both in service and out of service testing, and indicates the number of events permissible in a measurement period. For in service testing, it suggests how events should be interpreted in terms of G.821 parameters. This parallels the North American ANSI T1-231-1993 'Digital Hierarchy — Layer 1 In-Service Digital Transmission Performance Monitoring'.

8.3.6　In service measurement parameters and standards

In service measurements have become increasingly important as they allow long term performance monitoring and preventative maintenance without interrupting customer traffic. In the deregulated competitive environment, this is very desirable. In service measurements rely on detecting errors in fixed or allowed bit patterns within the data stream, or on computing parity/checksums on blocks of data:

1.　BPVs and Line Code Violations are of limited use as they apply to a single transmission section. Equipment will not retransmit code violations to subsequent sections and so this type of parameter cannot be used to indicate overall path performance. (BPV stands for Bipolar Violations in ternary codes such as HDB3, B8ZS, B3ZS, 4B3T etc.)

2. Frame Alignment Signal (FAS) Errors are detected by checking the bits in the repetitive frame alignment word. These form only a small part of the overall frame, and therefore provide only a sample or snapshot of error performance. Good for long term average error ratio (BER).

3. Parity Errors are detected by computing odd or even parity for blocks of data. Has the advantage of checking all payload bits, but can be fooled by even numbers of bit errors in the data block. Effective at low error rates (e.g. less than 10^{-4}). Used in DS-3 (44.736Mbit/s) transmission in North America, in the SONET/SDH frame standard, and in some line codes.

4. Cyclic Redundancy Checksum (CRC) is computed on blocks of data including payload bits and a CRC remainder sent to the receive end for comparison with the recalculated remainder. A discrepancy indicates one or more errors have occurred in the data block. Provides very reliable detection, giving a good indication of % Errored Seconds as per G.821. Currently used in T1 (1.544Mbit/s) ESF (CRC-6) and E1 (2.048Mbit/s) (CRC-4).

According to ITU-T Recommendation M.2100, system errors are classified as Anomaly Events (AE) such as frame errors, parity errors, code errors, and Defect Events (DE) such as loss of signal, loss of frame synchronisation etc. Table 8.10 shows the anomaly events detection processes available at the various telecommunication standard bit rates. (See M.2100 and ANSI T1.231-1993 for interpretation of these in service measurements.)

8.4 Data communications network measurement

Network measurement is no longer restricted to the trusty cable tester and a selection of rudimentary software utilities. Along with the wide variety of network installations now in existence, there is an equally

Table 8.10 In service anomaly events (M.2100) and performance primitives (T1M1.3)

BIP = Bit Interleaved Parity; FEBE = Far End Block Error
*Only when operating in these frame formats

Bit rate interface	Section/line	Path
T1, DS-1 1.544Mbit/s	BPVs (B8ZS, AMI) FAS error Line-code errors	CRC-6 errors[*] G1-G6 bits[*] (ESF data link)[*]
E1 2.048Mbit/s	BPVs (HDB3) FAS error Line-code errors	CRC-4 errors[*] E bits[*]
DS-3 44.736Mbit/s	BPVs (B3ZS) FAS errors Line-code errors M13 parity errors (P bits)	C-bit parity errors[*] FEBE bits[*]
34.368Mbit/s 139.264Mbit/s	BPVs (HDB3) FAS errors Line-code errors	
SONET/SDH	BIP-8 (Byte B1) (section overhead) BIP-8 (Byte B2) (line overhead)	BIP-8 (Byte B3) Path overhead FEBE (Payload path monitor e.g. DS-1, DS-3)

diverse range of measurement tools available, with features matched to the needs of the many potential users.

The simplest tool, the cable tester, uses Time Domain Reflectometry (TDR) to check for open or short circuits. Where a problem exists, the tester will indicate the distance from its connection to the fault. More sophisticated devices will passively monitor the traffic on the network, focusing on the electrical characteristics of the transmission.

A more complex tool, the protocol analyser, records conversations between devices on the network, and provides a detailed diagnosis of the protocols used to exchange information.

The most widely used measurement tool is the network monitor. The monitor continuously gathers information about the behaviour of the network, focusing on the data link and network layers. The monitor records the number and size of packets, the source and destination addresses, and uses this data to summarise the nature of traffic on the network.

Information gathered by network measurement devices may be useful to a great many people in an organisation. Each will require differing measurement facilities according to their respective roles.

Network maintenance engineers will concentrate on low level network characteristics, for fault detection and repair. Network managers will be more interested in security and control issues. Board level management will require reports on the usage and performance of the network to enable planning for future needs.

Many of the more common network monitors provide a rich set of functions that go some way towards satisfying the requirements of these groups. The more specialised tools are appropriate for specific tasks, such as installing a new network or development of new communication software.

8.4.1 Physical measurement

Cable testers work by first transmitting a pattern onto the network and then listening for a short period afterwards. The nature of the signal received during the listening period indicates the state of the cable. Analysis of the physical characteristics of the network is best performed by more sophisticated devices.

8.4.1.1 *Electrical characteristics*

Attaching an oscilloscope or logic analyser to a network enables an engineer to see exactly what the signals on the cable look like. A network analyser supplements the view of the electrical signals by comparing the characteristics against a table of technical specifications for that network technology. In particular, the analyser will look at voltage levels, the rise and fall times of signals and the presence of electrical noise. By comparing key parameters against expected values and tolerances, the analyser can perform a health check on the physical network.

The analyser can locate problems such as faulty connectors, improperly terminated cables or network devices operating out of specification. It can also alert the engineer to potential concerns such as cable degradation.

8.4.1.2 *Multiple attachments*

By attaching a network analyser and a number of subsidiary nodes on a single network segment, it is possible to form an even clearer picture of the physical behaviour of the network. If a network adapter board failed in such a way as to intermittently transmit garbled data onto the network, network measurement equipment operating at a higher level would be swamped with meaningless data. Whilst it would be clear that there was a problem with the network, there may be few clues as to the source of the disruption. However, by analysing the electrical signals at more than one point on the segment, it is possible to quickly and accurately locate the faulty device.

This sort of network troubleshooting is of greatest importance when a network is first installed. Additionally, periodic health checks can aid in pointing the engineer towards areas where corrective action is needed well before network users experience any significant disruption.

8.4.2 Statistical information

Network monitors continuously collect statistics about the traffic on the network, categorise the statistics, form tables, and finally present this information to the user in tabular or graphical form. The user will derive the most benefit from the results of this process if he can apply a significant degree of control over each stage.

8.4.2.1 *Categorisation*

Typically, network monitors will receive all packets transmitted on the network and extract the following details for each packet:

1.   The length in bytes.
2.   The physical address of the source of the packet.
3.   The physical address of the intended destination of the packet.

The monitor may optionally determine the following for each packet:

1.   Low level protocol type or identity.
2.   Logical network addresses for the source and destination.

Having extracted this information, the monitor may then record it in a form specified by the user. At its simplest, this could involve merely accumulating the total number of bytes transmitted on the network and then taking periodic samples of this total in order to form an indication of how the load on the network varies over time. This would then be displayed as a histogram.

By recording the total number of bytes transmitted in a table, with one entry for each network device, the monitor forms a more complete record of the traffic on the network. Some network monitors record even more information for each station:

1.   The number of packets sent or received.
2.   The number of bytes sent or received.
3.   How many of the packets were in some way erroneous, possibly with a breakdown of errors by type.

Such a detailed table may be displayed without further processing, or stored on disc to enable subsequent analysis. Alternatively, by taking periodic samples of, say, the total number of bytes transmitted by each station, the monitor can display a table or histogram showing how the relative activity of the stations on the network changes over time.

8.4.2.2 *Manipulation*

Network monitors can perform a limited amount of manipulation on the statistical data before recording it. This manipulation, under the control of the user, means that the monitor can focus on specific areas of concern.

A filter could be applied such that the monitor only records information for certain types of packets and discards the rest. For example, the filter could be programmed such that only packets of a particular type are noted. Where there are a number of protocols in use on a network, this facility enables the user to focus on each protocol in turn.

Another way in which the monitor can assist the user is by grouping pieces of information according to a user specified manner. The most typical instance of this is when monitors are used to look at communication between certain groups of stations. For example, this could be a server used by a number of client stations. The user would have to specify that the monitor should only gather statistics on packets in which the server was the source or the destination.

A more complex example requires the monitor to build a matrix to show which stations are communicating with which others. This would help the user to identify where to partition an overloaded network.

8.4.2.3 *Presentation*

It is common for network monitors to provide both tabular and graphical displays for a variety of statistical information. If the monitor has a windowing interface, it is possible to combine both sets of information on a single screen. The user has control over the scale and sampling period for histograms, and the method of ordering entries for tables.

8.4.2.4 *Further processing*

The more powerful network monitors provide sophisticated features for the user to control:

1.   Which statistics are to be collected.
2.   What filtering and manipulation is to be performed.
3.   How the data is to be stored and displayed.

However, it is still important for the user to be able to transfer statistical records and tables to disc to enable subsequent post processing. Most network monitors provide a mechanism to either record a snapshot of a table at the user's request, or periodically make a summary entry to a disc file.

Files of statistics may be processed by the user's own software to perform analysis specific to the user's needs. The files may even be in a form that enables them to be read into a standard software package for more generalised processing, such as report generation. The user is able to produce reports that are tailored to the needs of the target audience. One example would be an annual summary of the trends in usage of the network for the management team to forecast future purchasing requirements.

8.4.3 Reporting alarm conditions

The experienced user of a network monitor will be able to spot a fault or potential problem on the network merely by studying the various statistical displays. However, more effective use may be made of the monitor by configuring it to watch certain network parameters and raise an alarm if an invalid condition arises.

8.4.3.1 *Thresholds*

Network parameters that may be monitored include the network load and rate at which errors occur. Both of these parameters have a time component, and hence it is important that the user understands the sampling period used by the network monitor.

The bursty nature of networks means that the sampling period of the monitor can make it difficult to set a sensible threshold on which to base the alarm. Even a well behaved network can have brief periods of very heavy load. To illustrate the potential difficulty, consider the following example.

A network monitor produces a histogram to show the network usage for a working day, sampling the load every hour. From the resulting display it is clear that the load never exceeds 5%. So, the user specifies a load threshold of 5%, expecting the monitor to sound an alarm if the network suffers from an unusually high load.

However, the monitor takes samples of the network load every 30 seconds when checking for alarm conditions, and frequently during the course of the day the load appears to exceed 15%. Obviously the monitor alarm will be sounding all the time, with little benefit to the user.

8.4.3.2 *Station behaviour*

It is also possible for a network monitor to have alarm thresholds assigned to individual stations. This is useful for monitoring the use of a fileserver or a gateway, for example.

Where a monitor can associate alarm conditions with network stations, it is useful to detect:

1. When a new station appears on the network (sometimes called an intruder alarm).
2. When an important station, such as a server, seems to have stopped transmitting (a dead station).

For the latter, it is necessary to specify the requisite period of silence before the alarm should be generated. For client-server based communication that involves hello or uptime packets, it is quite straightforward to set this time. For less deterministic traffic, the user will probably have to specify quite a long time period.

When an alarm is detected, the network monitor will probably make an audible signal. It might also be possible to use the alarm to trigger some other action, such as packet capture.

8.4.4 Packet capture and decode

Traditionally, it has been the role of the protocol analyser to record conversations between stations on the network and present a chronological sequence of packets in an interpreted form. However, many network monitors will also provide a similar function, albeit restricted to the lower protocol layers, or with less detail in the analysis. For most users, the service provided by a network monitor is more than adequate, but for network protocol developers the added sophistication, and expense, of a protocol analyser is justified.

8.4.4.1 *Triggering and filtering*

Sometimes it will be necessary to record all of the traffic on the network for a period of time. However, it is more usual to require just a single conversation, or group of conversations, to be captured. The network monitor will have a number of filters that the user can use to specify patterns that must be matched before a packet is stored.

It is often possible to define a logical relationship between a number of patterns. For example, two patterns could be set up such that a server address is specified as the source in one pattern and the destination in the other. The monitor can then be instructed to capture only those packets that match one of the patterns. Hence, the sample of packets will record all packets explicitly sent or received by the identified server. Notice that to capture every packet associated with the server would also require additional patterns specifying appropriate broadcast and multicast, or functional, addresses.

In addition to providing a filtering facility, network monitors also allow the user to specify a condition, or combination of conditions, that must be satisfied before any packet capture commences. These may be dependent on a certain packet sequence occurring, or the raising of an alarm or even a specified time.

The ability to specify a time at which packet capture is to start is useful when the user is interested in the conversations that occur during scheduled events. A typical example of this is filesystem network backups. Backups are performed automatically at times of low activity, such as during the night.

The limit to the size of the capture buffer used to store conversations varies greatly between different monitors. Monitors with lower limits are restricted to storing captured packets in memory, either the network adapter's or that of the system. Devices with larger buffers achieve this in a number of ways:

1.   Copying captured packets directly to disc. Since the time to transfer data to the disc is quite long, this method restricts the speed at which packets may be received. Sensible use of the system memory for buffering will help to smooth out bursts of traffic.

2.   Using a RAM disc (a virtual disc that actually comprises a dedicated area of system memory). The buffer is not as large as for a real disc, but the limitation on the packet capture rate is eased.

3.   Packet slicing, a technique whereby only part of the captured packet is stored, the rest being discarded. This approach extends the limit at little cost, as long as the section of packet stored is sufficient for the user's needs. This may be true for lower protocol layers, but is much harder to achieve for higher layers.

8.4.4.2 *Presentation*

The standard of protocol decode performed on the captured packets varies enormously between network monitors. At its simplest, the display may comprise a sequence of packets with the protocol types identified and the important fields of the lowest network layers interpreted to show mnemonics with associated field values.

Sophisticated packet decode facilities may include a windowed display, with every packet shown in a variety of layouts, as specified by the user. The full name of every field will be given, along with the corresponding value and a suitable mnemonic. It may be possible to focus on one protocol layer, with higher and lower layers suppressed from the display. The monitor could even summarise each packet on a single line to enable rapid browsing.

With such diversification in the means of decoding packets it is worth considering the true merit of packet decode. The majority of protocol related faults that occur on networks are associated with the lower layers, and are frequently due to the improper configuration of a network device. For such problems, the packet capture and decode facilities provided by most network monitors are more than adequate. The more sophisticated features are only really of use in a development environment.

8.4.4.3 *Protocols*

Just as there is great variety in the display of interpreted packets, there are great differences between the range of protocols supported by network monitors. Most monitors will cope with the commonest low level protocols, such as TCP/IP. For higher protocol layers, or other protocol families, it is often possible to purchase additional software modules to extend the basic decodes provided by the monitor.

Some network monitors support a facility whereby users can write their own protocol decode functions. The user will write programmes using pre-defined library functions, and then link the code with that of the monitor. This will be particularly useful for protocol developers, or users of proprietary protocols.

The way in which most network monitors perform the interpretation of network protocols results in a fundamental limitation to the detail provided in higher protocol layers. This derives from the fact that the recording of conversations, and consequently the decode and display of the detail of those conversations, are all performed on a packet basis. This is different to the operation of the protocol implementation on the interacting stations.

The layering of protocols serves to conceal the packet oriented nature of low level network protocols from the higher levels. The higher protocol layers are concerned with transactions, conversations or sessions. Applications software on one machine will conduct a conversation with peer level software on another machine, oblivious to the way in which the conversation is broken up into packets, transmitted across the network and reassembled at the other end.

However, network monitors interpret protocol information on a packet by packet basis. Consequently, it is difficult to interpret high level protocol information in a packet in the midst of a conversation because the context in which that packet falls is unknown.

Network monitors compromise by either making semi-intelligent guesses, based on 'hints' in the lower level protocols, or just give up and display the data in hexadecimal and ASCII. The only effective means of overcoming this limitation is by copying a sequence of packets to a disc file and then using a specialised analysis package.

8.4.4.4 *Post processing*

Special purpose high level protocol decode software has a limited applicability, and so is not widely used. It overcomes the packet oriented approach to protocol decodes by behaving like the original protocol implementation on the network stations. Hence, every packet's context is meaningful.

The main audience for this type of software is protocol developers. In fact, the software results from a re-engineering of the original protocol implementation. To perform protocol decode, the software will have been changed to read packets from the disc rather than the network, and provide output to the screen instead of replying to received packets.

The advantage of using this type of software tool is the implicit validation of the operation of the protocol implementation being monitored. This is of greatest significance when using the packet to validate a new implementation of the protocol.

8.4.5 Monitors as active stations

Although most of the network monitor's functionality is concerned with passively watching all of the traffic on the network, and processing the data in ways already described, there are some features of a monitor that require it to participate actively in the communication on the network.

8.4.5.1 *Testing connections*

The role of a cable tester and the more sophisticated physical network analyser have already been discussed. Most network monitors also provide a limited cable test feature, but with poor accuracy. Some monitors also perform echo tests on stations specified by the user.

The echo test involves the monitor transmitting a special type of packet to a network station and then waiting for a reply. If a valid reply is received within the timeout period, this shows that the station is present on the network and that it understands the protocol to which the echo packet belongs. Such packets exist for ISO LLC and Xerox XNS protocols.

8.4.5.2 Representative loading

When a network monitor provides a packet transmission capability, there is usually the means to specify:

1.   The length of the packet.
2.   The data content of the packet.
3.   Whether the packet is to be repeatedly transmitted at a specified interval.

The purpose of re-transmitting the packet, with an interval specified by the user, is to enable the monitor to simulate additional loads on the network. By varying the other parameters, it is possible to generate a load that is representative of, say, adding another group of workstations and a fileserver. This allows the user to investigate the impact of expanding the use of the network. Particular areas of concern may be the effect on response times for other workstation users, or possibly whether a local bridge can cope with the additional load.

8.4.5.3 Traffic patterns

If a network monitor is able to transmit packets whose contents are defined entirely by the user, or copied from a packet captured from the network, then the monitor can be used to send out a series of different packets that together form a pattern or signature. By sending a particular series of packets to a single network station, it may be possible to stimulate it into behaving in a desired way. For example, a network server might respond with status information if sent an authentic request, which could be simulated by the monitor.

Alternatively, where the monitor is able to retransmit captured packets, the pattern might be suspected of having caused a network fault. Replaying the packet sequence will give the user the opportunity to monitor the effect more carefully.

8.4.5.4 *Test suites*

The process of using the network monitor to send sequences of packets to particular network devices in order to test their behaviour can be automated. The patterns of packets, together with details of the expected responses, form a suite of tests. Key parameters, such as the destination address, will have to be changed each time the test suite is applied, but this still forms quite a powerful testing facility.

A few network monitors now provide support for the use of test suites. The real benefit for the user comes from the level of analysis that the monitor performs on the results of applying a test suite. It is clear that the maximum benefit would arise from the use of artificial intelligence in the analysis of the results. At least one network analysis tool now attempts to provide a limited form of this.

8.4.6 Effective use

Network monitors are frequently used only in a troubleshooting capacity. So, for example, when users complain of sporadic interruptions in their service from a network server, the network monitor is wheeled out to solve the problem. At that time, the monitor is used to gather whatever information it can from the already faulty network.

By leaving the monitor permanently connected to the network, it may be used in a proactive role, gathering information about the operation of the network and providing early warnings of possible problems. Network monitors provide a means of recording the data that they produce. Compiling this data over a period of time enables network managers to observe the changing patterns of usage of the network. This facilitates forward planning of the growth of the network and can pinpoint areas of concern.

8.4.7 Larger networks

As the number and size of LANs continue to grow, it is increasingly necessary to partition individual networks and interconnect them to form multi-LANs. The connections between LANs filter out localised traffic, so that a network monitor at one part of the network cannot, by itself, report completely on the status of another part of the network.

8.4.7.1 *Remote monitoring*

Simplified remote monitoring devices may be attached to all segments of the network. These devices lack much of the sophistication of the monitors that have been described here. In particular, they possess no means of providing for direct user interaction.

A central monitoring station can interrogate each of the remote monitors and present the information as if it had been gathered locally. The communication with the remote devices may be in band, using the same network that is being monitored, or out of band, using an alternative route.

The central monitoring station, in addition to being able to act as if it were connected to a single monitor at another point of the network, will be able to summarise data gathered from all of the remote devices. In this way, the user can gain an overall view of how the network is operating.

8.4.7.2 *Network management*

More and more devices are becoming available with support for one of the network management protocols, such as SNMP (Simple Network Management Protocol). An increasing number of networks have a central management station to gather information from these devices. In such networks, the function of network monitors may be unclear.

Certainly, network management stations will be able to perform detailed analysis of how network devices are behaving by directly interrogating tables maintained by the device. By collating such information for all devices on the network, the management station will gain a detailed view of how the devices on the network are interacting.

However, the data supplied to the management station by network devices is only pertinent to each device, and only relates to how that device has interacted with the network. To gain a complete picture of the behaviour of the network requires access to the functionality provided by a network monitor.

A network monitor will continuously record information about all of the traffic that it sees on the network, including erroneous packets. Furthermore, the monitor can independently collect data about how the various network devices interact, forming the network's perspective of the communication patterns.

Remote monitoring devices, connected to all of the network segments, will provide information to the management station to complement that provided by the other network devices. In this way, the management station will be able to form a complete picture of how the network is operating.

8.5 ISDN test equipment

This section gives an overview to the testing requirements for ISDN, and the test equipment associated with carrying out such testing.

The structure of ISDN, including that of the interfaces of ISDN are examined, determining the types of tests that can be performed. The testing of ISDN interfaces is compared to that of traditional telephony testing and the differences and similarities are summarised.

Testing of ISDN is also examined for the following key areas:

1.   Physical testing.
2.   Transmission testing.
3.   Protocol testing.

8.5.1 Integrated Services Digital Network

The Integrated Services Digital Network is one evolving from a telephony Integrated Digital Network (IDN) that provides end-to-end digital connectivity to support a range of services, including voice and non-voice services, to which users have access by a limited set of standard multi-purpose interfaces. Two interfaces are defined by ITU-T for ISDN, the Basic Rate Access (BRA) (see Figure 8.13) and the Primary Rate Access (PRA) (see Figure 8.14).

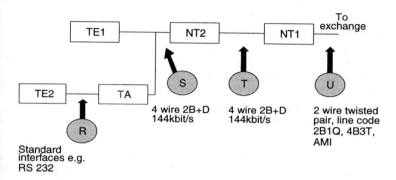

Figure 8.13 ISDN Basic Rate Access

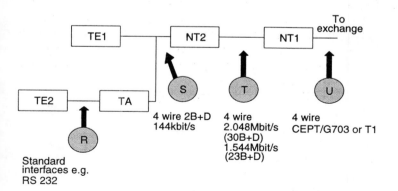

Figure 8.14 ISDN Primary Rate Access

8.5.1.1 *The interfaces*

The structure of ISDN is such that the two ISDN interfaces, the BRA and the PRA, are used for customer access; it is therefore apparent that the two interfaces are the most commonly tested component in ISDN (see Figure 8.15).

The two ISDN interfaces BRA and PRA are well defined by the ITU-T, a branch of the United Nations International Telecommunications Union. ISDN as defined by the ITU-T however is not just restricted to the interfaces but is defined as being a collection of components and functions: access types, devices, protocols and interfaces. Testing of ISDN is therefore not restricted to the interfaces of ISDN but encompasses the protocols and functions of the devices.

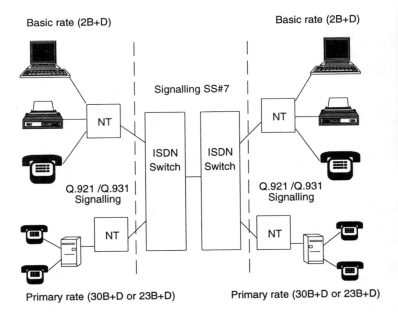

Figure 8.15   The Integrated Services Digital Network

8.5.1.2 *ISDN components*

The channel is the basic unit of service within ISDN, and is a fundamental component in its testing. The Basic and Primary rate interfaces are made up by a number of these channels. Three types of basic channel are defined, Bearer channels (B), Delta channels (D) and High capacity channels (H). A B channel is a 64kbit/s unit of clear digital bandwidth, based on the data rate required to carry one digitised voice conversation. B channels can carry any type of digital information (voice, data or video). A D channel is a signalling channel that carries the information needed to set up and tear down switched connections for the relevant B channels. Connections set up by the D channel are normally B channels that are within the same physical connection as the D channel, although in the case of Signalling System Number 7 this is not always the case.

The Basic Rate Interface is made up of two 64kbit/s B channels and a 16kbit/s D channel and is often referred to as 2B+D and is a worldwide standard. The Primary Rate Interface has two versions, one made up of 30 64kbit/s B channels and a 64kbit/s D channel (30B+D) that is found in Europe, Africa and South America and one made up of 23 64kbit/s B channels and a 16kbit/s D channel (23B+D) that is found in the USA, Japan and Canada.

8.5.2 ISDN testing compared

The Basic Rate Access is a new access method defined by ITU-T for ISDN and is based on the twisted copper pair used for the existing analogue telephone circuits. The Primary Rate Access is already used for transmission and was initially deployed in inter-local exchange networking for PCM systems.

Testing procedures for Primary Rate circuits already exist, although the testing methods used are normally restricted to physical and transmission and framing tests. Because ISDN makes use of the existing G.704 framing structure of the Primary Rate circuits the only extra requirement for ISDN testing is that of the signalling protocol that is carried in the D channel.

The testing of ISDN Basic Rate circuits has no historical precedence but yet can be split into three distinct categories as per the Primary Rate circuits and other non-ISDN circuits, as follows:

1. Physical testing, the testing of the physical parameters of the media used to carry the signals for the appropriate interface. These tests would normally be impedance, continuity, jitter, signal balance and electrical loading.
2. Transmission testing, the transmission test being designed to test the transmission capabilities of the physical media as well as the framing of the signal for the particular service. These tests normally check for errors on a transmitted signal, as well as checking for errors in framing.
3. Protocol testing, the protocol tests being used to check the logical flow of messages and information according to the rules of the protocols in use on the interface. These tests can operate in a functional and non-functional manner.

8.5.3 Different levels of test equipment

A wide variety of test equipment is currently available for ISDN, but the design of ISDN test equipment is still evolving. Most test equipment available for ISDN to date can be categorised by price and functionality.

The test products for ISDN have traditionally been split by testing capability such as protocol testers, physical line testers and transmission testers.

The fragmentation of ISDN testing in this manner suits the R&D laboratories where testing can be easily split into these disciplines. However for those who have to install and commission ISDN this methodology is both cumbersome and expensive.

A new generation of ISDN tester is now becoming available that combines elements of all three areas into a simple to use functional tester that can prove to be highly cost effective. Dedicated testers however still have their place to play in ISDN testing, as they can perform far more complex and detailed tests that cannot be achieved with the combinational simple testers.

8.5.4 Testing philosophies

8.5.4.1 *The effect of maturity*

The types of test which are carried out on transmission installations, and the ways in which the test equipment is connected, depend on the maturity of the service transmitted, as illustrated in Figure 8.16. In development, conformance with specification is of prime importance.

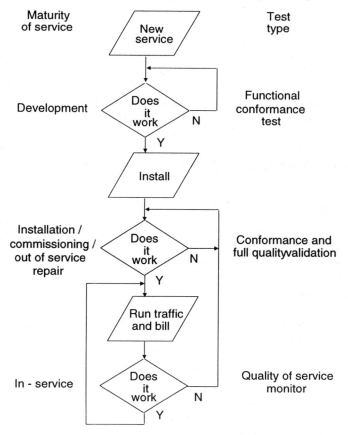

Figure 8.16   Type of test depends on stage of maturity

In installation and commissioning, transmission quality begins to play an important part, and in maintenance work, the specification is assumed, and long term performance is the issue. Therefore, as a particular installation or service matures, the trend is from conformance testing to transmission quality testing. Before the 1990s, ISDN was largely a developing technology, but as more real installations come into service, commissioning and maintenance performance testing is rapidly expanding.

8.5.4.2 *Transmission test connection methods*

A functional test of each transmission component, out of service, can prove the integrity of the component while reducing the risk of damage or impairment to the network due to the connection of faulty equipment. Tests are made in order to establish conformance to specification, in terms of correctly generated signals and the ability to receive, and respond correctly to, error free and errored data. A terminal equipment (TE), for example, may be tested by connecting it to a simulated network, and network terminating units (NTs), by connecting them between a simulated terminal and a simulated network.

A loop test through the network, with loops at strategic points to identify problem areas, or an end to end test through the network, verifies conformance and quality, and can be achieved without taking the equipment out of service. Full quality of service testing to ITU-T Recommendation G.821 involves the recording of periods of performance, within specified error ratio bands, for one month. This is normally only practical at the installation and commissioning phase.

8.5.5 ISDN Basic Rate transmission testing

8.5.5.1 *Basic Rate structure*

The ISDN Basic Rate signal is a time division multiplexed composite of two 64kbit/s channels, known as B channels, plus one 16kbit/s control channel, known as the D channel. Basic Rate transmission is used to connect subscribers to local exchanges, where ISDN line cards or ISDN multiplexers convert the basic rate for transmission over the network. The purpose of Basic Rate testing is to establish the quality of the transmission over the subscriber loop. This is achieved in three phases:

1.   Testing of the physical connection.
2.   Establishment of a call.
3.   Data or speech (voice) transmission testing.

8.5.5.2 *Basic Rate physical line tests*

The first step in Basic Rate testing is to establish the integrity of the physical connection between the subscriber's S interface, via the Network Terminator, to the exchange, or simply the U interface connection between the Network Terminator and the exchange.

The following physical parameters can be measured:

1.   Correct wiring polarity of the pairs, presence of out of specification hazardous voltages, and insulation resistance.
2.   Presence of phantom power, which is provided by the network as a common mode potential between the two pairs of the S interface. The level and polarity of this voltage can be measured.
3.   Presence of, and accuracy of, the clock which is provided by the network.
4.   Indication and manipulation of the information states by which the physical communication is set up.
5.   Impedance and insertion loss of the line.
6.   The relationship of the longitudinal balance of the circuit to the frequency of transmitted signals, for manual or automatic comparison with the limits specified by ITU-T I.430.
7.   The shape, balance, delay and jitter of transmitted pulses.

8.5.5.3 *Basic Rate test call set up*

In order to carry out transmission tests, a call has first to be established, either to a remote tester or to the other channel of the calling tester. If a speech call transmission test is required, the call has to be to another tester or ISDN telephone, because it is not permissible to have two simultaneous speech calls on one instrument. In the case of data calls, the following logical call connection schemes are possible:

1. One channel (B1 say) of a tester transmits, via the network, to the other channel of the same tester (B2), and B2 transmits, via the network, to B1, performing two full duplex tests using the full bandwidth of one Basic Rate circuit, as shown in Figure 8.17.

2. One channel (e.g. B1) of the tester transmits, via the network, to the other channel (B2) of the same tester, which loops the connection and retransmits, via the network, back to B1, performing one full duplex test using the full bandwidth of one Basic Rate circuit.

3. One channel (e.g. B1) of one tester transmits, via the network, to one channel (B2) of another tester, and B2 transmits to the

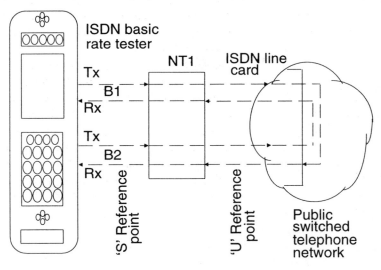

Figure 8.17 Logical connections for ISDN Basic Rate subscriber loop testing

first tester's B1 channel, performing a full duplex test using half the bandwidth of each of two Basic Rate circuits. The other half of the bandwidth can be simultaneously tested by setting up a similar data call or a voice call, for crosstalk testing or for supervisory communication between the two tester operators.

4. One channel of a tester transmits to the exchange which, by the sending of a special protocol command, is instructed to loop the connection back to the calling channel, performing a full duplex test using half the bandwidth of one Basic Rate circuit. The other half of the bandwidth can be simultaneously tested by setting up a similar data call, a data call to another circuit, or a voice call.

8.5.5.4 *Basic rate transmission tests*

Having achieved a successful call set up as above, the logical path established can be tested for transmission quality. For data calls this normally entails the sending of a pseudo-random binary sequence and the checking of a similar received sequence for errors.

The results measured can range from a simple count of bit errors and bits received, with a calculated Bit Error Ratio Test (BERT), to a full set of G.821 measurements, including errored and severely errored seconds, degraded minutes, and periods of unavailable time.

The duration of the test can range from a few seconds, sufficient to ensure that the call has been successfully established and data can be transferred, to many days for the gathering of G.821 statistics. These relate to the long term quality performance of the connection, and may be displayed in the form of histograms to assist in identifying periods of degraded service.

By setting up two simultaneous test calls, an assessment of crosstalk interference between channels can be made, either by using a voice call in one channel which may be degraded by a data call in the other, or by using two data calls which may mutually interfere.

In the case of voice calls set up, analogue measurements may be made by sending calibrated tones and measuring received level and frequency, to determine path loss and frequency response, signal to noise ratio etc.

8.5.6 ISDN Primary Rate transmission testing

8.5.6.1 *Primary Rate structure*

The 2Mbit/s framing structure defined by the ITU-T recommendation G.704 is the backbone of primary rate ISDN. It is a composite of 64kbit/s Basic Rate signals, and is itself a building block for the higher order multiplexed rates. The 64kbit/s signals, which can be data or pulse code modulated telephone channels, are each allocated a timeslot within the frame structure. Each frame consists of 32 time division multiplexed timeslots each containing 8 bits of data from one channel, with the data from each channel being identified by its position in the frame.

The first timeslot of each frame (timeslot 0) is used for frame synchronisation and frame supervisory functions, while timeslot 16 can be used for a variety of signalling methods. In ISDN, Common Channel Signalling (CCS) is used, and timeslot 16 carries supervisory signals controlling the status of the calls occupying the remaining timeslots, by the use of special protocols. Error detection can be achieved optionally by the use of a Cyclic Redundancy Check (CRC4), which groups 8 frames into sub-multiframes and 2 sub-multiframes into multiframes.

Clocks for the generation of frames and data are always locked to the master clock of the network. Terminal equipment therefore uses the clock recovered from the received signal to generate the frames and to produce 64kbit/s channel clocks to the tributaries.

Timeslot 0 of each frame is reserved for frame alignment or synchronisation. Alternate frames contain the Frame Alignment Signal (FAS) and the Not Frame Alignment Signal (NFAS). Bits 2 to 8 of the FAS, and bit 2 of the NFAS, are fixed and define frame synchronisation. Bit 3 of the NFAS is used to indicate remote end loss of synchronisation, and bits 4 to 8 are used for application specific signalling functions. Bit 1 of the FAS and NFAS is disregarded for the purposes of frame synchronisation, but can be used for CRC4 operation. Frame synchronisation occurs when 3 consecutive correct FAS (bits 2 to 8), and 3 corresponding correct NFAS (bit 1), are received, and is considered lost when 3 consecutive errored FAS are received.

The integrity of the data contained in the frames can be checked using a CRC4 in bit 1 of the FAS and NFAS. Multiframes are formed of two sub-multiframes, each of 8 frames. Bit 1 of each NFAS in the first sub-multiframe is set to the sequence 0010, and in the second sub-multiframe to 11XX, where X bits are 'don't care' as far as multiframe alignment is concerned, and are used to signal remote CRC errors. The four FAS bit 1s of each sub-multiframe form a four bit word corresponding to the CRC of the data in the preceding sub-multiframe. An error is detected when the received CRC word does not correspond to one locally calculated on the received data.

8.5.6.2 *Out of service Primary Rate tests*

The simplest method of out of service testing is a simple full bandwidth Bit Error Ratio Test (BERT) using, typically, a long pseudorandom pattern at 2.048Mbit/s, with no framing, to qualify the performance of transmission media. G.821 performance statistics can be applied at the primary rate, even though they are intended for use at 64kbit/s, provided that the system can be out of service for long enough to collect valid results. Time related events, or quality degradation periods, can be isolated by using time stamped stored or printed reports, and result histograms.

Alternatively the frames, with or without CRC4, can be generated by the tester for transmission to terminal, multiplexing or network equipment. In this case the tester can be set to corrupt the alignment signals in a pre-defined manner, in order to check the ability of the equipment to detect and recover from sync loss, according to the correct criteria. Testers can be set to replace the normal frame and multiframe alignment signal by programmable words, to exercise the facilities controlled by each word bit, for example distant alarm. At the same time a selection of the data fields (timeslots 1 to 15 and 17 to 31) can be filled with a pseudo-random sequence, performing a

BERT test to another similar tester, and CRC4 can be generated and checked to test CRC performance.

By substituting test equipment for network elements, or by using testers connected to individual transmission equipments in isolation, problems of incompatibility or specification interpretation can be resolved. The electrical characteristics of the transmission or terminal equipment, its characteristic impedance, pulse shape and encoding can be measured. When testing into the network, the transmitter of the tester is set to use, and to measure the frequency and jitter of, the clock recovered from the received signal. When testing terminal equipment, the tester has to look like the network, so it uses its own crystal controlled clock to generate the framed signal. The different connection methods are illustrated in Figure 8.18.

8.5.6.3 *In service Primary Rate tests*

In service testing is ideally carried out unobtrusively with minimum disruption to the traffic. Its objective is to assess the quality of the transmission and, where defects are found, to pinpoint the source of the problem.

In service testing can monitor a live network signal for correct frame alignment, condition of the distant alarm signals, CRC4 and signalling protocols. By regular monitoring of an installation, potential trouble can be spotted before it gets too serious. Connection to the network is normally made at a protected high impedance monitoring point, or by a bridge through the tester interface.

Intermittent, or time related, faults can be identified, using a tester with a printer facility to produce time stamped reports in response to error conditions. By comparing physical layer parameters, for example bipolar errors (infringements of the bipolar encoding scheme), with supervisory functions such as long term CRC4 performance, it is possible to differentiate between transmission and terminal equipment faults. It is also possible to intercept the frames, and either extract single, or multiple, timeslots for analysis, or to drop out timeslots and replace them with data inserted from a tester source. In this way selected channels of a live system can be tested without

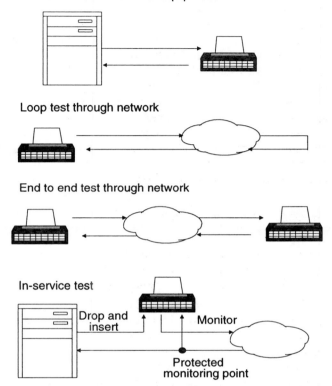

Figure 8.18 Connections for ISDN Primary Rate testing

disturbing the remaining channels, thereby proving the quality of capacity before it is brought into service.

8.5.7 Protocol testing

The level of testing that covers layers 2 and 3 of the OSI stack is commonly known as protocol testing. Protocol testing in ISDN is linked to the testing of the 'D' channel signalling protocol. Protocol testing at layers 2 and 3 as well as the layers above can be split into a number of different areas such as conformance testing, performance testing, interoperability testing and troubleshooting.

Protocol testing is normally carried out by dedicated protocol analysers with the appropriate ISDN interfaces fitted, although protocol analysers based on cards for use in PCs are becoming more popular. Some ISDN testers such as those that set up a path on Basic Rate connections, and then perform a transmission test, also have protocol support. This support however is only intended to perform a functional test and does not usually include the ability to decode or display protocol events.

8.5.7.1 *Interoperability testing*

Interoperability testing is designed to prove whether two ISDN devices or services can and will work together to specification. Any ISDN product has to be tested for interoperability with any other ISDN product that it may have to communicate with. A maxim in interoperability testing is that the commutative law does not apply. In other words, if A interoperates with B and B interoperates with C, A does not necessarily interoperate with C. ISDN products must be tested for interoperability and conformance at every major revision.

8.5.7.2 *Conformance testing*

Conformance tests are usually run automatically in a long series of short, very specific tests with pass/fail results provided along the way. Many ISDN providers, such as telecommunication ministries, require conformance testing before a given product or service can be operated on their networks; a given product or service is usually only ever tested once for conformance.

In Europe the Conference of European Post and Telecommunications Administrations (CEPT) has produced specifications collectively known as NETs (Norme Europeene de Telecommunications) covering various areas to promote type approval across Europe. NET3 covers the Basic Rate Access and NET5 the Primary Rate Access. Many manufacturers of protocol analysers have application programs available that allow them to carry out conformance tests for the NETs and other conformance specifications.

8.5.7.3 *Performance testing*

Performance testing requires the gathering and display of statistics on the numbers of protocol units (frames, packets, messages and so on) transmitted and received over a period of time between devices. The goal is to discover deviations from normal operation or from a pre-defined specification, that point to underlying problems in the terminal or switching equipment or in the operation of the protocols themselves.

For ISDN, degrading performance of the D channel protocols, such as longer set up times or a high number of unsuccessful calls, can indicate a number of problems ranging from error at the terminal, to traffic overloading on the ISDN network. Monitoring of the B channels can also indicate problems on the D channel, for example erratic traffic on the B channel may point to problems on the D channel signalling protocol. Performance testing can uncover day to day operating problems that might otherwise pass interoperability testing.

8.5.7.4 *Protocol troubleshooting*

If a problem is discovered protocol troubleshooting often finds the cause of the problem. ISDN defines new ways of performing routine tasks such as making a phone call. In order to trace the flow of protocol events, for a call being placed, a protocol analyser is often needed. Protocol analysers interpret protocol events by displaying to the user an 'English' breakdown of the protocol events that have occurred on the line (see Figure 8.19). The events displayed on the screen are usually marked with some form of identification indicating which device the message was received from. In addition each message will have a timestamp associated with it so that timing measurements or discrepancies can be determined.

ISDN also adds a new layer of complexity to protocol testing in that subtle effects of D channel call set up procedure can affect the

```
C SAPI=0 (CCP) TEI=66              Time: 12.30:00:1200
I 86 98 24
Q921: 00 85 AC C4
       PD=08 UCC REF=018
       M 05 SETUP
       I 04 Bearer Capability              Len=2
          58 Coding Standard               CCITT
             Transfer Capability           Unrestricted
          90 Transfer Mode                 Circuit
             Transfer Rate                 64Kbit/s
       I 18 Channel Identification         Len=1
             Interface                     Implicity Identified
          8A Interface Type                Basic
             Indicated Channel Exclusive   Yes
             Channel Indicator             Not D-Channel
             Channel Selection             B2
       I 70 Called Party Number            L=11
          80 Type                          Unknown
             Numbering Plan                Unknown
             Address Digits                0048885030
Q931: 08 01 18 03 04 02 88 90 18 01 8A 70
      0B 80 30 30 34 38 38 38 35 30 33 30
```

Figure 8.19   Typical display of a D Channel protocol from a protocol analyser

protocol events occurring on the B channel. For this reason dual port protocol analysers are very popular in monitoring dual processes simultaneously. In this way the user can simultaneously monitor the protocol events occurring on the same physical line but in different channels, for example the D channel and a B channel.

8.6 Introduction to cellular radio

Mobile telephone systems based on the cellular network concept are in use in most developed countries.

The key to satisfactory operation of these systems is a complex signalling arrangement by means of which a high level of accessibility and good transmission quality are achieved.

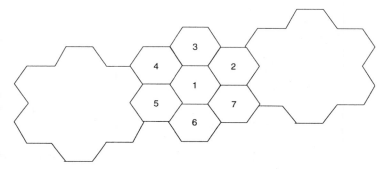

Figure 8.20   A seven cell cluster

Common to all systems is the use of a cellular structure for the optimal re-use of the available frequency channels. There are however significant differences in the signalling techniques and message formats used.

With this approach, each area served by a base station is called a cell, and these cells are arranged to cover the ground in a regular pattern. The service area of each station is roughly circular, but is normally drawn as a hexagon.

All the base stations are linked into a wired network which switches calls to a mobile as it moves about; the cellular arrangement has effectively made the radio link part of the network as short as possible. Figure 8.20 shows a typical 7 cell cluster.

For testing purposes cellular radio systems are divided into two major groups. Those systems which employ digital signalling and analogue speech transmission are generally referred to as analogue cellular systems, and those systems which use both digitised signalling and digitised speech transmission are referred to as digital cellular systems.

8.6.1 Data signalling

The management of the mobile network calls for information exchange between the mobiles and the base stations in each cell or cluster of cells. Among the procedures to be handled in this way we can identify:

1.   Selection of r.f. channels.
2.   Transfer of call numbers.
3.   Transmitter power level control.
4.   Handover of mobile between cells.
5.   Registration and call charging.

Depending on the system being considered, data signalling may take place on permanently allocated channels or on voice channels allocated from time to time as required.

For analogue cellular systems the signalling itself takes the form of a data message using typically fast frequency shift keying (FFSK) or phase shift keying (PSK). Digital networks use methods such as gaussian minimum shift keying (GMSK). Various forms of coding including high redundancy error correcting techniques are in use.

8.7 Analogue cellular test equipment

In addition to all the conventional r.f. and a.f. measurements, test equipment for cellular radio mobiles must also be capable of testing the various signalling procedures.

As a minimum requirement, it must be possible to simulate the base station function to the extent of opening the normal voice channel so that conventional measurements can be performed. It may also be necessary to analyse the actual bit streams of the messages in order to detect single bit errors in the transmitted data.

With a view to simulating the effects of interference in practical systems, the test equipment should also be capable of generating special code sequences, for example, with implanted errors. In the past this was done using discrete instrumentation controlled via computer. Today it is more commonly performed by integrated Radiotelephone Test Sets.

8.7.1 Analogue cellular test set

The cellular radio test set generates and analyses all data signals required to simulate the cellular base station. It must also provide all the facilities required for r.f. and a.f. measurements on the radio itself.

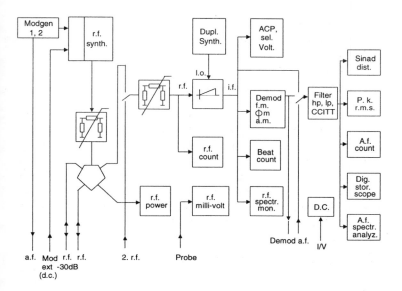

Figure 8.21 Radiotelephone test set block diagram

For example, the Rohde and Schwarz CMTA provides these functions. Special signalling firmware is installed for the common cellular systems. These are AMPS, TACS, Radiocom 2000, NMT450/900 and Network C.

A typical hardware configuration is shown in Figure 8.21. The individual instruments are controlled by a central microprocessor. Further system components may be integrated with the test set as required. These can be controlled by an external computer via the widely used IEEE bus. For example, users may wish to include a programmable power supply or a second signal generator for interference response testing.

8.7.2 Operation of the test set

During the test of the mobile radio all signalling functions (generation and analysis of data telegrams) are handled by the test set which must also make the r.f. and a.f. measurements. There are two main testing modes:

1.   Many mobile radios feature a service mode which may be accessed via the keyboard of the radio. For radios with special test interfaces, the necessary control signals may be generated by the test set using either the RS232C interface or a general purpose I/O interface. In this mode the functions of the radio (transmit, receive, channel, power) can be controlled directly and all the measurements required such as sensitivity, frequency response, distortion, transmitter power, modulation, signal to noise ratio, power consumption can be performed with the tester.

2.   Of much greater interest is the complete system test in which the mobile radio operates as if it were in the cellular network. The test set in this case forms a test system which simulates the base station, permitting calls to be sent from and received at the mobile station in real time via the r.f. connector. Once again the r.f. and a.f. measurements will also be handled by the test set, operated either in the manual mode or under programme control. The test set can also send the telegrams necessary for initiating channel handover or power level switching.

An extensive range of signalling and r.f./a.f. tests must be made as illustrated by the test menus taken from a modern test set, as in Table 8.12.

The table summarises the signalling procedures and measurements required for the three most common analogue cellular standards. A modern cellular radio test set is capable of storing test software for all of these standards plus Radiocom 2000 and C-NET.

8.8 Digital cellular test equipment

With respect to test equipment and methods, the main differences between conventional mobile radio and the new digital radio net-

Table 8.11   Test menus

NMT	AMPS	TACS/ETACS
Call mobile-base	Call mobile-base	Call mobile-base
Call base-mobile	Call base-mobile	Call base-mobile
Channel handover	Channel handover	Channel handover
Roaming	Registration	Registration
Response time	SAT 5.97/6.00/6.03kHz	SAT 5.97/6.00/6.03kHz
Tx power (3 levels)	Tx power (8 levels)	Tx power (8 levels)
Message analysis	Message analysis	Message analysis
Bit error implant	Bit error implant	Bit error implant
Transmitter	Power Frequency accuracy Modulation sensitivity Modulation frequency response Modulation distortion Adjacent-channel power (option)	

works (to which GSM belongs) can be categorised in the following way:

1.   The transmitted information is completely digitised and as-
      signed to time slots. Continuous analogue signals that were
      employed for testing in the past would obviously be out of
      place in digital environments.

2.   Modern digital modulation techniques affect the phase and amplitude of the r.f. carrier continuously over time. Generating digital signals of this kind, or analysing them, is beyond the capabilities of conventional test equipment such as signal generators, modulation analysers and power meters.

In 1992 CEPT established a special working committee called the Groupe Speciale Mobile (GSM) to formulate a new digital cellular standard. This was achieved and in 1992 the GSM (now renamed Global System Mobile) was launched.

8.8.1 Analogue and GSM test methods

The GSM system is one of a range of radio communication systems which use fully digital techniques.
    Other examples are:

1.   Cellular networks: D-AMPS, PCN.
2.   Paging systems: ERMES.
3.   Cordless telephone: CT2, DECT.
4.   Trunking networks.

Some of the techniques in GSM have been used in other systems. For example, military radios may use frequency hopping. Digital speech is widely used in telephony.
    The techniques that are used for GSM, the European digital mobile radio network, require test functions that cannot be handled by conventional equipment. The following section shows the test standards for GSM with special reference to the radio path or physical layer. The essential characteristics that this new generation of test equipment must have will then be derived.
    Table 8.12 compares conventional and GSM measurements.

8.8.1.1 *Time division multiple access (TDMA)*

In the GSM network the digital information is arranged in blocks and transmitted in precisely defined timeslots. An eight timeslot structure

Table 8.12   Comparison of conventional and digital mobile radio measurements

Conventional mobile radio measurements	GSM measurements
Measurement modes	
Continuous parameter settings	Time-limited settings
Continuous measurements	Time referenced measurements
Test tones	Data telegrams
Frequency division multiple access	Time division multiple access/frequency division multiple access
Bandwidth	
R.F. 10–25kHz	R.F. 200kHz plus frequency hopping
A.F. 3kHz	A.F. digital
Available test points on radio	
R.F.	R.F.
A.F.	Digital (no a.f.)
Acoustic	Acoustic
Need for co-ordination of test and measurement functions	
For convenience only	Essential for successful measurements
Signalling: limited, typical accuracy 10ms to 1s	Signalling: critical, accuracy 1μs

is used. Users are allocated a timeslot by the system during which data transfer takes place. The radio network, and hence the radio test equipment, must be capable of being synchronised together.

In order to measure timing parameters the test equipment must use sampling rates which are much faster than the data rate. The r.f. carrier power may be turned off between timeslots in a controlled manner. The test equipment must, therefore, be able to measure the power output over a wide dynamic range.

8.8.1.2 *Frequency hopping*

Frequency hopping is used within the GSM system. Each timeslot of information may be transmitted at a different radio frequency. The test equipment must, therefore, be able to generate and measure frequency hopping signals.

GSM employs a complex speech coder in order to reduce the data rate and hence bandwidth required by the system. The traditional 1kHz audio test tone is not considered a meaningful representation of speech. New test methods employing data sequences have, therefore, been developed.

8.9 The OSI model and GSM

The OSI model is a common method of describing any data transmission system. For GSM applications it is shown in Figure 8.22. A more graphical representation is shown in Figure 8.23.

8.10 The radio path or Physical Layer (Layer 1)

As can be seen from the OSI model Layer 1 contains the channel coding, error protection and interleaving. These processes are designed to ensure that data is transmitted correctly. If minor errors occur the decoder may be able to correct them. The interleaving process ensures that, if a signal is degraded for a short period of time, sequential data is not lost.

The following sections describe the testing of the radio link, the lowest part of Layer 1. The fundamental tools for receiver testing are

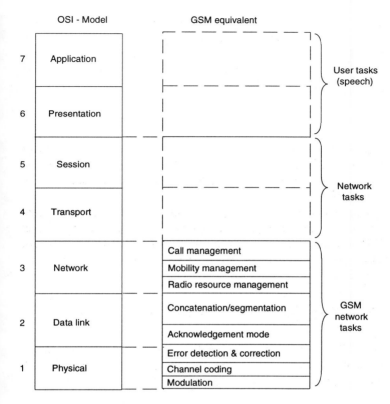

Figure 8.22   The OSI model as applied to GSM

described and the equipment required for transmitter testing is identified.

8.10.1 Receiver measurements

8.10.1.1 *Signal generator requirements*

Signal generators for GSM applications convert a given bit sequence into the corresponding modulated r.f. carrier signal. Conventional

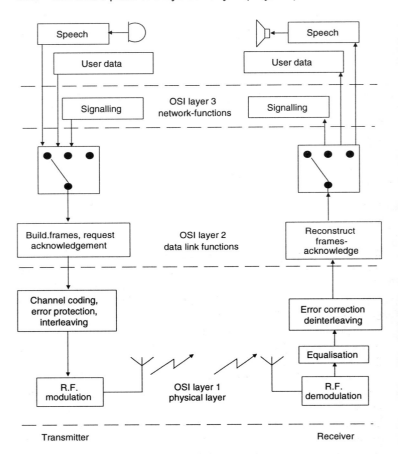

Figure 8.23   Symbolic representation of GSM transmit and receive functions based on the OSI layer model

signal generators are unsuitable for this because there is no direct way of controlling the phase of the carrier. Instead, I/Q modulators will provide this function (Figure 8.24).

As far as the magnitude of the frequency deviation and the stability of the centre frequency (for f.m. d.c. mode) are concerned, signal generators available at present are not completely satisfactory. The

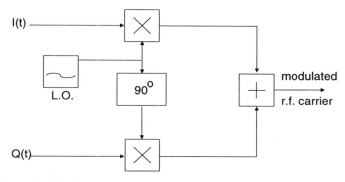

Figure 8.24 Q-I (vector) modulator

few signal generators on the market which have fast enough switching times are unattractive when their price is taken into consideration. Using this analysis as a basis, a short list of required features for a signal generator which would be suitable for GSM applications can be compiled, as in Table 8.14.

The principle of a typical GSM signal generator, such as that used in the Rohde and Schwarz GSM test set CMTA94, is shown in Figure 8.25. Digital signals are modulated by digital signal processing into their in phase (I) and quadrature phase (Q) components. These digital signals are then converted to analogue and modulated into the 900MHz frequency band using a frequency hopping local oscillator. The data is then transmitted in bursts of r.f. power with the amplitude profile of the bursts being shaped as specified by GSM. A fading simulator may be added at the output stage.

Fast digital signal processors are used to condition the (analogue) I and Q modulation signals. These processors replace classic 'analogue' functions such as filtering or integration by equivalent digital processes which increase precision and stability, as a function of time and temperature (Figure 8.26).

As the I/Q modulator itself is still analogue, this circuit largely determines the accuracy of the signal generator. In addition to the usual quality criteria for signal generators, three more must now be considered as in Figure 8.27.

Table 8.13   A signal generator for in band GSM measurements

Parameter	Value
R.F. carrier frequency range	890–960MHz
Frequency resolution	< 200kHz
Frequency switching speed	< 577µs (1 timeslot) to within < 4° of final phase
Frequency uncertainty	$\leq 50 \times 10^{-9}$
Output level range	–115 to 0dBm
Level uncertainty	< 0.5dB
Amplitude response	Pulse modulation with rise and fall times of ≈ 20µs
Modulation	Gaussian minimum shift keying (GMSK)
Modulation data rate	270kbit/s
Spectral purity,	
Phase noise	< 1°rms <4°pk measured in 1–100kHz band
Spurious signals	< –50dBc
Fading	Internal or external

If excessive imbalances are present they can be clearly seen in the generator output spectrum and may be detected as errors in the receiver under test.

8.10.1.2 *Simulation of radio channel*

The simulation of multipath reception (fading simulation) is becoming more and more important for digital radio systems. Fading simulators for GSM tests must be capable of electronically simulating the

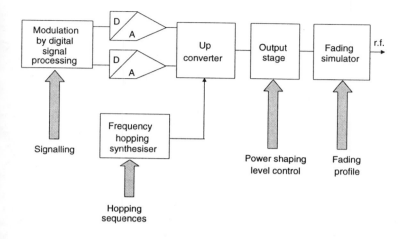

Figure 8.25 Principle of a typical signal generator

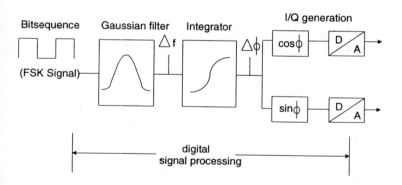

Figure 8.26 Use of digital signal processing

propagation conditions over various types of terrain. The effects of the speed of the vehicle must also be built into the simulation model.

The block diagram of Figure 8.28 shows the principle behind a fading simulator:

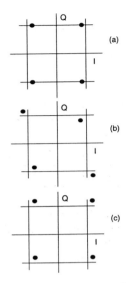

Figure 8.27 Some considerations for signal generators: (a) I/Q imbalance due to unequal gains in the two modulation paths; (b) skew since phase difference between the carriers is not 90°; (c) residual carrier components i.e. residual unmodulated carrier in the output signal

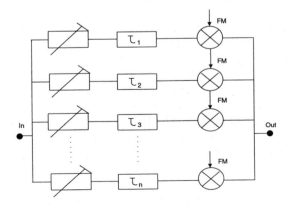

Figure 8.28 Principle of a fading simulator

Table 8.14   Fading simulator test requirements

Designation (km/h)	Speed (km/h)			
	3	*50*	*100*	*250*
Rural area (RA)				*
Hilly terrain (HT)			*	
Typical urban (TU)	*	*		
Equaliser test profile (EQ)				

1. The signal is split and fed along several paths.
2. Each path contains simulated loss, delay and spurious modulation (Doppler effect).
3. The signal is recombined.

Typical fading simulator requirements for GSM receiver tests are given in Table 8.14.

8.10.1.3 *Sensitivity measurements*

The sensitivity of the receiver is a crucial GSM parameter, as it is for other types of radio system. As measurements directly after the demodulator are, in general, not possible and would anyway give different results for different designs, GSM test methods which do not involve opening the radio set have been defined. The loop back method, in effect, makes the radio part of the test set up. If the decoder in the receiver detects an errored telegram (wrong parity), this fact is reported to the test set by the radio's own transmitter. This is indicated by the bad frame indication bit (BFI) in the transmit telegram, bit 58 acting as the BFI flag. This gives rise to three new test parameters which, depending on application, can be used as a measure of transmission quality (Figure 8.29).

1. BER; bit error rate, number of bad bits found in the transmission as a whole.

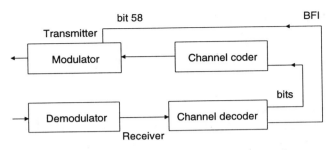

Figure 8.29   Recognising frame errors in the GSM mobile

2.   FER; frame erasure rate, number of bad frames.
3.   RBER; residual bit error rate, BER for 'good' frames.

As these measurements are carried out on the logical GSM channels (e.g. traffic channel, control channel), very long measurement times may result under certain circumstances because of the various data rates and the required BER values.

8.10.1.4 *Additional receiver measurements*

The quality criteria (BER, FER, RBER) described earlier replace the parameters S/N and SINAD in analogue radio systems. With regard to the reception quality, other well known receiver measurements are also carried out, such as co-channel rejection, adjacent channel rejection, blocking and spurious responses to 12.75GHz. In most cases, the interfering signal generator has to meet stringent spectral purity requirements. Depending on the test method, unmodulated or GSM modulated, static or frequency hopping interference generators are required.

.With adjacent channel measurements, a special requirement has to be taken into account. Because TDMA is used, there are adjacent channels in both the frequency domain and the time domain. Because of this, the expression 'adjacent timeslot rejection' has been introduced. This measurement is carried out implicitly by defining an appropriate level for the adjacent timeslots when sensitivity measurements are carried out.

8.10.2 Transmitter measurements

8.10.2.1 *Signal analyser requirements*

Conventional power meters and modulation analysers can only handle settled (static) test signals. This means they cannot be used to analyse signal packets (TDMA time slots). Even the latest display units for analysing digitally modulated signals (constellation analysers) have a limited use.

A precise analysis of dynamic behaviour can only be obtained by fast sampling of the r.f. signal or the corresponding I/Q signals (Figure 8.30). If the samples are stored in a memory of sufficient size, they can be post processed for comprehensive and flexible analysis of the transmitter, as shown in the GSM transmitter measurement flowchart of Figure 8.31.

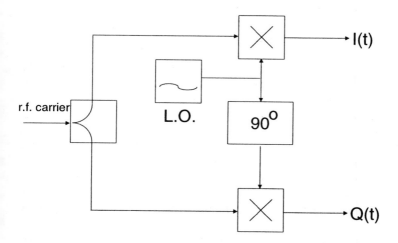

Figure 8.30 I-Q vector demodulator

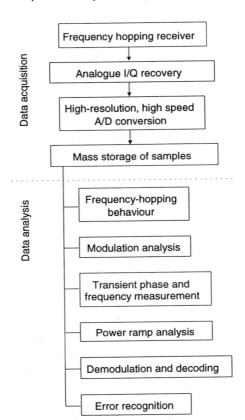

Figure 8.31   GSM transmitter measurement flowchart

8.10.2.2   *Principle of the signal analyser*

R.F. signals at the input of the analyser, shown in Figure 8.32, are attenuated to the correct level for the down converter. The signals are down converted to an i.f. frequency using a frequency hopping synthesiser. The signal is then divided into its in phase (I) and quadrature phase (Q) components. These baseband signals are digitised and stored for post processing.

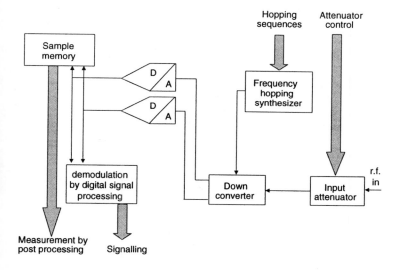

Figure 8.32 Principle of the signal analyser

8.10.2.3 *In channel measurements on transmitters*

Some of the most important measurements on transmitters using digital modulation are:

1.   Power levels, down to 13dBm for the mobile station.
2.   Power ramp up for ramp down using stipulated tolerance mask.
3.   Phase noise, measured as the deviation from the ideal phase trajectory.
4.   Frequency errors, also derived from phase data.

8.10.2.4 *Measuring spectral components*

The spectral components near the carrier are specified by the mask shown in Figure 8.33. The Tx signal is not continuous because of the TDMA used so that the measurement cannot be made by simply

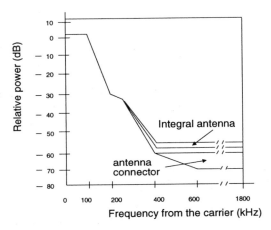

Figure 8.33   Mask used for measurement of spectral components

connecting up a spectrum analyser. This difficulty can be overcome by triggering the spectrum analyser in synchronism with the TDMA frames and displaying the results in zero-span mode. Further spectrum analyser settings are given in the specifications, a distinction being made between:

1. Measurements in the modulated section of the burst (spectrum due to modulation); resolution BW = 30kHz, video BW = 30kHz average mode.

2. Measurements at the edges of the burst (spectrum due to switching); resolution BW = 30kHz, video BW = 100kHz max-hold mode.

Spurious transmissions up to 12.75GHz must also be checked.

8.10.3 Simulation and analysis of Layer 1 coding

As the error free transmission of bits is a prime requirement, the binary data must undergo a certain amount of coding at this, the lowest level of the data transmission chain. In the GSM Specifications, these functions form part of the channel coding. The industry is attempting to implement the coding and decoding functions using VLSI semiconductors. However, great caution must be exercised when ICs of this kind are used in test equipment. If precise information about the error correction facilities of a mobile phone is required, for type acceptance for example, the test set must have facilities for injecting and detecting errors at different layers. Such facilities, however, cannot be realised, as VLSI circuits do not have the required interfaces.

When precise simulations and analyses are required, e.g. during development or for approval testing, it must be possible to access all levels of signalling.

By using the latest fast digital signal processors (DSP), test sets will be able to carry out real time simulations of GSM protocols on the one hand and perform test functions such as error injection, logging etc. on the other.

8.11 Data Link Layer (Layer 2)

The second layer of the OSI model deals with the correct transmission of well defined data blocks or telegrams. The trigger and synchronisation facilities are the most important features of test equipment for dealing at this layer. Special attention must be paid to skew problems which arise when a number of instruments are triggered externally. To solve problems of this kind at an acceptable outlay, it is necessary to design multifunction test equipment which is controlled via a common trigger.

Layer 2 of GSM is indeed a highly intelligent processor unit which must make a large number of decisions in real time. Equipment that can test these functions satisfactorily also requires a high degree of built in intelligence and automatic real time behaviour. Here, too, modern processors can provide a suitable solution. To simulate situations where errors occur, both layer 2 'error model' which can be modified by the user and an automatic model of correct behaviour are required.

8.12 Network Layer (Layer 3)

The network level of the OSI model also specifies an intelligent exchange of datagrams between communicating parties. Each datagram handshake causes the link to go into an appropriate well defined state. These states are the basis for handling the communication service such as speech, video or data transmissions.

In this context, one encounters terminology that is familiar from analogue cellular radio networks:

1. Registration.
2. Call set up by the mobile subscriber.
3. Call set up by the fixed network subscriber.
4. Call clear down.
5. Channel changeover within cell or to another cell.
6. Power control levels.
7. Queue mode.

Test sets require an enormous amount of memory to completely handle these processes as it is not just a question of simulation; these processes have to be monitored, and under certain circumstances logged, so that any errors can be analysed at a later date.

8.13 A.F. and speech codec measurements

The test procedures for acceptance testing make a distinction between a.f. measurements and r.f. measurements. The result is a new kind of measurement procedure, requiring acoustic and digital interfaces. It seems very likely that new definitions will emerge for testing the overall function of the transmit and receive path (r.f./acoustics). This kind of measurement will play an important role in the maintenance and repair of telephone handsets, and is illustrated in Figures 8.34 and 8.35.

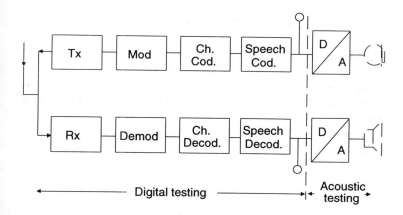

Figure 8.34 Division of measurements into r.f. (digital) and audio (acoustic)

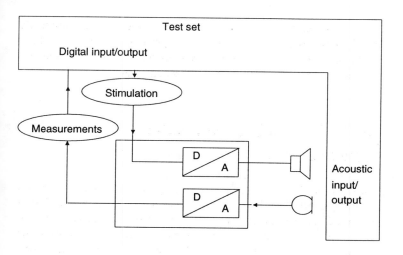

Figure 8.35 A.F. /acoustic measurements (GSM)

8.14 Test set up configurations

The set up for GSM will be configured so as to permit both data analysis (protocol checks, error rates etc.) and analogue measurements. As the measurements specified by GSM are nearly always made on closed radio sets, there is a need for test procedures which can supply information about the behaviour of the set using the signals that are available.

8.14.1 Mobile station measurements

The test set up for mobile station type approval measurements is fundamentally different from conventional (analogue) test set up, as shown in Figures 8.36 and 8.37. Because of the loop back technique

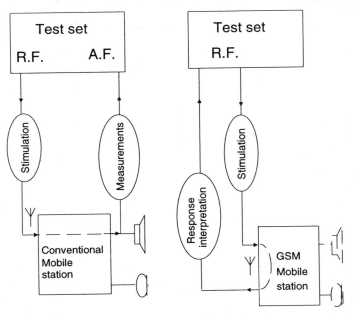

Figure 8.36 Comparison between conventional mobile and GSM measurements set up for receiver

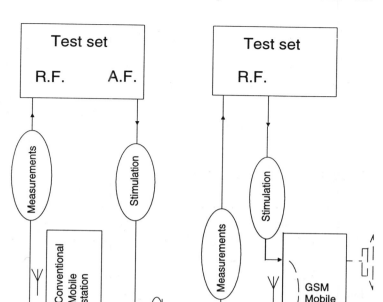

Figure 8.37   Comparison between conventional and GSM measurement set up for transmitter

used, the test set has to rely exclusively on the r.f. port without accessing the a.f. signals. The built in intelligence of the test set largely determines whether only r.f. parameters will be measured or the signalling behaviour of the mobile station will also be checked.

By using the service functions provided by the radio, it is possible to create simple test set ups which do not include expensive simulators. A controller sets the radio and remote controls the test set via a suitable interface, usually serial, as illustrated in Figure 8.38. When large batches are being manufactured, the controller also makes it possible to hook up the test system via a computer network to the factory control by means of standard interfaces such as Ethernet.

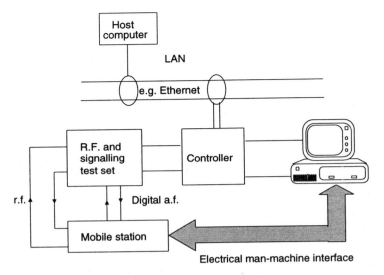

Figure 8.38 Configuration of a test set for r.f. signalling and digital audio measurements on GSM mobiles

8.14.2 Base stations

Because of the widespread use of modular techniques, the distinction between transmitter and receiver measurements is more marked in the base station than in the mobile station. To perform measurements on the modules, further interfaces in addition to the r.f. interface must be defined. After the r.f. interface, the first interface to be explicitly defined by the GSM is the Y/Y level, as in Figure 8.39.

Digital test signals can be fed in or tapped at these interfaces to check the functions of the transmitter and receiver at the physical layer (layer 1). Also, when base stations are being tested, base station functions can usually be controlled automatically by a computer so that the necessary test conditions are established.

If the complete base station is to be tested, the test set has to simulate a mobile station. This places great demands on the test set as far as real time characteristics and signalling facilities are concerned.

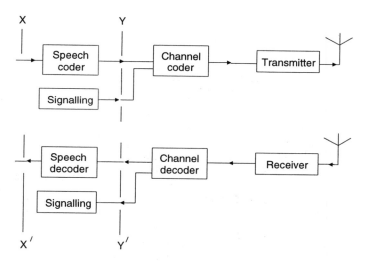

Figure 8.39 Internal interfaces of GSM basic station

As part of the network infrastructure, the base station is linked up with other network components via well defined interfaces. When tests are carried out using a simulated mobile station, it is assumed that these network interfaces are functioning correctly, or can be simulated by appropriate test signals. This is because the base stations exhibit transparent behaviour in many cases, for example are not able to support the protocols of the r.f. interfaces themselves.

8.15 References

Alexander, C. (1992) SONET testing — today and tomorrow, *TE&M*, 1 March.

Carolan, W. (1994) Layered approach eases B-ISDN testing, *Electronic Design*, 27 June.

Fields, J. (1995) ISDN moves testing into the networking domain, *Test & Measurement World*, April.

Flaherty, J.M. (1994) Fibre-optic system testing, *Test & Measurement World*, March.

Graham, G. (1993) When it comes to testing, less is more, *TE&M*, 1 July.

Hillman, A. (1994) Sonet test sets adapt to evolving standards with built-in measures, *Lightwave*, October.

Krucker, M. (1994) GSM testing between Phase 1 and Phase 2, *Mobile Europe*, December.

Lum, M. (1993) How to check for SDH compliance, *TEST*, May.

Lum, M. (1995) Making 'mid-fibre meet' a reality, *Communications International*, June.

Luttich, F. and Klier, J. (1989) Signal generators SMGU and SMHU — nothing but the best, *News from Rohde & Schwarz*, No. 126.

Maucksch, T. (1990) GSM test set CMTA94 for the European digital mobile radio network, *News from Rohde & Schwarz*, No. 129, pp. 4–7.

Novellino, J. (1994) Communications test presents a learning curve, *Electronic Design*, 27 June.

Owen, D. (1994) Fading and multipath simulation and testing, *Electronic Product Design*, May.

Reading, I. (1995) Developing an automated repair environment for GSM mobiles, *Mobile Europe*, April.

Rice, R. (1994) Testing PDH traffic on SDH networks, *Communications International*, November.

Romanchik, D. (1994) Cable testers offer more features, *Test & Measurement World*, March.

Rosar, W. (1994) Test approaches to GSM, *Telecommunications*, August.

Ruiu, D. (1994) Testing ATM systems, *IEEE Spectrum*, June.

Russell, J. (1994) ISDN testing: the next phase, *Telecommunications*, August.

Shanaham, H. (1995) Top ten measurements for GSM base stations, *Mobile and Cellular*, July.

Snodgrass, I. (1994) The testing challenges of DECT, *Mobile Europe*, May.

Sonnde, G. and Leutiger, M. (1994) Quality criteria for digital networks, *Electronic Product Design*, May.

Tomita, N. et al. (1994) Design and performance of a novel automatic fibre line testing system with OTDR for optical subscriber loops, *IEEE Journal of Lightwave Technology*, May.

Trezise, M. (1995) GSM mobile station testing, *Mobile and Cellular*, July.

9. Acronyms

Every discipline has its own 'language' and this is especially true of telecommunications, where acronyms abound. In this guide to acronyms, where the letters within an acronym can have slightly different interpretations, these are given within the same entry. If the acronym stands for completely different terms then these are listed separately.

AAN	All Area Networking. (Networking covering local and wide areas.)
ABM	Asynchronous Balanced Mode.
ACD	Automatic Call Distribution. (Facility for allowing incoming calls to be queued and distributed to waiting service operators.)
ACK	Acknowledgement. (Control code sent from a receiver to a transmitter to acknowledge the receipt of a transmission.)
ACSE	Association Control Service Element. (OSI application.)
ADC	Analogue to Digital Conversion.
ADC	Access Deficit Contributions.
ADDF	Automatic Digital Distribution Frame. (System used to replace manual distribution frames in plesiochronous transmission networks.)
ADM	Adaptive Delta Modulation. (Digital signal modulation technique.)
ADM	Add-Drop Multiplexer. (Term sometimes used to describe a drop and insert multiplexer.)
ADP	Automatic Data Processing.
ADPCM	Adaptive Differential Pulse Code Modulation. (ITU-T standard for the conversion and transmission of analogue signals at 32kbit/s.)

ADSL	Asymmetrical Digital Subscriber Loop. (Technique for providing broadband over copper.)
AE	Anomaly Events. (E.g. frame errors, parity errors, etc. ITU-T M.550 for digital circuit testing.)
AFC	Automatic Frequency Control.
AFRTS	American Forces Radio and Television Services.
AGC	Automatic Gain Control.
AIN	Advanced Intelligent Network. (Bellcore released specification for provision of wide range of telecommunication capabilities and services.)
AIS	Automatic Intercept System. (System which is programmed to automatically provide information to a telephone caller, who has been intercepted and routed to it.)
ALS	Alternate Line Service. (For example two different directory numbers associated with one line.)
ALU	Arithmetic Logic Unit.
AM	Amplitude Modulation. (Analogue signal transmission encoding technique.)
AMA	Automatic Message Accounting. (Ability within an office to automatically record call information for accounting purposes. See also CAMA.)
AMI	Alternate Mark Inversion. (Line code system.)
ANBFM	Adaptive Narrow Band Frequency Modulation.
ANBS	American National Bureau of Standards.
ANDF	Architecture Neutral Distribution Format. (Scheme from OSF to enable software to be produced in single code to run on any hardware.)
ANSI	American National Standards Institute.
ANI	Automatic Number Identification. (Feature for automatically determining the identity of the caller.)
AOS	Alternate Operator Services. (Companies, in the US, who provide operator services in competition with existing suppliers such as AT&T and the RBOCs.)
APNSS	Analogue Private Network Signalling System.

AP	Application Processes. (Processes within computer based systems which perform specified tasks.)
APC	Adaptive Predictive Coding.
APD	Avalanche Photodiode. (A semiconductor device used for fibre optic communications.)
API	Application Programming Interface.
APK	Amplitude Phase Keying. (A digital modulation technique in which the amplitude and phase of the carrier are varied.)
ARPA	Advanced Research Project Agency. (Agency operating within the US Department of Defence.)
ARQ	Automatic Request for repetition. (A feature in transmission systems in which the receiver automatically asks the sender to retransmit a block of information, usually because there is an error in the earlier transmission.)
ARS	Automatic Route Selection. (Facility in an equipment, usually a PABX or multiplexer, to automatically select the best route for transmission through a network.)
ASCII	American Standard Code for Information Interchange. (Popular character code used for data communications and processing. Consists of seven bits, or eight bits with a parity bit added.)
ASIC	Application Specific Integrated Circuit. (Integrated circuit components which can be readily customised for a given application.)
ASN.1	Abstract Syntax Notation One.
ASR	Automatic Send/Receive. (Operation usually carried out by an older type of teleprinter equipment.)
ASTIC	Anti-SideTone Induction Coil. (Hybrid transformer used in voice transmission systems.)
ASE	Application Service Element. (OSI application.)
ASK	Amplitude Shift Keying. (Digital modulation.)
ASVD	Analogue Simultaneous Voice Data. (ITU proposal for transmission of voice and data over conventional phone lines.)

ATDM	Asynchronous Time Division Multiplexing.
ATM	Asynchronous Transfer Mode. (ITU-T protocol for the transmission of voice, data and video.)
ATV	Advanced Television.
AU	Administrative Unit. (Term used in synchronous transmission. Ref: ITU-T C.709. It is the level at which circuit administration is carried out by the operator.)
AUSTEL	Australian Telecommunications authority.
AVDM	Analogue Variable Delta Modulation.
AWG	American Wire Gauge.

B-ISDN	Broadband Integrated Services Digital Network.
BABT	British Approvals Board for Telecommunications.
BASIC	Beginners All Symbolic Instruction Code. (Computer programming language.)
BBER	Background Block Error Ratio.
BCC	Block Check Character. (A control character which is added to a block of transmitted data, used in checking for errors.)
BCD	Binary Coded Decimal. (An older character code set, in which numbers are represented by a four bit sequence.)
BCH	Bose Chaudhure Hocquengherm. (Coding technique.)
BDF	Building Distribution Frame.
BELLCORE	Bell Communications Research. (Research organisation, incorporating parts of the former Bell Laboratories, established after the divestiture of AT&T. Funded by the BOCs and RBOCs to formulate telecommunication standards.)
BER	Bit Error Ratio. (Also called Bit Error Rate. It is a measure of transmission quality. It is the number of bits received in error during a transmission, divided by the total number of bits transmitted in a specific interval.)

BERT	Bit Error Ratio Tester. (Equipment used for digital transmission testing.)
BETRS	Basic Exchange Telecommunications Radio Service. (FCC)
BEXR	Basic Exchange Radio.
BHCA	Busy Hour Call Attempts. (Parameter used in the design of telephone exchanges. It is the number of calls placed in the busy hour. Also referred to as Busy Hour Calls or BHC.)
BIP	Bit Interleaved Parity. (A simple method of parity checking.)
BIST	Built In Self Test.
BISYNC	Binary Synchronous communications. (Older protocol used for character oriented transmission on half-duplex links.)
BMPT	Bundesministerium fur Post und Telekommunikation. (German telecommunication regulator.)
BnZS	Bipolar with n-Zero Substitution. (A channel code. Examples are B3ZS which has three-zero substitution; B6ZS with six-zero substitution etc.)
BOC	Bell Operating Company. (Twenty-two BOCs were formed after the divestiture of AT&T, acting as local telephone companies in the US. They are now organised into seven Regional Bell Operating Companies or RBOCs.)
BORSCHT	Battery, Overload protection, Ringing, Supervision, Coding, Hybrid, and Test access. (These are the functions provided in connection with a subscriber line circuit. The functions are usually implemented by an integrated circuit.)
BPON	Broadband over Passive Optical Networks.
BPSK	Binary Phase Shift Keying.
BPV	Bipolar Violation. (Impairment of digital transmission system, using bipolar coding, where two pulses occur consecutively with the same polarity.)
BRA	Basic Rate Access. (ISDN, 2B+D code.)

BRZ	Bipolar Return to Zero. (A channel coding technique, used for digital transmission.)
BSGL	Branch System General Licence. (Telecommunications licence in the UK.)
BSI	British Standards Institute.
BSM	Broadband Switched Mass-market.
BT	Formerly British Telecom. (UK.)
BTV	Business Tele Vision.
BUNI	Broadband User Network Interface.
CAD/CAM	Computer Aided Design/Computer Aided Manufacture.
CAMA	Centralised Automatic Message Accounting. (A centralised version of AMA, used in larger offices serving several smaller ones which may be too small to justify AMA on their own.)
CAP	Competitive Access Provider. (USA.)
CAS	Channel Associated Signalling. (ITU-T signalling method.)
CASE	Computer Aided Software Engineering (or Computer Aided System Engineering).
CBC	Canadian Broadcasting Corporation.
CBDS	Connectionless Broadband Data Service. (ETSI's version of SMDS.)
CBEMA	Computer Business Equipment Manufacturers' Association. (USA.)
CBS	Columbia Broadcasting System.
CBX	Computer Controlled PBX.
CCA	Cable Communications Association. (UK based association of cable TV operators.)
CCB	Coin Collection Box. (Pay phone.)
CCC	Clear Channel Capacity.
CCD	Charged Coupled Device. (Semiconductor device used for analogue storage and imaging.)
CCIR	Comite Consultatif Internationale des Radiocommunications. (International Radio Consultative Committee. Former standards making body within

the ITU and now part of its new Radiocommunication Sector.)

CCIS   Common Channel Interoffice Signalling. (North American signalling system which uses a separate signalling network between switches.)

CCITT   Comite Consultatif Internationale de Telephonique et Telegraphique. (Consulative Committee for International Telephone and Telegraphy. Standards making body within the ITU, now forming part of the new Standardisation Sector.)

CCR   Commitment, Concurrency and Recovery.

CCS   Cent Call Second. (100 call seconds. It is a measure of the traffic load and is obtained by the product of the number of calls per hour and the average holding time per call, expressed in seconds, and dividing the product by 100.)

CCS   Common Channel Signalling. (ITU-T standard signalling system. Also called CCSS.)

CCSS   Common Channel Signalling System. (ITU-T standard signalling system. Also called CCS or Number 7 signalling.)

CDDI   Copper Distributed Data Interface. (Name given to FDDI running over copper media.)

CDM   Code Delta Modulation. (Or Continuous Delta Modulation.)

CDMA   Code Division Multiple Access.

CDO   Community Dial Office. (Usually refers to an unattended switching centre serving a small community and controlled from a larger central office.)

CDR   Call Detail Recording. (Feature within a PABX for call analysis.)

CEC   Commission of the European Communities.

CFM   Companded Frequency Modulation.

CFSK   Coherent Frequency Shift Keying.

CICC   Contactless Integrated Circuit Card. (ISO standard for a smart card in which information is stored and retrieved without use of conductive contacts.)

CIM	Computer Integrated Manufacture. (General term covering the use of computers within the manufacturing processes.)
CIS	Commonwealth of Independent States. (Alliance of states following the collapse of the USSR.)
CIT	Computer Integrated Telephony.
CLASS	Custom Local Area Signalling Services.
CLI	Command Line Interface. (Usually refers to an interface which allows remote asynchronous terminal access into a network management system. Also referred to as Command Line Interpreter.)
CLI	Calling Line Identity. (Facility for determining identity of the caller. See also CLID.)
CLID	Calling Line Identification. (Telephone facility which allows the called party to determine the identity of the caller.)
CLIP	Connection-Less Interworking Protocol. (OSI Network Layer.)
CLTS	Connection-Less Transport Service.
CMI	Code Mark Inversion. (Line coding technique.)
CMIP	Common Management Information Protocol. (Protocol widely used in network management.)
CMIS	Common Management Information Service.
CMISE	Common Management Information Service Element. (Specific type of ASE.)
CMOS	Complementary Metal Oxide Semiconductor. (Integrated circuit technology.)
CMS	Call Management System.
CMT	Character Mode Terminal. (E.g. VT100, which does not provide graphical capability.)
CNN	Cable News Network. (USA.)
CO	Central Office. (Usually refers a central switching or control centre belonging to a PTT.)
COCOT	Consumer Owned Coin Operated Telephone. (Privately owned coin boxes linking to public telephone lines.)
CODEC	COder-DECoder.

CPE	Customer Premise Equipment.
CP/M	Control Programme for Microcomputers. (Operating system popularly used for microcomputers.)
CPFSK	Continuous Phase Frequency Shift Keying.
CPODA	Contention Priority-Oriented Demand Assignment protocol. (Multiple access technique with contention for reservations. See PODA and FPODA.)
CPSK	Coherent Phase Shift Keying.
CPU	Central Processing Unit. (Usually part of a computer.)
CR	Carriage Return. (Code used on a teleprinter to start a new line.)
CRA	Call Routeing Apparatus.
CRC	Cyclic Redundancy Check. (Bit oriented protocol used for checking for errors in transmitted data.)
CRT	Cathode Ray Tube.
CRTC	Canadian Radio, television and Telecommunications Commission. (Canadian government telecommunication regulatory body.)
CS	Central Station.
CSBS	Customer Support and Billing System.
CSDN	Circuit Switched Data Network.
CSMA	Carrier Sense Multiple Access. (LAN Multiple access technique.)
CSMA/CD	Carrier Sense Multiple Access with Collision Detection. (LAN access technique, with improved throughput, under heavy load conditions, compared to pure CSMA.)
CSTA	Computer Supported Telephony Applications. (Or Computer Supported Telecommunication Applications. For example, telemarketing applications.)
CSU	Channel Service Unit. (Subscriber line terminating unit in North America.)
CTA	Cable Television Association. (UK trade association of cable television suppliers.)
CTCSS	Continuous Tone Controlled Squelch System. (Method for calling in paging systems.)

CTR	Common Technical Regulation. (European Community mandatory standard.)
CTS	Clear To Send. (Control code used for data transmission in modems.)
CVSD	Continuous Variable Slope Delta modulation. (Proprietary method used for speech compression. Also called CVSDM.)
CW	Continuous Wave.
DAB	Digital Audio Broadcasting.
DAR	Dynamic Alternative Routeing. (Traffic routeing scheme proposed by BT in the UK.)
DARPA	Defence Advanced Research Projects Agency. (USA Government agency.)
DASS	Digital Access Signalling System. (Signalling system introduced in the UK prior to ITU-T standards I.440 and I.450.)
DASS	Demand Assignment Signalling and Switching unit.
DATV	Digitally Assisted Television.
DBMS	Database Management System.
DBT	Deutsche Bunderspost Telekom. (Also written DBP-T. German PTT.)
DCA	Dynamic Channel Allocation. (System in which the operating frequency is selected by the equipment at time of use, rather than by a planned assignment.)
DCC	Data Communication Channel.
DCDM	Digitally Coded Delta Modulation. (Delta modulation technique in which step size is controlled by the bit sequence of the sampling and quantisation.)
DCE	Data Circuit termination Equipment. (Exchange end of a network, connecting to a DTE. Usually used in packet switched networks.)
DCF	Data Communications Function.
DCN	Data Communications Network.
DCR	Dynamically Controlled Routeing. (Traffic routing method proposed by Bell Northern Research.)

DCS	Digital Crossconnect System. (See also DCX and DXC.)
DCS	Dynamic Channel Selection. (For example as used on call set-up in the CEPT 900MHz analogue cordless telephony standard.)
DCT	Discrete Cosine Transform. (Technique used in transform picture coding.)
DCX	Digital Crossconnect. (See also DXC and DSC.)
DDC	Data Country Code. (Part of an international telephone number.)
DDD	Direct Distance Dialling. (Generally refers to conventional dial-up long distance calls placed over a telephone network without operator assistance.)
DDF	Digital Distribution Frame. (Frame for physical connection of transmission lines. See also ADDF and MDDF.)
DDI	Direct Dialling In. (External caller able to dial directly to an extension.)
DDI	Distributed Data Interface. (Proposal to run the FDDI standard over unshielded twisted pair.)
DDN	Digital Data Network.
DDN	Defence Data Network. (US military network, derived from the ARPANET.)
DDP	Distributed Data Processing.
DDS	Digital Data Service. (North American data service.)
DE	Defect Events. (E.g. loss of signal, loss of frame synchronisation etc. ITU-T M.550 for digital circuit testing.)
DEDM	Dolby Enhanced Delta Modulation.
DEPSK	Differentially Encoded Phase Shift Keying.
DES	Data Encryption Standard. (Public standard encryption system from the American National Bureau of Standards.)
DID	Direct Inward Dialling. (PABX feature allowing an external caller to connect to an extension without first going through an operator.)

DIL	Dual In Line package. (Integrated circuit packaging. Also known as DIP.)
DIN	Deutsches Institute fur Normung. (Standardisation body in Germany.)
DIP	Dual In line Package. (Integrated circuit packaging. Also known as DIL.)
DIS	Draft International Standard.
DLC	Data Link Control.
DLS	Data Link Service.
DM	Degraded Minutes. (Any one minute period with a BER exceeding 10^{-6}, as per ITU-T G.821.)
DM	Delta Modulation. (Digital signal modulation.)
DMA	Direct Memory Access.
DN	Directory Number. (Of a customer in a switching system.)
DN	Distinguishing Name.
DNHR	Dynamic Non-Hierarchical Routeing. (Traffic routeing method implemented by AT&T.)
DNIC	Data Network Identification Code. (Part of an international telephone number.)
DOD	Department Of Defence. (US agency.)
DOS	Disk Operating System. (Popular operating system for personal computers.)
DOV	Data Over Voice. (Technique for simultaneous transmission of voice and data over telephone lines. This is a less sophisticated technique than ISDN.)
DPCM	Differential Pulse Code Modulation.
DPNSS	Digital Private Network Signalling System. (Inter-PABX signalling system used in the UK.)
DQDB	Distributed Queue Double Bus. (IEEE standard 802.6 for Metropolitan Area Networks.)
DQPSK	Differential Quaternary Phase Shift Keying.
DRG	Direction a la Reglementation Generale. (Directorate for General Regulation, in France.)
DS-0	Digital Signal level 0. (Part of the US transmission hierarchy, transmitting at 64kbit/s. DS-1 transmits at 1.544Mbit/s, DS-2 at 6.312Mbit/s etc.)

DSAP	Destination Service Access Point. (Refers to the address of service at destination.)
DSB	Double Sideband.
DSBEC	Double Sideband Emitted Carrier.
DSBSC	Double Sideband Suppressed Carrier modulation. (A method for amplitude modulation of a signal.)
DSC	District Switching Centre. (Part of the switching hierarchy in BT's network.)
DSE	Data Switching Exchange. (Part of packet switched network.)
DSI	Digital Speech Interpolation. (Method used in digital speech transmission where the channel is activated only when speech is present.)
DSM	Delta Sigma Modulation. (Digital signal modulation technique.)
DSP	Digital Signal Processing.
DSS	Digital Subscriber Signalling. (CCIT term for the N-ISDN access protocol.)
DSU	Data Service Unit. (Customer premise interface to a digital line provided by a PTT.)
DSX-1	Digital Signal Crossconnect. (Crossconnect used for DS-1 signals.)
DTE	Data Terminal Equipment. (User end of network which connects to a DCE. Usually used in packet switched networks.)
DTI	Department of Trade and Industry.
DTL	Diode Transistor Logic. (An older form of integrated circuit logic family.)
DTMF	Dual Tone Multi-Frequency. (Telephone signalling system used with push button telephones.)
DTP	Distributed Transaction Processing.
DTS	Digital Termination System. (Local radio loop provided by carriers in the US.)
DXC	Digital Crossconnect. (See also DCX and DCS.)
EB	Errored Block. (Measurement of transmission errors.)

EBCDIC	Extended Binary Coded Decimal Interchange Code. (Eight bit character code set.)
EC	European Commission.
ECC	Embedded Communication Channel. (Channel used within SDH to carry communication information rather than data.)
ECC	Error Control Coding. (Coding used to reduce errors in transmission.)
ECJ	European Court of Justice.
ECL	Emitter Coupled Logic. (Integrated circuit technology.)
ECMA	European Computer Manufacturers Association.
ECSA	Exchange Carriers Standards Association. (USA)
ECTF	Enterprise Computer Telephony Forum.
ECU	European Currency Unit. (Monetary unit of the EEC, created in 1981.)
EDI	Electronic Data Interchange. (Protocol for interchanging data between computer based systems.)
EDIFACT	EDI For Administration Commerce and Transport. (International rules for trading documents e.g. purchase orders, payment orders etc.)
EDP	Electronic Data Processing.
EEA	Electrical Engineering Association.
EEA	Electronic and business Equipment Association.
EEC	European Economic Community.
EEPROM	Electrically Erasable Read Only Memory. (Integrated circuit used to store data, which can be erased by electrical methods.)
EET	Equipment Engaged Tone. (Tone customer receives when there is no free line for his call.)
EFS	Error Free Seconds. (In transmitted data it determines the proportion of one second intervals, over a given period, when the data is error free.)
EFT	Electronic Funds Transfer.
EFTA	European Free Trade Association.
EFTPOS	Electronic Funds Transfer at the Point Of Sale.

EIA	Electronic Industries Association. (Trade association in USA.)
EIUF	European ISDN Users Forum.
ELT	Emergency Locator Transmitter.
EM	Element Manager. (First level network manager controlling elements.)
E-MAIL	Electronic Mail.
EMC	Electromagnetic Compatibility.
EMI	Electromagnetic Interference.
EMP	ElectroMagnetic Pulse. (Released by a nuclear explosion.)
EN	Equipment Number. (Code given to a line circuit, primarily in switches, to indicate its location on equipment racks.)
EOA	End Of Address. (Header code used in a transmitted frame.)
EOB	End Of Block. (Character used at end of a transmitted frame. Also referred to as End of Transmitted Block or ETB.)
EOC	Embedded Operations Channel. (Bits carried in a transmission frame which contain auxiliary information such as for maintenance and supervisory. This is also called a Facilities Data Link, FDL.)
EOC	Equal Opportunities Commission. (UK.)
EOT	End Of Transmission. (Control code used in transmission to signal the receiver that all the information has been sent.)
EOTT	End Office Toll Trunking. (US term for trunks which are located between end offices situated in different toll areas.)
EOW	Engineering Order Wire. (A channel for voice or data communication between two stations on a transmission line.)
ERL	Echo Return Loss.
ERM	Exchange Rate Mechanism. (Used within the European Community.)

ES	Errored Second. (Measurement of transmission errors.)
ESB	Emergency Service Bureau. (A centralised location to which all emergency calls (e.g. police, ambulance, fire brigade) are routed.
ESF	Extended Superframe. (North American 24 frame digital transmission format.)
ESN	Electronic Serial Number. (Usually refers to the personal identity number coded into mobile radio handsets.)
ESQL	Embedded Structured Query Language.
ESR	Errored Second Ratio. (Measurement of transmission errors.)
ESS	Electronic Switching System. (A generic term used to describe stored programme control exchange switching systems.)
ETB	End of Transmission Block. (A control character which denotes the end of a block of Bisync transmitted data.)
ETE	Exchange Terminating Equipment.
ETNO	European Telecommunications Network Operators. (Association of European public operators.)
ETS	Electronic Tandem Switch.
ETS	European Telecommunication Standard. (Norme Europeenne de Telecommunications. Standard produced by ETSI.)
ETSI	European Telecommunications Standards Institute.
ETX	End of Text. (A control character used to denote the end of transmitted text, which was started by an STX character.)
EVUA	European VPN Users Association.
FAS	Frame Alignment Signal. (Used in the alignment of digital transmission frames.)
FAX	Facsimile.

FCC	Federal Communications Commission. (US authority, appointed by the President to regulate all interstate and international telecommunications.)
FCS	Frame Check Sequence. (Field added to a transmitted frame to check for errors.)
FDDI	Fibre Distributed Digital Interface. (Standard for optical fibre transmission.)
FDL	Facilities Data Link. (See EOC.)
FDM	Frequency Division Multiplexing. (Signal multiplexing technique.)
FDMA	Frequency Division Multiple Access. (Multiple access technique based on FDM.)
FDX	Full Duplex. (Transmission system in which the two stations connected by a link can transmit and receive simultaneously.)
FEC	Feedforward Error Correction. (Also called Forward Error Correction. Technique for correcting errors due to transmission.)
FEXT	Far End Crosstalk.
FFSK	Fast Frequency Shift Keying.
FIFO	First In First Out. (Technique for buffering data.)
FITL	Fibre In The Loop. (Fibre optic cable access in the local loop to the subscriber.)
FM	Facilities Management.
FM	Forms Management.
FM	Frequency Modulation. (Analogue signal modulation technique.)
FMFB	Frequency Modulation Feedback.
FPGA	Field Programmable Gate Array.
FPODA	Fixed Priority Oriented Demand Assignment. (Medium multiple access method.)
FPS	Fast Packet Switch. (Standard for transmission based on frame relay or cell relay.)
FSK	Frequency Shift Keying. (Digital modulation technique.)
FT	France Telecom. (French PTT.)

FTAM	File Transfer and Access Method. (Or File Transfer Access and Management. International standard.)
FTP	File Transfer Protocol. (Used within TCP/IP.)
FTTC	Fibre To The Curb. (Method for implementing fibre optic access in the local loop, where the fibre is taken to street-side termination points and then dropped off to individual subscribers on copper.)
FTTH	Fibre To The Home. (Method of implementing fibre optic access in the local loop, where the fibre cable is taken all the way to the subscriber's premises.)
GAP	Groupe d'Analyse et de Prevision. (Analysis and Forecasting Group. A subcommittee of SOGT, part of the European Community.)
GATT	General Agreement on Tariffs and Trade.
GDN	Government Data Network. (UK private data network for use by government departments.)
GDP	Gross Domestic Product. (Measure of output from a country.)
GEN	Global European Network. (Joint venture between European PTOs to provide high speed leased line and switched services. Likely to be replaced by METRAN in mid 1990s.)
GHz	GigaHerts. (Measure of frequency. Equal to 1000000000 cycles per second. See Hertz or Hz.)
GMSK	Gaussian Minimum Shift Keying. (Modulation technique, as used in GSM.)
GoS	Grade of Service. (Measure of service performance as perceived by the user.)
GPS	Global Positioning System. (Usually refers to satellite based vehicle positioning.)
GPRS	General Packet Relay Service. (Data packet service in GSM.)
GSC	Group Switching Centre. (Part of the hierarchy of switching in BT's network. Also called the primary trunk switching centre by ITU-T.)
GVPN	Global Virtual Private Network.

HCI	Human Computer Interface.
HDB3	High Density Bipolar 3. (Line transmission encoding technique.)
HDLC	Higher level Data Link Control. (ITU-T bit oriented protocol for handling data.)
HDSL	High bit rate Digital Subscriber Line. (Bellcore technical advisory for the transmission of high bit rate data over twisted copper lines.)
HDTV	High Definition Television. (New television transmission standard.)
HF	High Frequency. (Radio signal.)
HFC	Hybrid Fibre/Coax. (Distribution network, for example as used in cable TV.)
HKTA	Hong Kong Telecommunications Authority.
HOMUX	Higher Order Multiplexer.
HRC	Harmonically Related Carrier. (Carrier system used in cable television.)
HRC	High Rupturing Capacity. (Usually refers to a type of electrical fuse used to break large values of current.)
HRDS	Hypothetical Reference Digital Section. (ITU-T G.921 for digital circuit measurements.)
HSE	Health and Safety Executive. (UK.)
HSSI	High Speed Serial Interface. (Specification for high data rate transmission over copper cable.)
HTML	HyperText Markup Language. (Language used to create hypermedia documents on the WWW.)
HTTP	HyperText Transfer Protocol. (Protocol used to transfer information over the Internet.)
Hz	Hertz. (Measure of frequency. One Hertz is equal to a frequency of one cycle per second.)
IA2	International Alphabet 2. (Code used in a teleprinter, also called the Murray code.)
IA5	International Alphabet 5. (International standard alphanumeric code, which has facility for national options. The US version is ASCII.)

IAB	Internet Activities Board.
IBC	Integrated Broadband Communications. (Part of the RACE programme.)
IBCN	Integrated Broadband Communications Network.
IBM	International Business Machines.
IC	Integrated Circuit. (Semiconductor component.)
ICA	International Communications Association. (Telecommunications users' group in the USA.)
ICAO	International Civil Aviation Organisation.
ICMP	Internet Control Message Protocol. (Protocol developed by DARPA as part of Internet for the host to communicate with gateways.)
IDA	Integrated Digital Access. (ISDN pilot service in the UK.)
IDDD	International Direct Digital Dialling.
IDN	Integrated Digital Network. (Usually refers to the digital public network which uses digital transmission and switching.)
IEC	International Electrotechnical Commission.
IEC	Interexchange Carrier. (US term for any telephone operator licensed to carry traffic between LATAs interstate or intrastate.)
IEEE	Institute for Electrical and Electronics Engineers. (USA professional organisation.)
IETF	Internet Engineering Task Force.
I-ETS	Interim European Telecommunications Standard. (ETSI.)
IF	Intermediate Frequency.
IFIPS	International Federation of Information Processing Societies.
IFU	Interface Unit. (Module interfacing to a crossconnect within the SDH.)
IGFET	Insulated Gate Field Effect Transistor. (A semiconductor unipolar transistor with a high input impedance.)
IKBS	Intelligent Knowledge Based System.
IM	Intermodulation.

IN	Intelligent Network.
INTUG	International Telecommunications Users' Group.
I/O	Input/Output. (Usually refers to the input and output ports of an equipment, such as a computer.)
IP	Internet Protocol.
IPC	Inter-Processor Communications.
IPC	International Private Circuit.
IPM	Inter-Personal Messaging. (Use of Electronic Data Interchange.)
IPR	Intellectual Property Rights.
IPVC	International Private Virtual Circuit.
IR	Infrared.
IRC	Incrementally Related Carrier. (Carrier system used in cable television.)
IRED	Infrared Emitting Diode.
IS	Intermediate System.
ISD	International Subscriber Dialling.
ISDN	Integrated Services Digital Network. (Technique for the simultaneous transmission of a range of services, such as voice, data and video, over telephone lines.)
ISI	Inter-Symbol Interference. (Interference between adjacent pulses of a transmitted code.)
ISLAN	Integrated Services Digital Network. (LAN which can carry an integrated service, such as voice, data and image.)
ISM	Industrial, Scientific and Medical. (Usually refers to ISM equipment or applications.)
ISO	International Standardisation Organisation.
IT	Information Technology. (Generally refers to industries using computers e.g. data processing.)
ITA	International Telegraph Alphabet.
ITC	International Trade Commission.
ITC	Independent Television Commission. (UK regulator.)
ITU	International Telecommunication Union.

ITU-T	International Telecommunication Union Telecommunication sector.
ITU-R	International Telecommunication Union Radiocommunication sector.
ITUSA	Information Technology User Standards Association.
IVA	Integrated Voice Application.
IVDS	Interactive Video and Data Services.
IVDT	Integrated Voice and Data Terminal. (Equipment with integrated computing and voice capabilities. In its simplest form it consists of a PC with telephone incorporated. Facilities such as storage and recall of telephone numbers are included.)
IVM	Integrated Voice Mail.
IVR	Interactive Voice Response.
IXC	Interexchange Carrier. (USA long distance telecommunication carrier.)
IXI	International X.25 Infrastructure. (Pilot backbone pan-European network used by Europe's academic community.)
JIS	Japanese Industrial Standard. (Product marking used in Japan to denote conformance to a specified standard.)
JISC	Japanese Industrial Standards Committee. (Standards making body which is funded by the Japanese government.)
JSA	Japanese Standards Association.
JTM	Job Transfer and Manipulation. (Communication protocols used to perform tasks in a network of interconnected open systems.)
KBS	Knowledge Based System.
kHz	KiloHertz. (Measure of frequency. Equals to 1000 cycles per second.)
KDD	Kokusai Denshin Denwa Co. Ltd (Japanese international carrier.)

LAMA	Localised Automatic Message Accounting. (The ability to use AMA within a local office.)
LAN	Local Area Network. (A network shared by communicating devices, usually on a relatively small geographical area. Many techniques are used to allow each device to obtain use of the network.)
LAP	Link Access Protocol.
LAPB	Link Access Protocol Balanced. (X.25 protocol.)
LAPD	Link Access Protocol Digital. (ISDN standard.)
LAPM	Link Access Protocol for Modems. (ITU-T V.42 standard.)
LASER	Light Amplification by Stimulated Emission of Radiation. (Laser is also used to refer to a component.)
LATA	Local Access and Transport Area. (Area of responsibility of local carrier in USA. When telephone circuits have their start and finish points within a LATA they are the sole responsibility of the local telephone company concerned. When they cross a LATA's boundary, i.e. go inter-LATA, they are the responsibility of an interexchange carrier or IEC.)
LBA	Least Busy Alternative. (Traffic routeing strategy defined for fully connected networks.)
LBO	Line Build Out. (The extension of the electrical length of a line, for example by adding capacitors.
LBRV	Low Bit Rate Voice. (Speech encoding technique which allows voice transmission at under 64kbit/s.)
LCD	Liquid Crystal Display.
LCN	Local Communications Network. (ITU-T.)
LCR	Least Cost Routeing. (Applies to the use of alternative long distance routes, e.g. by using different carriers, in order to minimise transmission costs.)
LDDC	Long Distance D.C. line signalling. (Method of d.c. signalling.)
LDM	Linear Delta Modulation. (Delta modulation technique in which a series of linear segments of constant slope provides the input time function.)

LEC	Local Exchange Carrier. (USA local telecommunication carrier.)
LED	Light Emitting Diode. (Component which converts electrical energy into light.)
LIFO	Last In First Out. (Technique for buffering data.)
LISN	Line Impedance Stabilising Network. (An artificial network used in measurement systems to define the impedance of the mains supply.)
LJU	Line Jack Unit.
LLC	Logical Link Control. (IEEE 802. standard for LANs.)
LPTV	Low Power Television.
LPC	Linear Predictive Coding. (Encoding technique used in pulse code modulation.)
LRC	Longitudinal Redundancy Check. (Error checking procedure for transmitted data.)
LSB	Least Significant Bit. (Referring to bits in a data word.)
LSI	Large Scale Integration. (Describes a complex integrated circuit semiconductor component.)
LSTR	Listener SideTone Rating. (Measure of room noise sidetone effect.)
LTE	Line Terminating Equipment. (Also called Line Terminal Equipment. Equipment which terminates a transmission line.)
MA	Multiple Access.
MAC	Media Access Control. (IEEE standard 802. for access to LANs.)
MAC	Multiplexed Analogue Components. (Television transmission system.)
MAN	Metropolitan Area Network.
MAP	Manufacturing Automation Protocol.
MASER	Microwave Amplification by Simulated Emission of Radiation.
MAT	Metropolitan Area Trunk. (A cable system which is used to reduce crosstalk effects in regions where

	there is a large number of circuits between exchanges.)
MATV	Mast Antenna Television. (Or Master Antenna Television. Local cable television system for a hotel or apartment block.)
MCM	Multichip module.
MD	Mediation Device. (ITU-T terminology for a device which carries out a protocol conversion function.)
MDDF	Manual Digital Distribution Frame.
MDF	Main Distribution Frame.
MDNS	Managed Data Network Service. (Earlier proposal by CEPT which has now been discontinued.)
MF	Multi Frequency. (A signalling system used with push-button telephones.)
MF	Mediation Function. (ITU-T term for a function involving protocol conversion.)
MHS	Message Handling System. (International standard.)
MHz	MegaHertz. (Measure of frequency. Equal to one million cycles per second.)
MIPS	Million Instructions Per Second. (Measure of a computer's processing speed.)
MITT	Minutes of Telecommunication Traffic. (Measure used by telecommunication operators for tariffing purposes.)
MMI	Man Machine Interface. (Another name for the human/computer interface or HCI.)
MoD	Ministry of Defence. (UK.)
MODEM	Modulator/Demodulator. Device for enabling digital data to be send over analogue lines.
MOS	Metal Oxide Semiconductor. (A semiconductor technology.)
MOSFET	Metal Oxide Semiconductor Field Effect Transistor. (A transistor made from MOS.)
MoU	Memorandum of Understanding.
MPEG	Moving Picture Experts Group. (Part of ISO.)
MPT	Ministry of Posts and Telecommunications. (Japan.)

MSDOS	Microsoft Disk Operating System. (Very popular operating system for PCs.)
MSI	Medium Scale Integration. (Usually refers to an integrated circuit with a medium amount of on-chip circuit density.)
MSK	Minimum Shift Keying. (A form of frequency shift keying, or FSK.)
MSO	Multiple Systems Operator. (A cable TV operator who is running more than one franchise area.)
MTBF	Mean Time Between Failure. (Measure of equipment reliability. Time for which an equipment is likely to operate before failure.)
MTS	Message Telephone Service. (US term for a long distance telephone service.)
MTTR	Mean Time To Repair. (A measure of equipment availability. It is the time between an equipment failure and when it is operational again.)
MUF	Maximum Usable Frequency.
NA	Numerical Aperture. (Measure of a basic parameter for fibre optic cables.)
NAFTA	North American Free Trade Association.
NAK	Negative Acknowledgement. (In data transmission this is the message sent by the receiver to the sender to indicate that the previous message contained an error, and requesting a re-send.)
NATA	North American Telecommunications Administration.
NBC	National Broadcasting Company. (USA.)
NBS	National Bureau of Standards. (USA.)
NCL	Network Control Layer.
NCTA	National Cable Television Association. (USA trade organisation representing cable television carriers.)
NDC	National Destination Code. (Part of numbering system.)
NE	Network Element.
NEP	Noise Equivalent Power.

NET	Nome Europeenne de Telecommunication. (European Telecommunications Standard, which is mandatory.)
NEXT	Near End crosstalk. (The unwanted transfer of signal energy from one link to another, often closely located, at the end of the cable where the transmitter is located).
NF	Noise Figure.
NFAS	Not Frame Alignment Signal. (In transmitted code.)
N-ISDN	Narrowband Integrated Services Digital Network.
NIST	National Institute for Standards and Technology. (USA.)
NLC	Network Level Control. (Or Network Layer Control.)
NMC	Network Management Centre.
NMI	Network Management Interface. (Term used within OSI to indicate the interface between the network management system and the network it manages.)
NNI	Network Node Interface. (Usually the internal interfaces within a network. See UNI.)
NOI	Notice Of Inquiry. (FCC paper for comment.)
NPA	Numbering Plan Area.
NPP	Network Performance Parameters.
NPR	Noise Power Ratio.
NRA	National Regulatory Authority.
NRZ	Non Return to Zero. (A binary encoding technique for transmission of data.)
NRZI	Non Return to Zero Inverted. (A binary encoding technique for transmission of data.)
NT	Network Termination. (Termination designed within ISDN e.g. NT1 and NT2.)
NTE	Network Terminating Equipment. (Usually refers to the customer termination for an ISDN line.)
NTN	Network Terminal Number. (Part of an international telephone number.)
NTT	Nippon Telegraph and Telephone. (Japanese carrier.)

NTU	Network Terminating Unit. (Used to terminate subscriber leased line.)
NVOD	Near Video On Demand (television).
OA&M	Operations, Administration and Maintenance. (Also written as OAM.)
OAM&P	Operations, Administration, Maintenance & Provisioning.
O&M	Operations & Maintenance.
OATS	Open Area Test Site. (Used for EMC measurements.)
OEM	Original Equipment Manufacturer. Supplier who makes equipment for sale by a third party. The equipment is usually disguised by the third party with his own labels.)
OFDM	Orthogonal Frequency Division Multiplexing.
OFTEL	Office of Telecommunications. (UK regulatory body.)
OKQPSK	Offset Keyed Quaternary Phase Shift Keying.
OLR	Overall Loudness Rating. (Measurement of end to end connection for transmission planning.)
OLTU	Optical Line Terminating Unit. (Or Optical Line Terminal Unit. Equipment which terminates an optical line, usually converting optical signals to electrical and vice versa.)
ONA	Open Network Architecture.
ONI	Operator Number Identification. (Operator used in a CAMA office to verbally obtain the calling number for calls originating in offices not equipped with ANI.)
ONP	Open Network Provision.
ONT	Optical Network Termination. (Termination point for optical fibre access system.)
OOK	On-Off Keying. (Digital modulation technique. Also known as ASK or Amplitude Shift Keying.)
OS	Operating System. (Or Operations System. ITU-T.)
OSB	One Stop Billing.

OSF	Open Software Foundation.
OSF	Operations System Function. (ITU-T.)
OSI	Open Systems Interconnection. (Refers to the seven layer reference model.)
OSIE	OSI Environment.
OSP	Operator Service Provider. (Company in the USA providing competitive toll operator services for billing and call completion.)
OSS	One Stop Shopping.
OTDR	Optical Time Domain Reflectometer.
PABX	Private Automatic Branch Exchange. (PBX in which automatic connection is made between extensions.)
PAD	Packet Assembler/Disassembler. (Protocol converter used to provide access into the packet switched network.)
PAL	Pulse Alteration by Line. (Television encoding system.)
PAM	Pulse Amplitude Modulation. (An analogue modulation technique.)
PANS	Peculiar And Novel Services. (Often used in conjunction with POTS.)
PBX	Private Branch Exchange. (This is often used synonymously with PABX.)
PC	Personal Computer.
PC	Private Circuit.
PCM	Pulse Code Modulation. (Transmission technique for digital signals.)
PCMCIA	Personal Computer Memory Card International Association.
PDA	Personal Digital Assistant.
PDH	Plesiochronous Digital Hierarchy. (Plesiochronous transmission standard.)
PDM	Pulse Duration Modulation. (Signal modulation technique, also known as Pulse Width Modulation or PWM.)

PDU	Protocol Data Unit. (Data and control information passed between layers in the OSI Seven Layer model.)
PEP	Peak Envelope Power.
PFD	Power Flux Density. (Measure of spectral emission strength.)
PFM	Pulse Frequency Modulation. (An analogue modulation technique.)
PIN	Personal Identification Number. (Security number used for items such as remote database entry.)
PIN	Positive Intrinsic Negative. (Semiconductor structure used for some types of diodes.)
PLC	Plant Level Controller.
PLL	Phase Locked Loop. (Technique for recovering the clock in transmitted data. Often performed by an integrated circuit.)
PLP	Packet Level Protocol.
PM	Payload Manager. (Within an SDH.)
PM	Phase Modulation. (Analogue signal modulation technique.)
PMBX	Private Manual Branch Exchange. (PBX with connections between extensions done by an operator.)
PMR	Public Mobile Radio.
POCSAG	Post Office Code Standardisation Advisory Group. (Name given by study group to UK digital paging system. Adopted by ITU-T as Radio Paging Code RPC No. 1.)
PODA	Priority-Oriented Demand Assignment protocol. (Multiple access technique. See also FPODA and CPODA.)
POH	Path Overhead. (Information used in SDH transmission structures.)
POL	Problem Oriented Language. (A term sometimes used to describe a high level computer programming language, such as Cobol or Fortran.)
PON	Passive Optical Network. (Technology for implementing fibre optic cable access in the local loop.)

POP	Point Of Presence. (Local access point into network, such as for the Internet. Also refers to the point of changeover of responsibility from the local telephone company, within a LATA, to the long distance or inter-LATA carrier.)
POSI	Promoting conference for OSI. (Japan and Far East users' group active in functional standards and interconnection testing.)
POTS	Plain Old Telephone Service. (A term loosely applied to an ordinary voice telephone service.)
PPL	Phase Locked Loop. (Component used in frequency stability systems such as demodulators for frequency modulation.)
PPV	Pay Per View (television).
PPM	Pulse Phase Modulation. (An analogue modulation technique. Sometimes called Pulse Position Modulation.)
PRA	Primary Rate Access. (ISDN, 30B+D or 23B+D code.)
PRBS	Pseudo Random Binary Sequence. (Signal used for telecommunication system testing.)
PRF	Pulse Repetition Frequency. (Of a pulse train.)
PRK	Phase Reversal Keying. (A modification to the PSK modulation technique.)
PROM	Programmable Read Only Memory. (Memory technology, usually semiconductor, where the data is written, or programmed, once by the user and thereafter can only be read and not changed. See also ROM.)
PSDN	Packet Switched Data Network. (Or Public Switched Data Network. X.25 network, which may be private or public.)
PSPDN	Packet Switched Public Data Network.
PSE	Packet Switching Exchange.
PSK	Phase Shift Keying. (Analogue phase modulation technique.)
PSN	Packet Switched Network.

PSN	Public Switched Network.
PSS ˙	Packet Switched Service. (BT data service offered.)
PSTN	Public Switched Telephone Network. (Term used to describe the public dial up voice telephone network, operated by a PTT.)
PTN	Public Telecommunications Network.
PTO	Public Telecommunication Operator. (A licensed telecommunication operator. Usually used to refer to a PTT.)
PTT	Postal, Telegaph and Telephone. (Usually refers to the telephone authority within a country, often a publicly owned body. The term is also loosely used to describe any large telecommunications carrier.)
PVC	Permanent Virtual Circuit. (Method for establishing a virtual circuit link between two nominated points. See also SVC.)
PWM	Pulse Width Modulation. (Analogue modulation technique in which the width of pulses is varied. Also called Pulse Duration Modulation, PDM, or Pulse Length Modulation, PLM.)
QA	Q interface Adaptor.
QAF	Q Adaptor Function.
QAM	Quadrature Amplitude Modulation. (A modulation technique which varies the amplitude of the signal. Used in dial up modems. Also known as Quadrature Sideband Amplitude Modulation or QSAM.)
QD	Quantising Distortion.
QoS	Quality of Service. (Measure of service performance as perceived by the user.)
QPRS	Quadrature Partial Response System. (Signal modulation technique.)
QPSK	Quadrature Phase Shift Keying. (Signal modulation technique.)
RA	Radiocommunications Agency. (UK body responsible for frequency allocation.)

RACE	Research and development in Advanced Communication technologies in Europe.
R&D	Research and Development.
RAID	Redundant Array of Inexpensive Disks.
RAISE	Rigorous Approach to Industrial Software Engineering. (Esprit project.)
RARE	Reseaux Associes pour la Recherche Europeenne.
RBER	Residual Bit Error Ratio. (Measure of transmission quality. ITU-T Rec. 594-1.)
RBOC	Regional Bell Operating Company. (US local carriers formed after the divestiture of AT&T.)
RCU	Remote Concentrator Unit.
RDA	Remote Database Access.
RDBMS	Relational Database Management System.
RDSQL	Relational Database Structured Query Language.
RF	Radio Frequency. (Signal.)
RFC	Request For Comment.
RFI	Radio Frequency Interference.
RFNM	Ready For Next Message.
RIN	Relative Intensity Noise. (Measure of noise in an optical source.)
ROIV	Remote Operation Invoke.
ROM	Read Only Memory. (Memory device, usually semiconductor, in which the contents are defined during manufacture. The stored information can be read but not changed. See also PROM.)
ROTL	Remote Office Test Line. (Technique for remotely testing trunk circuits.)
ROW	Right Of Way. (Usually refers to costs associated with laying cables.)
RPFD	Received Power Flux Density.
RPOA	Recognised Private Operating Agencies.
RTL	Resistor Transistor Logic. (An older integrated circuit logic family.)
RTNR	Real Time Network Routeing. (Dynamic traffic routeing strategy being implemented by AT&T.)

RTS	Request To Send. (Handshaking routine used in analogue transmission, such as by modems.)
RTT	Regie des Telegraphes et des Telephones. (Belgian PTT.)
RZ	Return to Zero. (A digital transmission system in which the binary pulse always returns to zero after each bit.)
SAB	Services Ancillary to Broadcasting.
SAC	Special Access Code. (Special telephone numbers e.g. 800 service.)
SAP	Service Access Point. (Port between layers in the OSI seven layer model, one for each of the layers e.g. LSAP, NSAP etc.)
SAPI	Service Access Point Identifier. (Used within ISDN Layer 2 frame.)
SCADA	Supervisory Control and Data Acquisition. (Interface for network monitoring.)
SCC	Standards Council of Canada.
SCPC	Single Channel Per Carrier. (A transmission technique used in thin route satellite communication systems. See also SPADE.)
SCVF	Single Channel Voice Frequency. (One of the signalling systems used in telex i.e. ITU-T R.20.)
SDH	Synchronous Digital Hierarchy.
SDL	Specification Description Language. (ITU-T recommended language for specification and description of telecommunication systems.)
SDR	Speaker Dependent Recognition. (Speech recognition technique which requires training to individual caller's voice.)
SDU	Service Data Unit. (Data passed between layers in the OSI Seven Layer model.)
SDXC	Synchronous Digital Crossconnect.
SEA	Single European Act. (Amendment to the Treaty of Rome.)

SECAM	Sequence Coleur a Memoire. (Sequential Colour with Memory. French television encoding system.)
SED	Single Error Detecting Code. (Transmission code used for detecting errors by use of single parity checks.)
SELV	Safety Extra Low Voltage circuit. (A circuit which is protected from hazardous voltages.)
SES	Severely Errored Second. (Any second with a BER exceeding 10^{-3}, as per ITU-T G.821.)
SESR	Severely Errored Second Ratio.
SFL	Service Level controller.
SHF	Super High Frequency.
SIM	Subscriber Identity Module. (Usually a plug in card used with a mobile radio handset.)
SIO	Scientific and Industrial Organisation.
SIP	Societa Italiana per l'Esercizio delle Telecomunicazion. (Italian PTT.)
SIR	Speaker Independent Recognition. (Speech recognition technique which does not need to be trained to individual caller's voice.)
SITA	Societe Internationale de Telecommunications Aeronautiques. (Refers to the organisation and its telecommunication network which is used by many of the world's airlines and their agents, mainly for flight bookings.)
SLC	Subscriber Line Charge. (USA term for flat charge paid by the end user for line connection.)
SLIC	Subscriber Line Interface Card. (Circuitry which provides the interface to the network, usually from a central office switch, for digital voice transmission.)
SMDR	Station Message Detail Recording. (Feature in a PABX for call analysis.)
SMDS	Switched Multimegabit Data Service. (High speed packet based standard proposed by Bellcore.)
SMX	Synchronous Multiplexer.

SNAP	Subnetwork Access Protocol. (IEEE protocol which allows non-OSI protocols to be carried within OSI protocols.)
SNI	Subscriber Network Interface.
SNMP	Simple Network Management Protocol. (Network management system within TCP/IP.)
SNR	Signal to Noise Ratio.
SNV	Association Suisse de Normalisation. (Swiss standards making body.)
SOH	Section Overhead. (Information used in SDH transmission structure.)
SOHO	Small Office Home Office (market).
SONET	Synchronous Optical Network. (Synchronous optical transmission system developed in North America, and which has been developed by ITU-T into SDH.)
SP	Service Provider.
SPADE	Single channel per carrier Pulse code modulation multiple Access Demand assignment Equipment. (As SCPC technique.)
SPEC	Speech Predictive Encoding Communications.
SQL	Structured Query Language.
SQNR	Signal Quantisation Noise Ratio.
SSB	Single Sideband.
SSBSC	Single Sideband Suppressed Carrier modulation. (A method for amplitude modulation of a signal.)
SS-CDMA	Spread Spectrum Code Division Multiple Access.
SSMA	Spread Spectrum Multiple Access.
SSTV	Slow Scan Television.
STD	Subscriber Trunk Dialling.
STDM	Synchronous Time Division Multiplexing.
STDMX	Statistical Time Division Multiplexing.
STE	Signalling Terminal Equipment.
STM	Synchronous Transport Module. (Basic carrier module used within SDH e.g. STM-1, STM-4 and STM-16.)

STMR	Sidetone Masking Rating. (Measure of talker effects of sidetone.)
STP	Shielded Twisted Pair. (Cable.)
STP	Signal Transfer Point.
STS	Space-Time-Space. (Digital switching method.)
STS	Synchronous Transport Signal. (SONET standard for electrical signals, e.g. STS-1 at 51.84Mbit/s.)
STX	Synchronous Transmission crossconnect. (Crossconnect used within SHD.)
STX	Start of Text. (Control character used to indicate the start of data transmission. It is completed by a End of Text character, or ETX.)
SVC	Switched Virtual Circuit. (Method for establishing any to any virtual circuit link. See also PVC.)
TA	Terminal Adaptor. (Used within ISDN to convert between non-ISDN and ISDN references.)
TA	Telecommunication Authority.
TAPI	Telephony Applications Programming Interface. (A standard for linking telephones to PCs.)
TASI	Time Assignment Speech Interpolation. (Method used in analogue speech transmission where the channel is activated only when speech is present. This allows several users to share a common channel.)
TC	Transport Class. (E.g. TC 0, TC 4 etc.)
TCM	Time Compression Multiplexing. (Technique which separates the two directions of transmission in time.)
TCM/DPSK	Trellis Coded Modulation/Differential Phase Shift Keying.
TCP/IP	Transmission Control Protocol/ Internet Protocol. (Widely used transmission protocol, originating from the US ARPA defence project.)
T-DAB	Terrestrial Digital Audio Broadcasting.
TDD	Time Division Duplex transmission.

TDD/FDMA	Time Division Duplex/Frequency Division Multiple Access. (Means of multiplexing several two way calls using many frequencies, with a single two way call per frequency.)
TDD/TDMA	Time Division Duplex/Time Division Multiple Access. (Means of multiplexing two way calls using a single frequency for each call and multiple time slots.)
TDM	Time Division Multiplexing. (Technique for combining, by interleaving, several channels of data onto a common channel. The equipment which does this is called a Time Division Multiplexer.)
TDMA	Time Division Multiple Access. (A multiplexing technique where users gain access to a common channel on a time allocation basis. Commonly used in satellite systems, where several earth stations have total use of the transponder's power and bandwidth for a short period, and transmit in bursts of data.)
TE	Terminal Equipment.
TEDIS	Trade Electronic Data Interchange System. (European Commission programme.)
TEI	Terminal Endpoint Identifier. (Used within ISDN Layer 2 frame.)
TELMEX	Telefonos de Mexico. (Mexican PTT.)
TELR	Talker Echo Loudness Rating. (Overall loudness rating of the talker echo path.)
TEM	Transverse Electromagnetic cell. (Code used for measuring characteristics of receivers such as pagers.)
TEMA	Telecommunication Equipment Manufacturers Association. (UK.)
TIA	Telecommunication Industry Association. (US based. Formed from merger of telecommunication sector of the EIA and the USTSA.)
TM	Trade Mark.
TMA	Telecommunication Managers' Association. (UK.)

TMN	Telecommunications Management Network.
TNV	Telecommunication Network Voltage circuit. (Test circuit for definition of safety in telecommunication systems.)
TOP	Technical and Office Protocol.
TOT	Telephone Organisation of Thiland. (Thai carrier.)
TPON	Telephony over Passive Optical Networks.
TR	Technical Report. (ISO technical document; not a standard.)
TRAC	Technical Recommendations Application Committee. (Comite Charge de l'Application des Recommendations Techniques. Part of CEPT.)
TSAPI	Telephony Server Applications Programming Interface. (A standard for linking servers to PABXs.)
TSI	Time Slot Interchange. (Switching system technique which switches between circuits by separating the signals in time.)
TTC	Telecommunications Technology Committee. (Japanese.)
TTE	Telecommunication Terminal Equipment.
TTL	Transistor Transistor Logic. (Integrated circuit logic family.)
TTLS	Transistor Transistor Logic Schottky. (Faster version of TTL.)
TTY	Teletypewriter. (Usually refers to the transmission from a teletypewriter, which is asynchronous ASCII coded.)
TU	Tributary Unit. (Part of SDH. Ref: ITU-T G.709.)
TUA	Telecommunications Users' Association. (UK.)
TUF	Telecommunications Users' Foundation. (UK.)
TUG	Tributary Unit Group. (Part of SDH. Ref: ITU-T G.709.)
TV	Television.
TVRO	Television Receive Only. (Domestic equipment for the reception of television via satellite.)
TWT	Travelling Wave Tube.
TWTA	Travelling Wave Tube Amplifier.

TWX	Teletypewriter exchange service. (Used in Canada.)
TeraFLOP	(Trillion Floating Point Operations per second. Measure of a super computer.)
UAP	User Application Process.
UART	Universal Asynchronous Receiver/Transmitter. (The device, usually an integrated cirucit, for transmission of asynchronous data. See also USRT and USART.)
UDF	Unshielded twisted pair Development Forum. (Association of suppliers promoting transmission over UTP.)
UDP	User Datagram Protocol.
UHF	Ultra High Frequency. (Radio frequency, extending from about 300MHz to 3GHz.)
UI	User Interface.
UL	Underwriters Laboratories. (Independent USA organisation involved in standards and certification.)
UN	United Nations.
UNCTAD	United Nations Conference on Trade And Development.
UNI	User Network Interface. (Also called User Node Interface. External interface of a network.)
UPS	Uninterrupted Power Supply. (Used where loss of power, even for a short time, cannot be tolerated.)
USART	Universal Synchronous/Asynchronous Receiver/Transmitter. (A device, usually an integrated circuit, used in data communication devices, for conversion of data from parallel to serial form for transmission.)
USB	Upper Sideband.
USITA	US Independent Telephone Association.
USRT	Universal Synchronous Receiver/Transmitter. (A device, usually an integrated circuit, which converts data for transmission over a synchronous channel.)
USTA	US Telephone Association.
USTSA	US Telecommunication Suppliers Association.

UTP	Unshielded Twisted Pair. (Cable.)
VAD	Voice Activity Detection. (Technique used in transmission systems to improve bandwidth utilisation.)
VADIS	Video Audio Digital Interactive System.
VADS	Value Added Data Service.
VAN	Value Added Network.
VANS	Value Added Network Services.
VAS	Value Added Service. (See also VANS.)
VASP	Value Added Service Provider.
VBR	Variable Bit Rate.
VC	Virtual Container. (Transmission mechanism used in SDH, ITU-T G.709. Its signals are never presented outside the network.)
VCO	Voltage Controlled Oscillator. (Component used in frequency generating systems.)
VCX	Virtual Container Crossconnect. (Synchronous crossconnect at the VC level. Used within the ITU-T SDH hierarchy.)
VDT	Video Dial Tone. (System in which subscriber can obtain variety of video services by dialling through the PSTN. Also referred to as VOD or Video on Demand.)
VDU	Visual Display Unit. (Usually a computer screen.)
VF	Voice Frequency. (Signalling method using frequencies within speech band. Also called in-band signalling. Also refers to the voice frequency band from 300Hz to 3400Hz.)
VFCT	Voice Frequency Carrier Telegraph.
VHF	Very High Frequency. (Radio frequency in the range of about 30MHz to 300MHz.)
VHSIC	Very High Speed Integrated Circuit.
VLF	Very Low Frequency. (Radio frequency in the range of about 3kHz to 30kHz.)
VLSI	Very Large Scale Integration. (A complex integrated circuit.)
VMS	Voice Messaging System.

VNL	Via Net Loss. (The method used to assign minimum loss in telephone lines in order to control echo and singing.)
VOA	Voice Of America.
VOD	Video on Demand. (Also known as VDT or Video Dial Tone.)
VPN	Virtual Private Network. (Part of a network operated by a public telephone operator, which is used as a private network.)
VQ	Vector Quantisation. (Encoding method.)
VQL	Variable Quantising Level. (Speech encoding method for transmission of speech at 32kbit/s.)
VRC	Vertical Redundancy Check. (Parity method used on transmitted data for error checking.)
VSB	Vestigial Sideband modulation. (A method for amplitude modulation of a signal.)
VSWR	Voltage Standing Wave Ratio.
VT	Virtual Tributary. (SONET terminology for a virtual container.)
VTP	Virtual Terminal Protocol.
WACK	Wait Acknowledgement. (Control signal returned by receiver to indicate to the sender that it is temporarily unable to accept any more data.)
WAN	Wide Area Network.
WATTC	World Administrative Telephone and Telegraph Conference. (Of ITU.)
WBLLN	Wideband Leased Line Network.
WDM	Wavelength Division Multiplexing. (Multiplexing technique used with optical communications systems.)
WIMP	Windows, Icons, Mouse and Pointer. (Display and manipulation technique for graphical interfaces e.g. as used for network management.)
WS	Work Station.
WSF	Workstation Function.
WTO	World Trade Organisation.

WWW	World Wide Web. (Client-server system used for the Internet.)

ZVEI	Zurerein der Electronissches Industrie.
ZZF	Zentrasamt fur Zulassungen im Fernmeldewessen.

Index